The Voice of Egypt

Chicago Studies in Ethnomusicology
Edited by Philip V. Bohlman & Bruno Nettl

For Jim

Contents

Preface

This book addresses the issue of agency in society, particularly the role of the exceptional individual in expressive culture. Theoretically, it rests on the rather large literature that has become known as practice theory as well as the literature associated with cultural studies. I am particularly indebted to the work of Raymond Williams, whose *Culture and Society* accounts successfully in broad social terms for a good number of English literary "stars."

My book draws from more than five years of fieldwork in several places in Egypt coupled with a reading of a substantial portion of the copious discourse on music and musicians in Egypt. Information has been readily available; however, answers to my questions are scattered throughout many sources and have been pieced together from literally hundreds of tiny announcements, short reviews, and interviews collected and evaluated over a period of years. I am grateful to the Fulbright-Hayes programs in Egypt, to a postdoctoral fellowship sponsored by the Rockefeller Foundation at the Institute for the Study of Religion, Literature, and Society in the Contemporary Middle East, University of Texas at Austin, and to the College Library at Harvard University for the years of support these institutions provided. The Douglas W. Bryant Fellowship at Harvard University underwrote the costs for obtaining rights and preparing illustrations.

While in Egypt, I worked among musicians, "culture brokers," and listeners from many walks of life in Cairo, Alexandria, and al-Minyā. I was particularly fortunate to have lived for two years in al-Minyā, for there I was led into more ordinary social circles than those in the cosmopolitan environment of Cairo and in the rather extraordinary world of musicians. My social role and obligations in al-Minyā were perhaps as normal as a foreigner can hope to have. In this environment I learned a great deal about Egyptian attitudes and values concerning expressive culture.

Most academics benefit from the support of their colleagues, and I am particularly rich in this regard. Jihad Racy of the University of California-Los Angeles and Dr. Buthayna Farīd of the Institute for Music Education at Helwan University in Egypt helped me launch my research in Egypt and have remained for years mentors and friends. The musicology faculty at the University of Illinois gave unstintingly of their considerable expertise, especially Professors Alexander Ringer, Bruno Nettl, and Lawrence Gushee. Without Kamāl Ḥusnī and his family I would never have developed a grasp of the texture of entertainment in early twentieth-century Cairo. Ḥasan Shams patiently explained the workings of Egyptian Radio to me, and Medhat Assem gave me hours of time talking about musical patronage in Cairo. Sāmī al-Laythī and Muṣṭafá Nabīl, editor in chief of *al-Hilāl* magazine, graciously provided assistance at the publishing house Dār al-Hilāl. The personnel at the archives of Dār al-Akhbār were also very forthcoming, and I am grateful for the opportunity to use the periodical rooms at Dār al-Kutub and the American University in Cairo. Umm Kulthūm's family was more than helpful, especially considering the volume of journalists and writers they have endured over the years.

Countless musicians and listeners taught me Arab music and helped me understand the numerous subjects that came under discussion. Sayyid Haykal, now dean of the Higher Institute for Arab Music, was among the first of them, and he showed great patience with my general ignorance of his milieu. Balīgh Ḥamdī, Aḥmad al-Ḥifnāwī, ʿAbd al-Munʿim al-Ḥarīrī, Mansī Amīn Fahmī, Maḥmūd ʿIffat, and Ḥasan Anwar were especially helpful. Counsel and information from Sayyid al-Maṣrī and ʿAbd al-ʿAzīz al-ʿAnānī have been constants in my life for fifteen years. Conversations with Ratība al-Ḥifnī, Maḥmūd Kāmil, Manār Abū Hayf, ʿĀdil ʿAbū Zahra, Mīnū Raghab, and Martha Roy greatly helped my understanding of music in Egypt. I owe an indescribable debt to Aḥmad Ramzī ʿAbd al-Shāfī Ismāʿīl and to his wife, my best friend Fātin Muḥammad Aḥmad, in the company of whose extended families I lived happily for more than two years in al-Minyā. They have been a constant source of friendship and help ever since.

Patty Tang's work refining my musical transcriptions improved them greatly; Stephanie Treloar's proofreading was invaluable; and Ruth Ochs ably assisted with countless tasks related to the production of this book. The generosity and assistance of Mahmoud Arif, Farouk Ibrahim, Hisham Farouk, and Meissa Mohie el-Din Ingram enabled the inclusion of many of the illustrations. David Brent, Matthew Howard, Susan Olin, Claudia Rex, and Robert Williams at the University of Chicago Press have been at all times patient, encouraging and very helpful.

Everett Rowson devoted many hours to meticulous review of my translations and transliterations. The depth of his understanding of Arabic literature and Egyptian society has been indispensable, and he has patiently endured my endless and often last-minute queries. I have benefited from the advice and encouragement of Salwa El Shawan Castelo-Branco, Michel Goldman, Scott Marcus, Lorraine Sakata, George Sawa and Suzanne Meyers Sawa, Philip Schuyler, Kay Kaufman Shelemay, and Jane Sugarman. I am grateful to the staff of the Loeb Music Library who made room for this work in our daily lives; I appreciate the friendship and support of my colleagues at the Harvard College Library and Music Department and especially to John Howard, Kay Kaufman Shelemay, and Christoph Wolff who have offered me an extraordinarily stimulating intellectual place to live.

Steve Blum's friendship, scholarship, and critical eye have guided me for many years. His mentorship began the day I crossed the threshold of the University of Illinois and has never failed me since. More than to any other scholar, this work owes its existence to him.

My husband, Jim Toth, has shared much of the experience of this narrative with me. He now knows more about singers than he ever hoped to know. My travels and my understanding have been enriched by his interests and companionship, and this book is for him.

Technical Note

Transliteration of Arabic words has followed the system used by the *International Journal of Middle Eastern Studies,* except for colloquial Egyptian texts for which I have adapted the system used in Hinds and Badawi's dictionary. The distinction between colloquial and formal texts is not always clear-cut. Well-known words such as *Cairo* and *Beirut* have been left in their familiar forms. Personal names have been transliterated in literary Arabic insofar as practicable.

To estimate dollar values, I have used the rates of exchange published monthly by the International Monetary Fund in *International Financial Statistics* since 1948, and, for earlier years, the rates published in various editions of the *World Almanac* and Baedeker's guide books to Egypt. In all cases, the dollar amounts are contemporary with their equivalents in Egyptian pounds: 50 £E in 1928 is equivalent to $250 in 1928.

The musical transcriptions do not necessarily reflect the actual pitch sung (which, in some cases, is very difficult to determine because of recording quality); instead they have been located in the appropriate *maqām* (or a reasonable transposition thereof). The key signatures are not intended, of course, to indicate keys but rather to facilitate the reading of the notated example.

One

"The Voice and Face of Egypt"

Umm Kulthūm was unquestionably the most famous singer in the twentieth-century Arab world. Her performing career lasted over fifty years, from about 1910, when she sang with her father at weddings and special occasions in villages and towns in the eastern Delta of Egypt, until her final illness in Cairo in 1973. She recorded about three hundred songs. For almost forty years her monthly, Thursday night concerts were broadcast live over the powerful Egyptian radio waves. As a result, her audience consisted of millions, reaching far beyond the concert-going public of Cairo to households all over the Middle East where people gathered to listen to the broadcasts. Many who could well afford tickets preferred sitting with friends and family in coffeehouses and homes. Part of listening to Umm Kulthūm was a long evening of tea and camaraderie. Listeners remember this entire experience along with the sound.

By way of describing the impact of her Thursday concerts, many stories circulated: "Such-and-such a military leader postponed a manoeuvre because Umm Kulthūm was singing." "Life in the Arab world came to a stop." Detractors complained that "You couldn't read about anything else in the newspaper that day except the color of Umm Kulthūm's dress and what jewelry she would wear." On those Thursdays, "we lived in her world all day."[1]

She was a cultural leader in a general sense, as a public personality, seven-year president of the Musicians' Union, member of governmental committees on the arts, and cultural emissary of Egypt to other Arab nations. When she died in 1975, her funeral was described as bigger than that of President Jamāl ʿAbd al-Nāṣir. She was, for many years, "the voice and face of Egypt."[2] She remains today an inescapable figure in Arab musical life.

Umm Kulthūm's story is that of a successful musician in a complex society: it is multifaceted. It is the story of a village girl who grew up to become the cultural symbol of a nation. It is also that of a competent professional woman, whose career depended negotiating a demanding and difficult path through the institutions of musical performance in Cairo. She sought and found ways to influence and even control the institutions and processes that affected her career. And her story is that of the development of a wonderfully accomplished musician whose singing was and still is viewed as a contemporary exemplar of an old and deeply valued Arab art.

In all aspects of her public life she asserted values considered to be indigenous. She helped to constitute Egyptian cultural and social life and to advance an ideology of Egyptianness. Her most powerful medium of expression was her musical style. She developed a personal idiom from antecedents considered to be Arab and Muslim. Umm Kulthūm and her repertory are widely viewed as *aṣīl,* authentically Egyptian and Arab. She helped to constitute several different styles, and her performances contributed to two important formations in contemporary Egyptian expressive culture—one neoclassical, the other populist. That this repertory may be justly viewed as her own, and not the result of independent creations of poets, composers, and technicians, results from her extensive involvement in the selection and composition of the poetry and music she sang, as well as the conditions of her performances.

Her thousands of performances over a long period of time were the subject of much reportage, criticism, and ordinary talk. She produced musical culture in a general sense. And, over the course of years, she herself was created by the fame she attained. Listeners evaluated her style and those of other performers and responded to changes she and others made in the musical practices they had learned. Her musical choices, and ultimately her place in Egyptian society, depended on the society's reception of her art. She was a participant in the society that she affected with her performances; she experienced and responded to her audience and to the artistic, social, and political forces surrounding her. Her career, artistry, and dominant presence in the culture offer an impressive entrée into Arab expressive culture.

Some Questions

Knowing a few facts about her life, I approached the study of Umm Kulthūm with the simple questions of why and how an individual could sustain such popularity for so long. Why was *this* individual, among many other entertainers, so important? My view, of course, was and is that of an outsider: unlike my Egyptian friends and colleagues, I did not grow up loving the voice of Umm Kulthūm, nor did I harbor the fatigue or even resentment some of them felt toward her pervasive presence. Unlike many ethnomusicologists, I did not approach Umm Kulthūm's repertory from instinctive love of the music. In fact, like many Western listeners, I did not understand it. I came into the society of musicians in Cairo as one who had to be taught why Umm Kulthūm's singing was good singing. I did not become, in the course of my years in Egypt, an objective observer of cultural expression: my story, and the language of my interpretation of Umm Kulthūm's story, is that of a Western musician and academic who learned to love and value Arabic singing.

I began, in the early 1980s, with lessons and conversations with musicians. In answer to my fundamental questions about why Umm Kulthūm was so important, why audiences thought her performances were so good, and why she was so much more highly regarded than anyone else, they talked predominantly about her musical style, her vocal skills, her habits and preferences in rehearsals and performances, and her treatment of others. As my circle of acquaintances widened I spoke with critics and writers, journalists, teachers, Umm Kulthūm's friends and family, and her associates, as well as personal friends and casual acquaintances of my own. My women friends in al-Minyā and the surrounding villages, their husbands and children and their large extended families; my acquaintances among professionals, shopkeepers, and students there; intellectuals from Alexandria; friends and neighbors in Cairo; in short, the people who constituted my experience of daily life in Cairo and provincial Egypt over the years all talked about Umm Kulthūm and vastly broadened the understanding I developed from her musicians and colleagues.

My questions about a single person quickly led to larger questions about Egyptian and Arab culture and society. What were the material circumstances of a commercial singer's life? How did she make her way? In what respects was Umm Kulthūm's career typical? How was she affected by the operations of institutions such as record companies and theaters? What was her effect on musical life and in what ways were her actions informed or constrained by precedents? Where were her performances situated in the larger processes of social life?

Umm Kulthūm's career unfolded during two world wars, the Egyptian Revolutions of 1919 and 1952, the Great Depression and the momentous sociopolitical changes of the 1950s and 1960s—events that affected her as a citizen of Egypt and as a working musician, just as they commanded the attention of her listeners. She was constantly identified as a truly Egyptian artist—she was *aṣīl,* "authentic." In this larger realm why did Umm Kulthūm and her emblematic authenticity, her *aṣāla,* become so important?

Why did this category emerge in musical expression and the surrounding discourse?

Initially, I found the explanations and evaluations attached to Umm Kulthūm's repertory redundant to the point of seeming incomprehensible: it was as though listeners had learned the talk along with the tunes. When Egyptians talked about Umm Kulthūm they often said, "She was good because she could recite the Qur'ān," leaving me to wonder what exactly that meant. "She never sang a line the same way twice"; but they sounded remarkably similar to me at the time, especially when compared to the florid melodic invention in instrumental improvisations. "She sang naturally," people repeated, "not like Europeans," or "she sang naturally because she could read the Qur'ān." And when she performed, "she depicted the state [*ḥāl*] of the people exactly." "Her voice was full of our everyday life."

"She does not just sing the 'Rubā'iyyāt,'" a violinist commented about a translation of 'Umar Khayyām's famous poem that Umm Kulthūm recorded, "she infuses it with meaning." "You must understand the words. You can't like this music if you don't understand the words." But, I thought, instrumental improvisation is a high art in Arab music—why can't I hear Umm Kulthūm's music the same way—melodically?

I was told that this well-spoken, richly bejeweled woman was "really a country woman." "She was a daughter of the Egyptian village," "a *bint il-riif*."

"It wasn't only her voice—her *character* was the reason for her success." "Egyptians not only like her voice, we respect *her*. . . . We look at her, we see fifty years of Egypt's history. She is not only a singer." Then who is she? What role did musical sound play in the construction of her persona and in public perceptions of her? And is it possible that "fifty years" in Arab societies, where women appear to outsiders to be oppressed, silent, and veiled, could be represented by the life and work of a woman?

My questions multiplied. More sophisticated listeners made more extensive and complex comments, but the essential points they made were usually the same and were points that would not be relevant to many other artists.

Speech about Music

"We have much to learn," Stephen Blum writes,

> about the ways in which people talk about the dialogues in which musicians and listeners are engaged. All of the talk relies on tropes, as

> Goethe recognized: "We think we are speaking in pure prose and we are already speaking in tropes; one person employs the tropes differently than another, takes them farther in a related sense, and thus the debate becomes interminable and the riddle insoluble."[3]

People talked to me readily, repeating, elaborating, and embellishing their tropes. "Talking," an anthropologist friend observed, "is a national pastime in Egypt." All sorts of topics are subject to detailed discussion, evaluation, and comment. Radio and television broadcasts, for example, are not merely to be absorbed, they are to be discussed. They provide a starting point for argumentation of views.

I began to pay increasing attention to speech about music in its various manifestations. Clearly this talk, this evaluation, was as much a part of musical practice as performance itself.[4] But what did the tropes mean? I tried to find ways to hear talk about music that I "neither constrained nor controlled"[5] and to look at the terms of the published discourse surrounding Umm Kulthūm from the beginning of her career.

This task was formidable. A great deal has been written about music in twentieth-century Egypt, much of it dealing with musicians in commercial domains. Brief accounts of Umm Kulthūm's career and commentary on her performances, as well as those of the other entertainers in commercial venues, appeared frequently in the relatively large number of periodicals and columns devoted to music and theater published in Cairo. Many magazines were given entirely to entertainment, music, and theater, and others contained regular articles on performances.[6] *Al-Rādyū al-Miṣrī* (and its successors) published broadcasting schedules including names of performers, songs, and durations of performances.[7] The autobiography became a popular genre for public figures of all sorts beginning during the 1920s. Stars of music and theater published memoirs, including actresses Rūz al-Yūsuf, Badīʿa Maṣabnī, Faṭma Rushdī, actor Najīb al-Rīḥānī, playwright Badīʿ Khayrī, and musicians Muḥammad ʿAbd al-Wahhāb and Zakariyyā Aḥmad. Umm Kulthūm's autobiographical statements began in 1937, with a series of articles in the magazine *Ākhir Sāʿa*. The autobiography she published in 1971 with Maḥmūd ʿAwaḍ is similar in content to the 1937 memoir, with ancillary chapters added by ʿAwaḍ.[8] Biographies of the most famous stars were published. Following the establishment of Egyptian National Radio in 1934, interviews with musicians were broadcast and, beginning in the 1940s, some were kept in sound archives and collected on tape by those aficionados who had the necessary equipment.

The central question here is not only what is performed alone but also what is heard. Speech (and discourses, broadly conceived to include action)[9] constitutes the means by which musicians and listeners locate sound. Their talk helps to constitute identities of musical styles. Blum described this by saying,

> The definition of stylistic norms evolves from both the actual practice of performing musicians and the verbal statements, evaluations, justifications which attach themselves to practice. Non-specialists participate in several aspects of this process: one chooses what he will listen to, what he will attempt to reproduce, and what he will say about it. . . . Recurrent traits or patterns which result from such procedure for music-making might be said to constitute a style.[10]

Listeners' interpretations of similarity and difference, of transformations and contrasts, define styles. These depend, as Richard Middleton writes, on what is heard and how it is heard.[11] Listeners' interpretations connect with their attempts "to make sense of a changing world in terms of past experience."[12] Assuming that musical meaning is coproduced by listeners and that, as Middleton argues, "acts of 'consumption' are essential, constitutive parts of the 'material circuits' through which musical practice exists—listening, too, must be considered a productive force."[13] Thus our interest properly resides in historically situated performers and listeners who produce, respond to, reproduce, and reuse music and so constitute a practice of music.

Musical practice in Egypt includes three behaviors: the performing itself, listening to performance, and speaking about music and performances. As the mass media proliferated in Egypt, beginning with commercial recording in about 1904 and radio in the 1920s, listeners could exercise greater choice in what to hear. The behavior of choosing became a part of musical practice. The discourse of listeners is constituted by listening behaviors and also by speech about music. This discourse helps to produce the musical style as a cultural conception and identifies its place in social life. Musical meaning resides in the process of the production of sound, the subsequent interpretation of the sound, and the ensuing re-production of sound and interpretation.

The character of speech about music in Egypt varies with the interests and competence of the speakers and their social situations. The discourse of experts is often technical in nature to the extent of being almost incomprehensible to the ordinary listener. The speech of musicians themselves is often opaque, vague, and contradictory, for the musician's principal mode of expression is rarely speech. The talk of ordinary listeners often depends on analogies, images, and relationships for explanation of sound or feeling. However, the general themes of the discourse about song in Egypt are remarkably consistent; patterns of thought, criticism, and association emerge as fragments of discourse that are widely shared, attached to similar musics and believed to be true.

In musical practices over time, talk, along with musical sound, operates in a transformative capacity as well. In the career of a popular star such as Umm Kulthūm, speech about music affects further performances and new productions. Listening practices carried her music into new places and times. The discourse of listeners helps to create a "changing space in which certain possibilities for action emerge, are exploited, and then are abandoned."[14]

"Archival knowledge" forms part of the discourse.[15] Historical collections made by listeners give indications of what was important to them, what not, and, sometimes, why. Historical resources permit comparison of interpretations of events as they occurred with later reflections on the same events and offer a view of the usages of events from the past to illustrate larger ideas or trends and to explain and shape the present. One sees the role of the performer in the production of the discourse, the emergence of "attitudes" as "sentiments become habitual"[16] and, ultimately, the construction of strong cultural formations.

As a practice, discourse is discontinuous and neither uniform nor stable.[17] People in Egypt, whether writing, speaking, or listening, did not do so in order to advance a single goal, promote a particular result, or necessarily for similar reasons at all. Nevertheless, taken together, the printed discourse and bits of speech about music and the explanations and discussions that I continued to have during the years of my work in Egypt made sense. The talk of the 1980s took its place in a larger corpus of commentary about music having particular characteristics. What motivated this talk? and what, if we can know, did it displace?

Listening

Sound, often nondiscursive, textures daily life in Egypt. Twentieth-century Cairo has been frequently characterized by outsiders and residents alike as increasingly noisy. The "noise" proceeds from motor vehicles, sometimes from animals, from construction equipment and processes, from people and their electronic gadgets. Even in elite residential districts one can still hear vendors of mint or grape leaves singing out their wares and manual laborers chanting as an aid to applying their strength together to moving heavy objects.

Music forms a significant part of this aural environment. For almost a hundred years the playing of sound recordings has been a part of life. Recordings have been available since the turn of the century and have been played in public places almost constantly since then. Radio garnered an important corner in public life beginning in the 1930s. Ibrahim Abu-Lughod's description of a typical Delta grocery shop of the 1960s illustrates common use of radio in daily life:

> Small in size, limited in stock to the very basic staples, presided over by the proprietor assisted by a young boy, usually a relation, it is open to the street, equipped with the necessary counter, a few chairs and a kerosene burner to boil water for coffee and tea. It inevitably contains a radio in constant operation. This radio is a standard prop not only in the grocery store but in the offices of the seed merchant, the grain dealers, the cotton agent, etc. The radio plays constantly not only to entertain the proprietor, for whom business is always slow, but as a service to his friends and customers. Those with business to transact, and even those with no pressing business at all, will stop leisurely to listen for a while, discuss the programs, exchange pleasantries, news and gossip.[18]

By the 1960s "the mass media [had become] a part of the everyday life of all but a few of the citizens of Egypt."[19] The transistor radio vastly increased the listening audience. Cassette tapes and tape players further expanded the opportunities available to musicians and listeners. While Egyptians might complain that the pace of life is now faster than in Abu-Lughod's description, that no one's business is leisurely anymore, the music plays on.

In the 1980s and 1990s, in a single block one might hear Western rock music, young Egyptian and other Arab stars, and the recitation of the Qur'ān. At 5 P.M., particularly in places where small shops open into the street, in the grocer's, in the shop of the *makwagi* (the professional ironer of clothes), in parking garages under apartment buildings where doormen and attendants watch over their tenants' vehicles, in the auto mechanic's workshop and electrical supply shop, radios are often still tuned to the

Umm Kulthūm station. Established by President ʿAbd al-Nāṣir in the 1960s, this all-music station begins and ends its nightly broadcast with a tape of a song from one of her concerts. Sound helps to characterize the location and the time of day. The use of the sound forms part of social practice.

Listening begins with the choice to pay attention to certain sounds rather than others. In its immediate context, listening, in Egypt, is usually participatory: audience members call out subtle compliments or loud encouragement to performers. Silence is interpreted as disinterest or dislike. Some audiences express vociferous displeasure as well. Performances are ultimately shaped by repetitions encouraged by audience requests. Listening to broadcast performances, as indeed listening to broadcast programming of any kind, involves reaction and evaluation among those listening together.

The number of listeners to any performance expanded almost continuously throughout Umm Kulthūm's career, beginning with fewer than a hundred and growing to fourteen hundred in the concert halls of the 1960s. The broadcast audience expanded with the constant strengthening of Egyptian Radio to reach throughout the Arab world, especially after the proliferation of transistor radios in the early 1960s. Listeners also heard the songs through commercial recordings that were broadcast over the radio.

This entire audience certainly did not share a single subjectivity. In fact, Egyptian listeners often talked of highly idiosyncratic responses to individual performances. The same music was understood by different listeners as having a range of meanings or by a single listener in several different ways.[20]

Thomas Turino's "metaphorical notion of *context* as an ever-expanding series of concentric rings with pathways that cross and connect them"[21] provides a useful means to understand listening: listeners may grasp a performance most immediately in terms of the pleasure of the aesthetic experience; they may also associate the performance with a more general social identity: with habitués of dance halls, with "foreigners," with pious Muslims or sophisticated multilingual intellectuals, for instance; their comprehension may widen further to include awareness of constraining and enabling factors influencing the sound such as governmental sponsorship of performance, censorship by broadcasting committees, and the relative influence of the performer with the relevant commercial and political authorities.

The engagement of the listener continues through use of recordings. Listeners replay abbreviated and complete performances and move them into new contexts at different times. This practice continues today as aficionados at the Umm Kulthūm Coffeehouse replay fading complete concert tapes, and middle-class audiences hear short skeletal renditions of Umm Kulthūm's songs by the chorus of the national Arab music ensemble. Listeners both understand and modify the concepts by which musical styles are defined and located within their society. Musical expressions are relatively open codes. "Specific musical elements," Middleton writes, "are usually less firmly embedded in particular syntactic and semantic structures than are, for example, words, and . . . those conventions of meaning and syntax which do exist are more general, less precise, leaving greater freedom to make specific orientation in specific contexts." His notions of "articulation," the "docking" of a performance at a particular "place," allow us to see how the same performances carried different meanings at different times.[22] The uses of Umm Kulthūm's performances change and give rise to new points of social articulation as conditions change. Thus, following Anthony Giddens, "the most seemingly 'powerless' individuals are able to mobilise resources whereby they carve out 'spaces of control' in respect to their day-to-day lives and in respect of the activities of the more powerful."[23] The meaning of Umm Kulthūm's work is not simply expressed, it is produced (and re-produced) by performers and listeners. In this way listeners in their everyday lives contribute to structures of feeling that may become widespread. They manifest attitudes informed by aspects of life that lie beyond the domain of expressive culture—the explicitly political or economic, for instance. "To enter into [such a] history, we have to learn to understand the specific elements—conventions and notations—which are the material keys to intention and response, and, more generally, the specific elements which socially and historically determine and signify aesthetic and other situations."[24]

Performing

Egyptian conceptions of verbal art exist along a continuum from the spoken (in which music is never present) to the sung in which melody overwhelms text.[25] Sermons and oratory move speech toward melody; Qur'anic recitation is variously melodic; religious song and *mawāwīl* are melodic with careful attention to the articulation of the text; songs "in the Turkish style" are virtuosic, and melody may obscure the text; *layālī,* or vocal improvisations, rely on only three words (*ya leel, ya ʿeen*), the meanings of which may be completely irrelevant. A distinction is useful between forms that are fundamentally and essentially musical and those that are not. Song forms, such as *adwār, ṭaqāṭīq,* and *aghānī,* do not exist as such without melody. Qur'anic recitation and the *ghinnāwas* of the Awlād ʿAlī Bedouin, on the other hand, do.[26] Some genres such as *qaṣā'id* exist in two distinct forms: as poetry, in which cases they are printed texts or recited words (moving toward melody), and as song, in which cases the texts are usually abbreviated and substantial melodic "enhancement" is expected. Verbal art in Egypt is commonly regarded as individual performance; it is less often participatory or communal.[27]

The singer and sung poetry have been central to Arab musical life for centuries. This preference has many manifestations in the twentieth century. The singer is often the main attraction in plays and films, for instance. Public and private performances are structured around favorite singers.

"Song" is a broad concept. Kamāl Ḥusnī, the son of Egyptian composer Dāwūd Ḥusnī and himself a *ḥāfiẓ al-turāth* (a custodian of the musical heritage frequently called upon as a teacher), articulated five major components of traditional song: text (*al-naṣṣ*), composition (*al-laḥn*), rendition (*al-adā'*), instrumental accompaniment (*al-ālāt al-muṣāḥiba*), and audience (*al-jumhūr*). These reflected the ideas of noted authorities. In his *Kitāb al-Mūsīqá* (ca. 1904), Kāmil al-Khulaʿī wrote that song consisted of composition (*al-talḥīn*) based on proper use of the melodic and rhythmic modes bound together by a poetic text and usually cast in one of the classical genres. To that he added qualities of voice, proper delivery, and demeanor for the singer, and proper listening incumbent upon the audience as essential to a good performance. According to musicologist Maḥmūd al-Ḥifnī, the four pillars of the modern musical renaissance were poetry (*al-ta'līf*), composition (*al-talḥīn*), rendition (*al-adā'*), and listening (*al-istimāʿ*). Lines of songs, songs as whole entities, musical styles, and memories of performances as social events are all units of meaning. These teachings have old precedents.[28] The history of the transmission of these ideas through the ages is not well known, but clearly the musical cognoscenti of the early twentieth century knew and valued them. What is more, many less musically educated Egyptians responded to musical performances using similar categories and terms.

A good singer is a *muṭrib* (f., *muṭriba*), one who creates an environment of *ṭarab* with his or her performance. Excellent rendition generates *ṭarab,* literally "enchantment," the sense of having been deeply moved by the music. In early twentieth century Egypt, *ṭarab* was

> most frequently induced by a solo vocalist's skill in manipulating the laḥn by adding zakhārif [ornaments], ḳaflāt [cadences], and ḥarakāt [literally movements, here varied repetitions or improvisations], a solo vocalist's ability to express the text's meaning; and a performer's ability to create an improvised structure . . . in which he/she demonstrated his/her understanding and original treatment of the maḳām.[29]

Ṭarab is the ultimate goal of performance and essentially the responsibility of the singer. *Ṭarab,* a listener told me, comes from the singer, not the composer. It is part of rendition (*adāʾ*). Words conveying a poignant meaning delivered using the particular qualities of a singer's voice create *ṭarab.* "But the words," I was told, "do not contain all the meaning." *Ṭarab* requires the singing voice.

Musical performance, certainly for a professional musician, is closely entwined with social practices and material circumstances. Raymond Williams argues persuasively that cultural "products" result from individuals working with cultural materials.[30] With specific reference to music, performance is, in Blum's words, "a mode of human labor. A performer works within the constraints imposed by a particular set of social relations. He learns, elaborates, exercises, and refines the techniques which make it possible for him to act as a performer within one or more (changing or stable) contexts." The musical "product" thus "carries traces of the processes through which the performer has effected and realized his choices, has established his personal (and social) 'stance' or position."[31] Christopher Waterman suggests that musical structures, and, one might add, styles, are "learned configurations of habit, knowledge, and value predicating a range of performance strategies." Performance is "the contingent, dialectical realization of musical structure in social action."[32]

Analysis of sound presents the first viable option for understanding musical performance, but what kind of analysis? and with what tools? Structural analysis, in this case, by melodic and rhythmic mode (the systems of *maqāmāt* and *īqāʿāt*) is an obvious starting point. It has a strong foundation in Arab music theory dating back to the ninth century and has been for many years the tool of scholars. For Umm Kulthūm's repertory, this type of analysis yields certain information: one learns, for instance, that during the 1920s Umm Kulthūm sang in a wide variety of *maqāmāt*—twenty-three, in fact, and some were very unusual. In the 1960s, she sang in only eight, all basic. Cognoscenti often characterize her late repertory as inferior and boring, and this is one reason why.

But one inevitably reaches a point in each and every performance (and often a point of overwhelming audience response) where musical structure fails to account for the response. And my structural explanations were only rarely interesting to Egyptians. This was not the language with which many Egyptian listeners—even sophisticated musicians—evaluated Umm Kulthūm. It failed to account for her impact. Linking structural musical analysis to analysis of discourse historically opens windows on the dynamics of performance. It allows us to see performance and reception as parts of an ongoing musical process embedded in social practice.

Performance in the twentieth century often employed the mass media. Umm Kulthūm's career coincided with the burgeoning of institutions of commercial music including the media in Egypt. She "got in on the ground floor" of almost every medium and used all of them extensively. In many instances development of these media involved a major shift in the means of musical production from patronage by individuals and small institutions to larger capitalist ones. One of the questions of the time and for decades to follow was how institutional patronage should work.

A critical problem for Umm Kulthūm and her contemporaries was that of control, artistic and financial, over the circumstances of their work. This was a subject of their talk and of commentary: at the beginnings of their careers, professional performers were invariably subject to the authority of recording companies, theatrical companies, and agents. But performers failed in the commercial environment when they lost financial control. Successful performers, particularly forceful individuals such as Umm Kulthūm, Munīra al-Mahdiyya, and Badīʿa Maṣabnī, resisted governance of the artistic and financial results of their work by external agencies. Egyptian banker Ṭalʿat Ḥarb's various investments in entertainment and Setrak Mechian's Egyptian recording company manifested resistance, widely shared, to control by foreign companies. Grasping the economics of cultural production became essential.

This engagement—by no means a simple domination of the individual by the institution—links artistic expression with material process in Egyptian society. As an increasingly powerful individual, Umm Kulthūm helped form the institutions of musical performance. The careers of Umm Kulthūm and her contemporaries show paths through a period of major change and offer a means to analyze the interactions of individuals with emerging institutions over a period of decades.[33]

"Popular" Music

Words such as *aṣīl* (authentic), *turāth* (heritage), *klasīkī* (classical), and *mutaṭawwir* (advanced or developed) are used in discussions of Umm Kulthūm's repertory. They are significant, for most of them carry associations with social groups: *klasīkī* with elites, *aṣīl* with those who manifest commitment to behavior and principles considered to be indigenously Egyptian or Arab. Umm Kulthūm's songs were clearly "popular," but only in the most general sense of the word, that which is widely disseminated and well liked by a large number of people, as differentiated from repertories intended for specific occasions or designed to attract the attention of listeners with special training, connoisseurs, or smaller audiences defined by geographic region or occupation, for instance.

Racy gives no name for the category of music to which Umm Kulthūm's repertory appears to belong, positing instead a "central domain" that draws from the musical styles of other repertories present in the Arab world but having smaller or occasional audiences. These repertories include Western popular music, Western art music, Arab folk music, religious music, and "old Arab music (from before 1919)." Salwa El-Shawan found the categories of Arab music to be widespread music (exemplified by light music from films or commercial recordings), the recitation of the Qur'ān, religious song, folk song, and Western music. These categories overlap and draw upon each other.[34]

This situation casts into relief the Western scholars' problematic of categorizing, and coping with the concepts of "tradition" and "authenticity." Umm Kulthūm's repertory illustrates the difficulty of applying the Western categories of "art," "popular," or "folk" to non-Western repertories. In particular, her repertory challenges concepts of the nature of popular culture.

The Individual

The position occupied by Umm Kulthūm as a commercial musician is not unusual in twentieth-century culture: a talented individual, a seeker of fame and fortune who develops her skills and, in addition to attaining the status and wealth she initially sought, also becomes a spokesperson for or representative of a large population. What effect do such people have on their societies, if any? What is the role of the extraordinary individual, the "star" musician?

Anthropologists have long recognized that the lives of individuals offer inroads into societies. But the scholarly reconstruction of life histories has often fallen short of its mark and has, as many have observed, revealed more about the scholar than the individual whose life is represented. Ethnomusicologists have rarely studied individuals (although their fieldwork may depend primarily on contact with one or a small number of people); perhaps this tendency represents an effort to avoid interpretations of culture based on the works of "great men," so long in vogue in the history of European classical music. When individuals appear at the forefront of ethnomusicological or folkloric studies, they are rarely famous stars.[35] In studies of popular music, the successful performer has become alternatively the subject of a biography in which his or her society is largely ignored, or the object of a diminution in which his or her success is attributed to "marketing." Thus the sophisticated and the dull are lumped together under the assumption that anything can be sold.

To say that talented performers working in commercial domains are simply marketed to the unsuspecting public seems naive. As Middleton observed,

> Composers, performers and other productive agents are not either wholly "manipulated" or wholly "critical" and "free"; their subjectivity—or the positions being continually constructed for that subjectivity—is traversed by a multitude of different, often conflicting lines of social influence, bringing them into multiple, often overlapping identities and collectivities. Neither for them nor for their music are the simple categories of "mass" or "individual" appropriate.[36]

One wants to account for the impact of exceptional performers—John Lennon, Elvis Presley, Duke Ellington, Carlos Gardel, Ravi Shankar, Joseph Shabalala, Edith Piaf, Umm Kulthūm, and others—on the culture of their societies without losing track of them as participants affected by their societies. Large numbers of people responded to them avidly. They were (and in some cases still are) strong symbols. Simon Frith correctly argues that, for such very bright stars, one wants to grasp not only the life behind the myth, as many journalists and biographers try to do, but the myth at the heart of the life. Examining these myths offers a way of understanding what is shared between stars and their audiences.[37]

What is wanted is, as Giddens has written, a theory of the subject that will at the same time decenter the subject. For Umm Kulthūm, we need an approach that comprehends not only the production of music but also its reception, subsequent productions and reuses of her songs. Practice theory offers a good model for this sort of inquiry. Giddens, for instance, treats the individual as a "reasoning, acting being," while explaining individual actions with reference to society: neither the actor nor the society has primacy but "each is constituted in and through recurrent practices." Stars, as social actors, "reproduce or transform [systems], remaking what is already made in the continuity of *praxis*."[38] The influential individual may thus be seen, as Turino sees Natalio Calderón, the creator of an impressive Peruvian ensemble, as one who made history "but on the basis of political-economic conditions . . . [and] aesthetics *not* of his own making."[39] The exceptional individual does not operate outside of the practices of his or her society. Following Williams, "even while individual projects are being pursued, what is being drawn on is trans-individual, not only in the sense of shared (initial) forms and experiences, but in the specifically creative sense of new responses and formations."[40]

The professional musician chooses musical and other social gestures from any number of precedents, articulating a pattern. Listeners respond in a variety of ways, confirming or challenging the integrity and acceptability of the performance. Their responses presumably (and apparently) condition the performer's next engagement with them. In the course of these actions, as Waterman observed, music plays a role in "the enactment of identity" and operates as a "potentially constitutive factor in the patterning of cultural values and social interaction."[41] This nonverbal sound as a cultural production does not "reflect" social or cultural values but rather helps to constitute them. As Williams writes,

> The most damaging consequence of any theory of art as reflection is that, through its persuasive physical metaphor (in which a reflection simply occurs, within the physical properties of light, when an object or movement is brought into relations with a reflective surface—the mirror and then the mind), it succeeds in suppressing the actual work on material—in a final sense the material social process—which is the making of any art work.[42]

Artistic work advances larger cultural formations. Expressive formations are "conscious movements and tendencies (literary, artistic, philosophical or scientific)" that are "by no means . . . wholly identified with formal institutions . . . and which can sometimes even be positively contrasted with them."[43] Williams discards the related word "trend" as suggesting the following of a movement or fashion that misleadingly characterizes disparate works by unrelated artists in different fields in complex societies.

Viewing Umm Kulthūm's works from this perspective helps to place them in Egyptian society. The affect of her singing might be grasped through its close connections to "meanings and values as they are actively lived and felt," or structures of feeling:

> characteristic elements of impulse, restraint, and tone; specifically affective elements of consciousness and relationships: not feeling against thought, but thought as felt and feeling as thought: practical consciousness of a present kind, in a living and interrelating continuity. We are then defining these elements as a "structure": as a set, with specific internal relations, at once interlocking and in tension. Yet we are also defining a social experience which is still in process, often indeed not yet recognized as social but taken to be private, idiosyncratic, and even isolating, but which in analysis (though rarely otherwise) has its emergent, connecting, and dominant characteristics, indeed its specific hierarchies.[44]

Cultural work is "related to a much wider area of reality than the abstractions of 'social' and 'economic' experience . . . people using their physical and material resources for what one kind of society specializes to 'leisure' and 'entertainment' and 'art.'" They are elements of "an inclusive social and cultural formation which indeed to be effective has to extend to and include, indeed to form and be formed from, this whole area of lived experience." Artistic conventions, understood through performance and discourse, are established relationships.[45] These aural components of social life offer a counter to the bias of the visual in the constitution of "cultural facts"[46] and add new dimensions to explanations of social practice.

Social Issues

As part of social practice, the constitution of musical styles, the evaluation of performances, and the development of music-related institutions formed part of a larger problematic of modernization in Egypt, whether technological, social, economic, political, or cultural.

Discussions were often sophisticated, rife with complicated conditions and caveats. The fundamental question was not "whether" but "how." Most took the usefulness of foreign resources (for musicians, such devices as saxophones, clarinets, electronic instruments, and musical notation) for granted. Few advocated the abandonment of some Egyptian "essence." Laila El-Hamamsy's presentation of the roots of the problematic exemplifies many others written in Egypt:

> By the ease of [the French] military victory [in 1798] and by the display of their science and technology, they had undermined the complacency of Egypt's traditional society. By exposing the Egyptians to new administrative methods, as well as political beliefs and educational concepts, they had generated the first signs of a mood of self-questioning and self-doubt which acted as an important stimulus for change.[47]

The mood of questioning, not simply accepting, permeated the ensuing discourse as Egyptians sought to invent their own solutions to the imperative of modernization, to wrest and retain control of their lives and society in the face of economic, political, and potentially cultural domination. To this day these problems have not admitted definitive solutions. "Modernization," "Westernization," and related matters of change must be interpreted as foci for discussion rather than as acts or processes accomplished or in progress.

We have been correctly warned against preoccupation with the Western influence at the expense of overlooking other sources of invention. Years ago Jacques Berque observed that by emphasizing the impact of the West on the Middle East we "leave out the heart of the matter."[48] Recent scholarship demonstrates the strength of his point. In her introduction to a collection of essays on the history of Middle Eastern women, Nikki Keddie wrote that "in the past two centuries those Muslims who became Westernized tended to be those in the middle and upper classes who had profitable contact with Westerners. For larger if less visible groups, Westernization was generally unpopular."[49] Preoccupation with the use of Western resources guides our gaze toward only a small segment of the population, usually the urban or the elite.

We risk overlooking the actual role of the foreign when it is adopted, adapted, or integrated into local life. Speaking in terms of feminist issues, anthropologist Cynthia Nelson points out that the strategies even of relatively Westernized women were "not so much imported as they were the result of an actual historical encounter between Egypt and the West."[50] The simple adoption of Western techniques, especially technologies considered to be beneficial, did not automatically produce "Westernized" music in the views of Egyptians. Rather, the resulting musical styles take "specific path[s] through modernity."[51] Similarly, the Awlād Alī Bedouin with whom Lila Abu-Lughod lived

> wore shiny wristwatches and plastic shoes, listened to radios and cassette players, and traveled in Toyota pickup trucks. Unlike me, they did not regard these as alarming signs that they were losing their identity as a cultural group . . . because they define themselves not primarily by a way of life, however much they value pastoral nomadism and the rigors of the desert, but by some key principles of social organization.[52]

Examining the "heart of the matter" reveals important principles, practices, and valuations of the materials of cultural expression.

What emerges in this discussion bears upon the ordering of social life as a whole. In his convincing discussion of premodern Cairo, Timothy Mitchell characterizes it as an "order without frameworks":

> The city was the spacing of intervals or enclosures forming a continuous materiality. Its order was a question of maintaining, within such enclosures, the proper relationships between directions, forces and movements, not its ability to reveal in material form the determining presence of a non-material plan or meaning. It was an order without frameworks.[53]

Mitchell argues that physical and conceptual "enframing" was (and possibly still is) fundamental to the foreign domination of Egypt.[54] Erving Goffman's frame analysis and Steven Feld's interpretation of music listening address similar processes. Feld's language of "frames," "boundaries," and "interpretive moves" suggests definition and deliberateness on the part of the listener and seems to place limitations on listeners' interpretations.[55] On the other hand, Mitchell perceives, correctly I think, a more fluid order than the language of boundaries, borders, and frameworks of thought, common to anthropology and ethnomusicology, seems to allow. Applying a similar perspective to musical life, we will perceive a comparable fluid order, the order of *ṭarab* culture, with the forces, movements, and relationships of performer and audiences predicating a musical product that is—despite its orchestras and electronics—quite unlike a Western concert.

Finally, this "voice of Egypt" was female. Indeed, the careers of Umm Kulthūm and her female contemporaries fly in the face of popular conceptions of Arab women as submissive, sheltered, silent, and veiled. Those unfamiliar with the Middle East may ask how a woman could represent cultural achievement there.

The authority and accomplishments of women in Arab societies have been studied by many other scholars.[56] Star performers supply the social fabric with a few glittering threads; they form a small and extraordinary but highly visible segment of the population in the twentieth century. However, in many societies musicians, male or female, constitute a marginal population: one would generalize from information about them only with the greatest care. A look at the careers of the female singers of Cairo (and for that matter female patrons and entrepreneurs) adds color to the emerging picture of the activities of Arab women, the scope of their undertakings, their influence, and their often forceful presence in daily life. The realm of performers discloses information relative to gender within its ranks and in public life generally.

The tropes or "conceptual wires"[57]—the ideas woven throughout Umm Kulthūm's performances—underlay important evaluations. They do not necessarily define a structure nor are all available threads that constitute the fabric of musical judgment present in discourse about her. But just as "one can describe a particular configuration of styles and practices as 'Italian' without presupposing an underlying cultural unity,"[58] one can see threads that form fabrics of "Egyptianness" or "Arabness" that serve their societies for some period of time. Umm Kulthūm's idiom lends a congruence to certain principles; it manifests stylistic integrity recognizable within the culture, and her repertory thus contributes to musical and cultural formations that have links to social and political institutions.

This study joins the interpretation of sound and aesthetic judgment with the material circumstances of life for performers and listeners that help constitute reasons for actions and explain musical results. I hope to achieve a credible reading of musical practice lodged in social practice with emphasis on the role of the star performer as a participant and constituent of both.

Two

Childhood in the Egyptian Delta

My childhood was not different from that of many children of my country.[1]

"Min al-Mashāyikh"

Umm Kulthūm was born in a small rural village to a poor family. Her date of birth is not known for certain, but a reasonable possibility is May 4, 1904, given on a page from the Daqahliyya provincial birth records for Ṭammāy al-Zahāyra.[2] Her father, al-Shaykh Ibrāhīm al-Sayyid al-Baltājī (d. 1932), was the leader (*imām*) of the local mosque, and her mother, Faṭma al-Malījī (d. 1947), was a housewife.[3] Upon meeting al-Shaykh Ibrāhīm in 1917, the composer Zakariyyā Aḥmad remarked that he was "an extremely devout and pious man," and so he seemed to many others who saw him later in Cairo.[4] Umm Kulthūm's mother cared for the children: Umm Kulthūm, her sister, Sayyida, who was about ten years older, and her brother, Khālid, who was one year older. Umm Kulthūm was the last child, and she described her mother as a woman who lived simply and taught her children the importance of truth, humility, and trust in God.[5] Her words express an ideal of a good Egyptian woman.

The family lived in the village of Ṭammāy al-Zahāyra near the city of al-Sinbillawayn in the Delta province of Daqahliyya. The village consisted of about 280 homes for 1,665 people, or about six people per house.[6] As Umm Kulthūm later described it,

> It was a humble village. The highest building in it did not exceed two stories. The greatest display of wealth was the ʿumda's carriage pulled by one horse. . . . And there was only one street in the whole village wide enough for the ʿumda's carriage. . . . I sang in the neighboring villages, all of which were small. I thought that the city of al-Sinbillawayn was the biggest city in the world and I used to listen to news about it the same way one would listen now to news about New York or London or Paris.[7]

The family house was a small one made of mud brick; they owned no other property.

When she was about five years old, Umm Kulthūm entered the *kuttāb,* or Qur'ān school, that her older brother Khālid attended in their village. Upon the death of their teacher, the children were sent to the school in a neighboring village several kilometers away. Umm Kulthūm remained a student there for three years.[8]

The education she received in the *kuttāb,* common to those working-class children of her generation who were sent to school at all, included first and foremost the memorization of the Qur'ān. She and her classmates acquired an ability, however basic, to enunciate Qur'anic Arabic. More than the skill itself, they learned the value attached to Qur'anic learning and to correct pronunciation and phrasing of the text.

The Qur'ān is almost always read aloud. Even rudimentary instruction trains one to carefully enunciate words and even individual letters. As Kristina Nelson explains in her excellent study of the subject, "the basic structural unit of the recitation performance is the phrase followed by a pause," and the single-breath phrase is an important characteristic of recitation.[9] Correct reciting requires careful attention to the structure of phrases and pauses for breath at appropriate times to preserve the sense of phrases and sentences without distortion. The rules for reciting (*tajwīd*) mandate particular pronunciation of vowels following emphatic consonants such as *ḥ, ḍ,* or *ṣ.*

These values, elementary skills in reading and writing, and the daily life with the *shaykh* of the *kuttāb* formed a common fund of experience for many of Umm Kulthūm's contemporaries. Education for girls was by no means the norm, but neither were they excluded from the life of the *kuttāb.* Umm Kulthūm attended school with at least two other village girls, and accounts dating from the late nineteenth century mention female students.[10]

Umm Kulthūm's father augmented his meager income from the mosque by singing religious songs for weddings and other celebrations in his own and neighboring villages. He performed with his son Khālid and his nephew Ṣabr. Umm Kulthūm said she overheard him teaching the songs to her brother and learned them by rote herself. When al-Shaykh Ibrāhīm discovered what she had done and heard the unusual strength of her voice, he asked her to join the lessons.

She later described her learning process as imitation of her father, his inflections and his pronunciation, as a child would learn multiplication tables, without understanding: "I sang like a parrot," she said.[11]

Umm Kulthūm began performing in her own village at the house of the *ʿumda,* the village leader, on an occasion when Khālid felt ill. She participated as a male would have. The family's repertory consisted primarily of religious songs, including those that constituted the story of the Prophet's life (al-Qiṣṣa al-Nabawiyya). During Umm Kulthūm's childhood, singers formed this "story" from a large corpus of recitations and sung poetry in the genres of *tawshīḥ* (pl., *tawāshīḥ*) and *qaṣīda* (pl., *qaṣāʾid*) relating to the life of Muḥammad. The performer chose a number of items to make his or her own rendition. The style of performance used by the singers was at that time in flux, moving toward relatively melodic from more prosaic recitation, apparently under the impetus of two well-known religious singers from the old and famous Azhar University in Cairo, Ibrāhīm al-Maghrabī and his younger colleague, Ismāʿīl Sukkar. Their performances were popular and well respected, and they directed other renditions toward increased melodic elaboration.[12] Arabic musical practice rewarded such innovation. Replication or representation of artistic models from the past paled in comparison to the importance of developing a performer's own distinctive, contemporary voice.

Religious songs were usually sung by men. But women also became accomplished religious singers and performed, sometimes veiled, for male and female audiences.[13] Vocal accompaniment was the norm, and performances commonly featured alternation between the principal singer and a small group of male vocalists.[14] The religious singers of Cairo began using instruments such as the violin and the *qānūn* in place of or in addition to vocal accompaniment.

These religious songs were considered appropriate to many different occasions: Muslim religious holidays, including the evenings of the holy month of Ramadan and the large public festivals commemorating the birthday of the Prophet or that of another saint, as well as weddings, circumcisions, namings of babies, and celebrations of the inundation of the Nile. Performers were often people like Umm Kulthūm's father, professional musicians in the sense of being recognized and compensated for a special skill, hired locally or brought from a neighboring village or town or from Cairo for the occasion.

Recitation of the Qurʾān occupied a central place in Egyptian culture in public contexts and, less formally, as a source of comfort and as part of religious expression and instruction everywhere. Descriptions of these events abound, such as the following:

> My grandfather was a Qur'ān reader in a village. The reading of the Qur'ān is a marvelous and beautiful art in the view of the peasants [*fallaḥiin*]. They love to hear it. When someone finds a reader with an especially good voice and brings him for some occasion, the village in its entirety rushes to hear him, the men surrounding him and the women sitting on the roofs of the houses or in any other place where they can hear the beautiful voice that reads the Qur'ān.[15]

In her description of Egypt during the first half of this century, Afaf Marsot writes that "to listen to a good chanter [of the Qur'ān] is a universal treat," adding that, along with a few other local musical entertainments, it was "one of the few means at the fallah's disposal which was not censored, punished, taxed, or confiscated, unlike everything else he owned."[16] As Nelson writes,

> The pervasive sound of recitation becomes basic to Muslims' sense of their culture and religion even before they can articulate that sense, and by listening to Quranic recitation they participate in an experience with meaning far beyond the immediate sound or occasion.[17]

Thus Qur'anic recitation and religious song, the music Umm Kulthūm learned from her father, were familiar to virtually all Egyptians, regardless of socioeconomic background or the region in which they lived. Many people, although unable to articulate the particular rules of recitation, could recite correctly, and many more were familiar with the correct sound.[18] The sound of recitation and religious song was an important part of the cultural expression shared, in one way or another, by virtually all Egyptians.

Maḥmūd al-Ḥifnī writes that "Qur'anic recitation, religious song and praise of the Prophet had stars who exceeded at that time the highest ranks of fame and celebrity."[19] Many of the singers who worked in Cairo had been trained originally as reciters of the Qur'ān and worked professionally in both areas, singing amorous *qaṣā'id* as well as religious *tawāshīḥ*. These included some of the most famous performers of their time, such as Yūsuf al-Manyalāwī and Salāma Ḥijāzī.[20] A number of aspiring singers sought training from the religious singers of Sufi groups, in particular the al-Laythī order which was known for the beauty of its musical expression.[21]

Whatever the relationship of an individual singer to a Sufi order may have been, the stronger socioreligious connection was to the various forms of popular Islam, consisting of behaviors neither orthodox nor clearly Sufi, shared by whole communities and associated with traditional life in Egypt generally.[22] Persons with this type of background were identified as *min al-mashāyikh,* individuals possessed of a common educational and religious experience. Presumably the *shaykh* could recite the Qur'ān properly, understood literary Arabic, and knew a portion of the heritage of Arabic poetry and literature. From her sound and appearance Umm Kulthūm was immediately recognized by her early audiences as *min al-mashāyikh,* reared among the shaykhs.

The title *shaykh* (pl. *mashāyikh*) was accorded to various public figures. Although it has been used in secular contexts (for instance, *shaykh al-balad* for a village political leader), it usually carried religious overtones. The feminine *shaykha* was an educated religious woman, perhaps a female reciter of the Qur'ān. The title was accorded a wide variety of people from humble villagers such as Umm Kulthūm's father to the scholars of the Azhar University, the thousand-year-old bastion of Islamic learning. The background of Aḥmad ʿUrābī, leader of the Egyptian resistance effort against the British in 1881–82, manifests the reach of the *mashāyikh* and concepts about them in Egyptian society: ʿUrābī was commonly characterized and remembered as a professional army officer who had been educated at the Azhar University and was the son of a village *shaykh.*[23]

During the eighteenth and nineteenth centuries, Marsot points out, religious leaders were

> teachers, scholars and the intelligentsia of the day. They were scientists and mystics, humanists and artists. They comforted the bereaved, advised the high and the mighty, and on occasion protected the poor and the downtrodden. In brief they were ubiquitous, and fulfilled functions on all social levels. . . . Most of the prominent ulama were of fallah, peasant, origin.[24]

Marsot argues that their influence waned in the later nineteenth and twentieth centuries. However the figure of the Muslim religious leader remained powerful in the minds of many Egyptians, often as teachers in an environment where colonial authorities severely limited educational opportunity. The figure was aural as well as visual: the *mashāyikh* had a distinctive sound.

Two famous performers who won the acclaim of many and whose careers illustrate the concept of *min al-mashāyikh* in a musical context were Darwīsh al-Ḥarīrī (1881–1957) and ʿAlī Maḥmūd (1881–1946). Both lived and worked in the traditional neighborhoods of Cairo. As children, both learned to read the Qurʾān and later entered the Azhar University, where they studied grammar, theology, the rules of recitation, and Islamic law. Both supported themselves as reciters of the Qurʾān. Al-Ḥarīrī went on to study principles of music with a composer of musical plays and then embarked on the composition of *muwashshaḥāt.* He taught many of Umm Kulthūm's colleagues including Zakariyyā Aḥmad and Muḥammad ʿAbd al-Wahhāb. ʿAlī Maḥmūd continued as a Qurʾān reader and also became a famous singer of all types of religious songs and amorous *qaṣāʾid,* many of which he recorded and performed on the radio.[25]

Despite the patina of religion, the *mashāyikh* were not always viewed favorably. While they commanded respect in a general sense, the faults of some made them subject to criticism and ridicule. An example was the Arabic adaptation of Molière's *Tartuffe,* which featured as its central character al-Shaykh Maṭlūf, literally "the spoiled shaykh." The autobiographies of Umm Kulthūm and Ṭāhā Ḥusayn contain critical observations of the *mashāyikh,* and such views were common. Al-Khulaʿī, for one, denounced the ignorance and bad manners of the musical *mashāyikh,* describing them as "disgusting theologians who leave work with the Qurʾān and take up singing about which they know nothing at all," who were prone to error and apt to "lean forward . . . moving their hands and feet, swaying and so exerting themselves that their veins swell and eyes bulge."[26]

Nevertheless the performances and general demeanor of the *mashāyikh* were familiar and valued by many from all walks of life, even among non-Muslims. When queried by his colleagues at the 1932 Conference on Arab Music about the encroachment of Western influences, the Jewish composer Dāwūd Ḥusnī answered "As long as there is the Qurʾān, Arab music will always live." Similarly, Christian violinist Sāmī al-Shawwā viewed the *tawāshīḥ* and religious *qaṣāʾid* as exemplars of traditional Egyptian music, part of the culture shared by all Egyptians.[27]

The musical *mashāyikh* were not the only performers in Umm Kulthūm's milieu. Alongside them at public events were singers of the *mawwāl* (pl. *mawāwīl*), a multifarious type of colloquial song often associated with rural musical culture.[28] Performance of a *mawwāl* was often preceded by improvisation on the words "Ya leel, ya ʿeen" ("Oh night, oh eye," the usual text for vocal improvisation) called a *layālī*. The *mawwāl* itself was accompanied by drums, hand-clapping, the double reed *mizmār* or *urghūl*, or a combination of these. These instruments also played music for the dances of the countryside such as the men's stick dance, part of many public celebrations. Recitation of the old Arabic epic tales such as that of the Bani Hilāl, often with accompaniment by drum or spike fiddle (*rabāba*), described by Lane in the mid-nineteenth century, retained vitality into the twentieth century.[29]

Egyptians had been trained to play European military music in the army since the days of Muḥammad ʿAlī. The brass instruments and, to a lesser extent, the martial style of playing were transformed in the hands of the local players and attained their own popularity. In 1913, foreign observers noticed a "standard military band" and a bagpipe orchestra as part of the entertainment for the huge saint's day celebration for al-Sayyid Badawī held in the city of Tanta. During the 1910s and 1920s, an instrument dealer in Cairo named Ḥasab Allāh formed ensembles of brass players to entertain at public events and large private parties all over Egypt. This repertory, known as "mūsīqá Ḥasab Allāh" (Ḥasab Allāh's music), became extremely popular for a number of years.

These musics all formed part of Umm Kulthūm's childhood. In addition, musical performance became mediated. Umm Kulthūm and her friends listened to phonograph records. She learned songs from the records she heard at the home of her schoolmate, the *ʿumda*'s daughter. The commercial recording industry became established in Egypt early and grew quickly, becoming a popular means of musical entertainment.[30] Local newspapers carried advertisements for phonographs and recordings available to Egyptians via mail order from London as early as 1890. Recordings of Egyptian repertories were being made by 1904, and, in its 1913–14 catalog, the Odeon company advertised over 450 locally recorded discs, including Qur'anic recitation and various types of song. The Gramophone recording company was active in Egypt beginning in 1903 and by 1910 had released over 1,100 Egyptian recordings. Pathé, Columbia, and the Lebanese Baidaphon company appeared in the first decade of the century, and an Egyptian firm was established by Setrak Mechian.[31]

The price of phonographs gradually decreased so as to make them generally accessible to the middle classes.[32] More importantly, record players were shared. They appeared in coffeehouses and other public places where those who could not afford a machine themselves could hear new records.

Families who owned a phonograph invited friends to come and listen.[33] Audiences, even in villages as small as Umm Kulthūm's, listened to records.

She recalled hearing *qaṣā'id* recorded by al-Shaykh Abū 'l-ʿIlā Muḥammad, who would become her principal mentor and teacher in Cairo, and she also learned some of the popular love songs of the day. She remembered "Abuuya Zaraʿ li Gineena Kullaha Burtuqaal" (My father planted me a garden full of oranges) and Sayyid Darwīsh's "il-Baḥr Biyiḍḥak."

Performing Experience

Umm Kulthūm's debut at the home of the *ʿumda,* when she was between five and eight years old, was immediately followed by an invitation to perform for a celebration in a neighboring village. For this she was given ten piasters (about fifty cents) by the host. It was equivalent to half of her father's monthly wage from his position at the village mosque. Among the audience were people from the nearby city of al-Sinbillawayn who asked her father to bring her for their parties, and word spread about the little girl with the powerful voice who sang the songs of the *mashāyikh.*[34] Because of her youth and exceptionally strong voice, the child became an attraction for the group.

During the nineteenth century, new roads had been built, old ones improved, and a far-reaching railroad system completed in Egypt. The wealthy traveled from rural to urban areas for business and social purposes, as did their emissaries and entourages. These occasionally included entertainers, hired to travel from Cairo to country estates (or even the reverse) to perform for special occasions. Musicians followed the regional tours conducted by royalty or high officials and offered performances, public and private, at the stops along the way. Whole theatrical troupes toured the provincial cities: their performances took place in tents erected on public land, and tickets were sold through village leaders and rural notables.[35] Lesser musicians, like the young Umm Kulthūm and her family, traveled to villages and towns throughout the eastern Delta, fulfilling invitations to perform.

At first the family walked to the places where they performed, returning late at night. Umm Kulthūm described one of their later trips as follows:

> We walked several kilometers from our village to al-Sinbillawayn; then we took a train to al-Manṣūra; then we took a boat across the Nile to

> Ṭalkhā; then we took another train to Nabrāwa and walked to the village where the wedding was supposed to be held.[36]

Umm Kulthūm later reflected that it seemed to her they walked the entire Delta before they ever set foot in Cairo (see map 1).[37] As they traveled farther and earned more, they were able to use public transportation and, occasionally, to insist that donkeys be provided by the host.

She acquired a large audience. A journalist in the 1920s wrote that, like a local Qur'ān reciter, she developed a good reputation for singing in villages for a small fee.[38] She herself attributed her early popularity to curiosity:

> Of course, [the audiences] did not consider my singing as real singing, rather they heard it as a novelty: a little girl, seven years old, who sings with her high voice the religious songs and hymns to the Prophet that a man with a husky voice would sing, as people now listen to a little boy giving a speech in literary Arabic. They will not listen for his expression of new meaning but as a novelty because the speaker is a young boy.[39]

She became the family star. Patrons asked specifically for her, and family decisions began to be made with her career in mind.

Having noted her success, a local merchant proposed that Umm Kulthūm give a public concert and organized one in the town of Abū Shuqūq (see map 1). Tickets were sold for one to five piasters each ($.05 to $.25). The evening began with confusion among audience members and an argument that lasted almost an hour. After Umm Kulthūm began to sing, the argument resumed and she sang for only one-half hour of the four-hour event.[40]

Such events were relatively new to Egypt at the time. The audiences were largely if not exclusively male, and the social constraints that normally governed behavior at familial gatherings loosened in the context of the public event. Sometimes alcohol was served and inebriated audience members caused disturbances. When Umm Kulthūm was about fourteen years old, her family performed at a concert in a public house in Zaqāzīq during which her father became concerned about drunkenness among audience members. After negotiation with a reluctant manager, he elicited a promise that no alcohol would be served while his daughter was singing.[41] In another instance at al-Qarshiyya near Ṭanṭa the villagers invited Umm Kul-

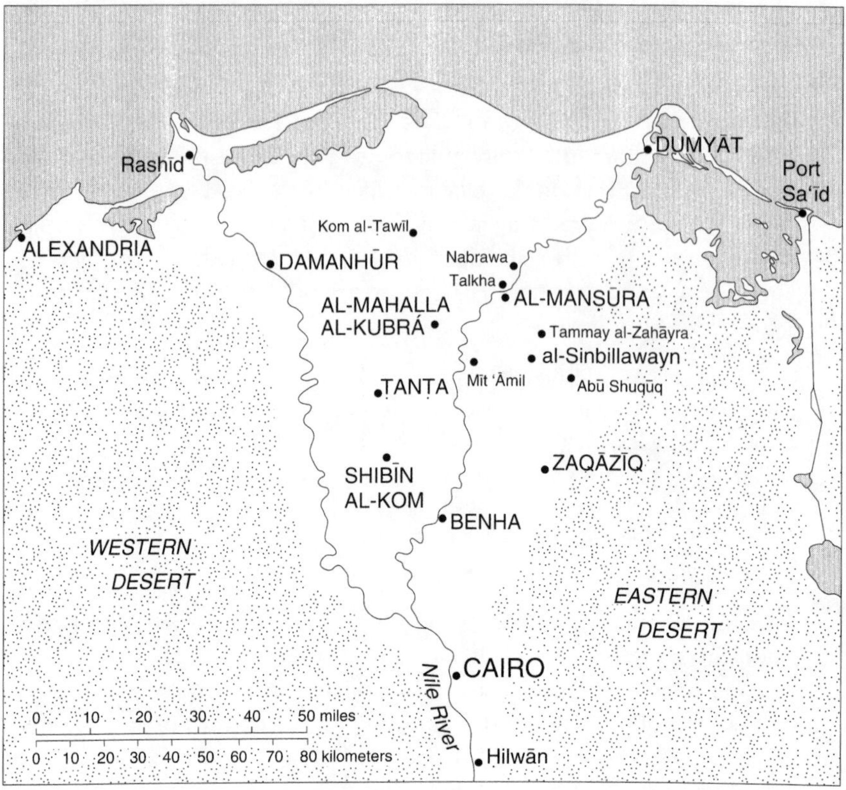

Map 1. The Egyptian Delta

thūm to sing, knowing that she was popular enough to attract people from a neighboring village whom they wanted to ambush.[42] The constant presence of her father and relatives was undoubtedly a great help in these situations. On the other hand, these occurrences contributed to al-Shaykh Ibrāhīm's anxiety at risking his daughter's reputation by allowing her to appear before public audiences, a problem he addressed in part by requiring that she dress in a boy's coat and Bedouin head-covering.

Al-Shaykh Ibrāhīm's misgivings must have been exacerbated by the low esteem with which their compatriots regarded musicians, male or female.[43] While most Egyptians patronized some form of public or private entertainment and entertainers lived and worked almost everywhere in Egypt, young people were not encouraged to take up these professions nor to consort with others who did. Aside from the notorious difficulty of earning a living as an entertainer and the frequently hard conditions confronting the beginner, the prevailing attitude seems to have been based on concepts of personal dignity. Displaying oneself publicly as an actor on stage, as a singer of love songs, or, worst of all, as a dancer, was seen as an unworthy use of time not commensurate with dignified behavior.[44] By becoming a star performer one could overcome these prejudices. However, successful musicians recalled the initial resistance of their families to their public performances. Umm Kulthūm's contemporary, composer Muḥammad ʿAbd al-Wahhāb, remembered being physically dragged off the stage and home through the streets by his older brother. Another colleague, the composer Zakariyyā Aḥmad, remembered his father exclaiming, "You're a son of a respected family and you're going to become one of those whose lives [consist of] 'Oh night, oh my eyes'?!"[45]

An objectionable aspect of musical performance was its association with vices such as the consumption of drugs and alcohol, gambling, and prostitution. These associations were particularly strong in the arena of commercial entertainment that Umm Kulthūm was about to enter. The presence of foreign soldiers at entertainment venues in cities exacerbated the situation as these men had relatively large amounts of money to spend and few restraints.[46]

So, Umm Kulthūm continued her progress toward commercial performance cautiously and dressed as a boy. Her initial steps toward the entertainment districts of Cairo were made as a result of her growing renown, by way of requests for her from the houses of wealthy, titled notables. She sang for Tawfīq Bey Zāhir al-Qāḍī near Damietta, and Tawfīq Bey became one of several Delta notables credited with having "discovered" her.[47]

Strong connections of elite families with rural Egypt and provincial cities as well as Cairo resulted in lines of communication between cities and rural estates that formed an important conduit for entertainers to reach patrons and new audiences. An estate employee usually connected the aspiring entertainer with the potential patron. For instance, the administrator for the property of al-Shināwī Pāshā,[48] near al-Manṣūra, hired Umm Kulthūm for the Pāshā's brother's wedding. A similar instance brought Umm Kulthūm and her family to ʿIzz al-Dīn Yakan Bey to participate in a celebration of Laylat al-Miʿrāj at his palace in Ḥilwān (see map 1).[49] ʿIzz al-Dīn was a member of a large landowning family with property near Ṭammāy al-Zahāyra. Its overseer knew of Umm Kulthūm and suggested that ʿIzz al-

Dīn invite her to participate in his annual celebration, which he did, without having seen or heard her himself. After discussing the matter with Umm Kulthūm's father, the overseer reported the following to ʿIzz al-Dīn:

> al-Sinbillawayn
>
> His Highness the Pāshā
>
> I have the honor to communicate to Your Grace what follows: As Your Grace ordered, I met today with al-Shaykha Umm Kulthūm and her father. It appears that some others made contracts with her some time ago, more than ten days, for the night of the celebration of al-Miʿrāj, but we, by means of some acquaintances, were able to nullify the first agreement and we drew up with her father the enclosed documents.
>
> Her father found the payment of 3 £E [$15.00] small, because from that he must pay the train fare, coming and going, of 120 piastres [$6.00]. But we surmounted this difficulty also, leaving the matter to Your Grace's discretion . . .
>
> [Signature unclear]

The overseer enclosed a written contract, confirming the arrangements:

> I, the undersigned al-Shaykh Ibrāhīm al-Sayyid of Ṭammāy al-Zahāyra, Markaz of al-Sinbillawayn, father of al-Shaykha Umm Kulthūm, confirm that I and my daughter have agreed to go to the palace of His Grace Muḥammad ʿIzz al-Dīn Bey in Ḥilwān on the coming 26 Rajab 1335 [May 19, 1917] to read the Story of the Noble Prophet on Laylat al-Miʿrāj for 3 Egyptian pounds as payment and for expenses. If I am late I acknowledge that I will be obliged to pay a fine of ten pounds.[50]

When the family arrived at the palace, ʿIzz al-Dīn was so shocked at Umm Kulthūm's youth that he immediately sent for a replacement, the well-known religious singer Ismāʿīl Sukkar, and dispatched the girl to the basement with the servants. Later, after ʿIzz al-Dīn was satisfied that everyone had been properly entertained, he asked for her and she sang.[51]

By such means Umm Kulthūm and other rural singers entered elite circles and, if they were lucky, acquired wealthy and influential patrons. ʿIzz al-Dīn's willingness to chance an unknown but highly recommended performer, probably for the sake of novelty, was not uncommon, nor was his choice of a singer *min al-mashāyikh,* especially for a religious holiday.

Written contracts such as that given above stipulated the terms of agreement between patron and performer, especially between parties not previously known to each other. Al-Shaykh Ibrāhīm negotiated these on his family's behalf. Another example follows:

> On the date shown below and by my signature, I, Ibrāhīm al-Sayyid from the village of Ṭammāy al-Zahāyra in the Markaz of al-Sinbillawayn, Daqahliyya, agree with Aḥmad Ismāʿīl from Kūm al-Ṭawīl, Markaz Kafr al-Shaykh, Gharbiyya, to come with my daughter, al-Sayyida Umm Kulthūm, to read the noble Life of the Prophet on Thursday night, 4 Dhū al-Ḥijja, 1338 Hijrī (which is 1920 Mīlādī) for the fee of 9 1/2 £E [$47.50], of which we have already received 4 £E as a deposit, the remainder of 5 1/2 £E to be paid to us later. Both signatories hereby confirm this.

Throughout the period from about 1910 to 1920, Umm Kulthūm's fee changed dramatically, from the 10 piastres she received at one of her first village performances to 25 piastres, then to 1 £E. When the family could charge 1.5 £E ($7.50) per concert, they felt themselves to be well-off.[52] Prosperity at the time often depended on the price of cotton, the country's most important cash crop. With the rise in cotton prices in 1919, a number of singers, including Umm Kulthūm and her family, raised their fees. Her father asked 8 £E ($40), then 10 £E ($50) per performance. In addition, gifts of money, silk, or jewelry were given to the performers.[53]

As their income grew, Umm Kulthūm later said, al-Shaykh Ibrāhīm commenced behaving in the way he thought appropriate to his family's new status. He took his children to be photographed. He stipulated in contracts that Umm Kulthūm was to be offered a bottle of soda water at the expense of the host, as he had heard other famous singers required. He asked that hosts transport them to and from the train station with donkeys and eventually purchased his own. The family began to ride first class, instead of third, on trains.[54]

As Umm Kulthūm's singing career in the Delta flowered, numerous people encouraged her father to move to Cairo in order to advance her career. He was reluctant to do this, for he did not know the city and had no close relatives nor any assurance of work there.[55] The subject of Cairo remained under discussion for several years. Practical assistance that was credible to al-Shaykh Ibrāhīm was first offered by al-Shaykh Abū ʾl-ʿIlā Muḥammad, Umm Kulthūm's recording favorite. In 1919 or 1920, al-Shaykh Abū ʾl-ʿIlā and Zakariyyā Aḥmad came to al-Sinbillawayn to entertain during several evenings of Ramadan.[56] Umm Kulthūm attended their performances with her brother and urged her father to invite Abū ʾl-ʿIlā to their home where she sang for him.

Zakariyyā reported that he and Abū ʾl-ʿIlā were both very impressed with her voice, her energy, and her sense of humor. She wanted to be taught all the songs he had sung and Zakariyyā tried to oblige, saying later that she was "very clever for her age which was about 15." He and Abū ʾl-ʿIlā tried to persuade her father that a move to Cairo was feasible. Pursuing this aim herself, Umm Kulthūm seems to have initiated correspondence with Zakariyyā following his visit, requesting his assistance in the move.[57]

Shortly after the visit to al-Sinbillawayn, probably with the aid of Zakariyyā, Umm Kulthūm's father contracted for her to sing at a wedding in Cairo, and this seems to have been her first performance there. Zakariyyā and Abū ʾl-ʿIlā invited their colleagues to attend, and in this way she met religious singers ʿAlī Maḥmūd and ʿAlī al-Qaṣabjī (whose son Muḥammad would compose many of her songs and play in her ensemble for over forty years), as well as Muḥammad Abū Zayd and Ṣiddīq Aḥmad, both entertainment agents.[58]

At about the same time, during the first years of the 1920s, Umm Kulthūm was invited to sing at the Cairo home of one of the elite families of Upper Egypt, the ʿAbd al-Rāziqs.[59] The women entertained visitors separately from the men, and it was to the women that Umm Kulthūm was sent to sing. Surprised and amused by the strong voice coming from a young girl, they sent her into the men's parlor where she left an indelible impression on Medhat Assem, then a young boy who had come to the house with his mother, a friend of ʿAbd al-Rāziq Pāshā's wife:

> The choice men of Egypt were there. I remember ʿAdlī Pāshā Yakan, ʿAbd al-Khāliq Tharwat, ʿAlī Māhir, al-Ustādh Luṭfī al-Sayyid. The girl entered the room—the women literally pushed her—all by herself, wearing a country dress, embarrassed in front of the rich clothes that the ladies of the house wore. I remember the disdain of those present for this simple country girl. She proceeded between the rows of guests, her black scarf hiding her head except for her eyes and her mouth, until she stood in the place made for her and started to sing. In the beginning the guests turned away from her to conversations with their neighbors. But her voice had hardly left her throat when conversations stopped and a deep silence fell on the place for several seconds. Umm Kulthūm sang religious words. The audience turned their attention to her and requested repetitions and returns.[60]

Afterward, Umm Kulthūm sang for one of the nights preceding a wedding in a tent in a street near the ʿAbd al-Rāziq house. Her family considered the patronage of the ʿAbd al-Rāziqs extremely auspicious and later viewed them as mentors.[61]

Agents Abū Zayd and Ṣiddīq Aḥmad as well as Zakariyyā Aḥmad arranged additional performances for Umm Kulthūm in the working-class neighborhoods of Cairo. Between 1920 and 1922 Umm Kulthūm made a number of successful appearances in downtown theaters, at benefit concerts, in homes of wealthy patrons, and for weddings.[62] By mid-1922, she was an established performer in the city.

The Audiences

How is it that peasant villagers and elite politicians could have similar artistic tastes? What motivated an elite family to tolerate—even support—an unsophisticated singer from the countryside? What in Egyptian society enabled her travels from the *ʿumda*'s house in Ṭammāy al-Zahāyra to the ʿAbd al-Rāziq palace in Cairo? We look now at the character of her early audiences and patrons and the attitudes they shared that helped her move from place to place and ultimately assured her success in Cairo.

The vast majority of Egyptians were, like Umm Kulthūm's family and many of her village audiences, peasants or landless poor. Those who owned a plot of land usually held one *faddān* (approximately one acre) or less. In cities, there were a growing number of urban industrial workers, typically landless although better paid than agricultural workers.[63]

These lower classes suffered at the hands of most governors: in the mid-nineteenth century from heavy taxation and expropriation of land and later, under the British, from control of crop prices, severely limited opportunity, and the heavy hand of British military authority. The Dinshawai Incident (1906) was a case in point long remembered: a number of villagers were executed in retaliation for the death of a British soldier who had been attacked while hunting pigeons belonging to a local farmer.

The difference in circumstances between the lower and upper classes was great, and it has become commonplace to characterize Egyptian society as highly stratified. Little if any opportunity for education, one of the mechanisms for upward mobility, was open to the poor other than the local Qur'ān school or convent school of varying quality and efficacy.[64] Under the British colonial authority, little or no effort was made to encourage education of Egyptians, and indeed this was one of the many sources of resentment against the British. The literacy rate, especially among the rural poor, was very low.[65]

A certain amount of upward mobility was possible. Talented individuals could enter the salons of the upper classes as Umm Kulthūm did.[66] As the century wore on, merchants and bureaucrats as a group gained increasing power in political and economic life, creating new spheres of influence.

Families such as the Yakans and the ʿAbd al-Rāziqs, whose bases of power developed during the nineteenth century, lived what were in many respects wildly different lives. In that century, the elite stratum was constituted by the Turco-Circassian ruling class, many of whom had come to Egypt with Muḥammad ʿAlī, had acquired substantial holdings of land, and been appointed by him to positions of authority in government.[67] An excellent example was ʿIzz al-Dīn Yakan's family, which retained its high status well into the twentieth century. Two Yakan brothers, contemporaries of Muḥammad ʿAlī, came to Egypt with him and were given large tracts of land. The family became involved in cotton production and later invested in ginning equipment. They diversified further, joining with banker Ṭalʿat Ḥarb in support of the first Egyptian owned and operated bank in the 1920s. They assumed positions of political power as well: the erudite ʿAdlī Pāshā Yakan became a prominent figure in politics and government in the 1920s and 1930s, serving for a time as prime minister.[68]

Near the end of the nineteenth century, some of the wealthier local Egyptian families were able to augment their land holdings through purchases of royal lands sold to pay debts. As a result, "the status and interests of many rural notable families approximated those of the descendants of Turco-Circassians."[69] As these Egyptians gained in wealth and status, they intermarried with the Turco-Circassian families, thus blurring the lines between local and foreign elites. By 1918, "the distinction had ceased to have any practical significance."[70]

The ʿAbd al-Rāziqs were one such family. They had served as religious leaders at the Azhar mosque and university throughout the nineteenth century while also maintaining substantial plantations which they enlarged by purchasing khedival lands both near their ancestral home in al-Minyā and in the Egyptian Delta. During the early twentieth century they were among the leaders of the Liberal Constitutionalist political party to which many of the more conservative wealthy landowners also belonged. Muṣṭafá ʿAbd al-Rāziq became the head of the Azhar University and later a cabinet minister.

He was described by Jacques Berque, who based his account on contemporary journalism, as follows:

> Mustafa al-Raziq was born in 1882, at the village of Abu Girg in the district of Bani Mazar, 300 kilometres south of Cairo; he was a Saʿidi [someone from Upper Egypt]. As they said at the time, "the Saʿid pervaded his voice and his whole being." He had kept the grave bearing, the restrained dignity of his people, a sort of general polish, *masqul,* in his gestures and thoughts. He still wore the caftan and the characteristic clerical turban, *amama;* yet he had abandoned the traditional sandal of the shaikh, the *markub,* for European-style shoes. He corrected this disparity by other factors in his costume; he dressed in attractive, somewhat daring, colours, and with discreet elegance. His features were pleasing and yet venerable and his whole person radiated kindliness and distinction. Stories were told of his edifying clemency.[71]

A later description of the father of Medhat Assem—the young boy who listened to Umm Kulthūm in the ʿAbd al-Rāziq house—manifests similar terms of valuation:

> Ismāʿīl Bey ʿĀṣim . . . was a man of letters, a translator and playwright who studied at the Azhar, then in France in a manner similar to Saʿd Zaghlūl's. Perhaps the most important high point in the history of Ismāʿīl ʿĀṣim as a lawyer is his defense of the victims of Dinshawai. He was also one of those who called for the establishment of a native Egyptian university. At the same time he was among those who advocated joining in the procession of international civilization. He himself undertook the translation of the play "Tosca" into Arabic and presented it at the Royal Opera House. He produced it himself and acted in the leading male role. With that he was the first Egyptian amateur from a noble family to enter the realm of theater. He was a pioneer for other sons of elite families, preceding the lawyer and actor ʿAbd al-Raḥmān Rushdī.[72]

This description uses events and circumstances from Ismāʿīl ʿĀṣim's life to construct tropes with which he (and others of his class and generation) were and are characterized and remembered. His title ("Bey"), his status as a lawyer and multilingual writer, his identity as one educated at the foremost Islamic university in the world and also in Europe, his interest in the foreign and his defense of the peasants of Dinshawai against the British, his recognition of the status difference between wealthy elites and professional performers, and his successful crossing of that boundary combined to form an integrated character who became familiar to Egyptians. The new Egyptian elite combined local and foreign learning and elegance with social values believed to be shared by all Egyptians.

The various interests of such families provided them with strong roots in rural Egypt (often represented by at least one large plantation home, and one or more town houses in provincial cities) as well as important links with the political processes that took place in Cairo (where each family typically maintained an imposing residence). Unlike their Turkish predecessors, these families viewed the lands they controlled as their primary or only homes. Some, for instance the ʿAbd al-Rāziqs and ʿUmar Sulṭān, spoke principally Arabic rather than Turkish and deliberately identified themselves, vis-à-vis the Turco-Circassians, as Egyptians.

Landownership was essential among the elite and constituted a sign of affluence for most Egyptians. To the peasants who lived and worked on the land, owning even part of a *faddān* meant increased security, a sense of belonging in a particular place, and enhanced personal status. As Marsot observed, "For men of social pretensions, possession of land was a sine qua non. In a country that was predominantly rural in mentality, those who were rich but landless were made in some subtle way to feel their lack of solid worth."[73] "To be 'respectable,'" according to Eric Davis, "landownership was a necessity."[74]

Rural notables of lesser station than the ʿAbd al-Rāziqs but with similar attitudes toward the land contributed to the political leadership of Egypt, among them the great nationalist hero, Saʿd Zaghlūl, and the eminent journalist, later president of the Egyptian University, Luṭfī al-Sayyid. And a multifaceted urban professional class developed, consisting of lawyers, doctors, teachers, journalists, merchants, and government officials, some of whom had been educated in Europe. They were considered to be the most Westernized of Egyptians, judging by clothing and behavior, although Berque cautions that this "by no means implies their adherence to an alien code of values."[75] Instead, it may have indicated the interest in new technology that, in many cases, their professions required. Members of this group were younger sons of village notables or children of urban merchants. As their affluence increased, many strove "to purchase an estate, intermarry with the landlord class and merge socially and politically with it."[76]

A key problematic in this society was the "foreign"—predominantly the European—with its perceived powers, potentials, and evils. Discourse of the time was saturated with negative views of the foreign presence in Egypt. The male characters in Najīb Maḥfūẓ's famous trilogy of novels think and speak about the troublesome and even fearsome presence of British soldiers in the streets of Cairo. Egyptians of all strata shared a resentment of the foreign presence in their country and of the economic and political control exercised by foreign powers.

The roots of these attitudes reach well back into the nineteenth century, to the time of Muḥammad ʿAlī whose education and training of Egyptian students "set the stage for the emergence of a new class of Egyptians, imbued with a new national consciousness which expressed itself in a desire to improve society and to secure for themselves a greater share in its control and development."[77] Increasing numbers of Egyptian civil servants, army officers, and landowners fed this current. The entry of imperial Britain into Egypt in the late nineteenth century galvanized nationalistic attitudes and resistance.[78]

"An antagonistic relationship" developed "between a large segment of the Egyptian upper class and foreign capital," leading to an active resistance to European economic control of Egyptian resources among elites.[79] Despite the prestige they derived from foreign travel and education, and despite the common association of the generally desirable process of modernization with Westernization, numerous upper- and middle-class families identified their interests with those of Egypt. As Berque observed, "An aristocrat such as Adli [Yakan], a landowning magnate such as Muhammad Mahmud were undeniable patriots. . . . Misr [Egypt] won the support of all the privileged."[80] Similarly, Zayid observed that,

> By the seventh decade of the nineteenth century the socially advanced Egyptians had developed a sharper awareness of their identity, a genuine concern for their country and a strong desire to be their own masters. In 1877 "Egypt for the Egyptian" was unmistakably the "national" aspiration. The extravagance of Ismaʿil Pasha, leading to bankruptcy and to foreign interference and control, greatly stimulated the patriotic feelings of the Egyptian.[81]

Under the British Protectorate that ensued, the urban middle class, "the most Europeanized section of the community . . . formed the natural vanguard of the national movement." Equipped educationally and professionally for responsible positions, this group "felt itself cramped both economically and politically by the British."[82] Alongside frequently admired

European technology, learning, and liberal thought, these Egyptians saw what Jean Lacouture and Simonne Lacouture described as the "auctioning of Egypt by a Europe whose thieves were disguised as diplomats and the diplomats as thieves."[83] Occurrences such as the Dinshawai Incident, settled in the Mixed Courts where foreigners were not subject to local law, fed what Berque called the "slow wrath" of the general population.[84] An entire generation of Egyptians grew up living with the collective memory of Dinshawai.

The circumstances brought about by World War I fused various resentments against foreign authorities. Landowners complained of the restriction of cotton acreage, the urban middle class of the foreign military presence, the large numbers of British officials, and the concomitant inflation. The British stationed over 100,000 imperial troops in Egypt in the years 1914–15, "partly to intimidate the Egyptian nationalists." Aside from the threatening nature of their presence, the behavior of the men when on leave was often mentioned as having a corrupting influence on Egypt's youth and a degrading effect on public life in Cairo.[85] Unskilled workers were afflicted with a fall in real earnings. The rural population suffered as the British commandeered their grain and animals at low prices, conscripted their young men, forced contributions of money, and engendered terrible feuding by compelling village leaders to administer unpopular policies.[86] Support for the proposition "Egypt for Egyptians" was strong and widespread.

Audiences from all socioeconomic classes sought what was "modern" or *ḥadīth*—that is, new, useful, and, if necessary, imported—yet authentically Egyptian-Arab, or *aṣīl.* These attitudes informed patronage of arts. For some it was a matter of familiar practice and local pride. "I'm an Egyptian, noble of race," sang a character on Sayyid Darwīsh's stage at the time, touting his heritage.[87] For some, support for Arabic art became an overt political statement. Many of the feminist Hudá Shaʿrāwī's fundraising events featured traditional Egyptian musical entertainments. She commissioned a number of works from Badīʿ Khayrī and Zakariyyā Aḥmad, often folkloric in theme. She supported what she perceived as truly Arabic theatrical productions. "She was," according to Badīʿ, "devoted to what was Arab." Despite her upbringing, which was conducted largely in French and Turkish, "her house was Arab, her taste was Arab."[88]

"It is interesting," El-Hamamsy writes, "that, concomitant with the strong desire to modernize the nation, which involved the wider adoption of foreign ideas and foreign techniques, there developed a powerful counter-balancing mood demanding the reassertion of Egyptian cultural traditions and values."[89] The sustained appreciation for arts perceived to be culturally authentic lodged for the most part among audiences of working-class Egyptians. However, the *aṣīl* attracted significant support from members of the middle and elite classes as well. As the century wore on, the people and practices *min al-mashāyikh* came to represent local values, historically Egyptian culture, and the authentic.

In the early 1920s, on the basis of her successful performances and the patronage of the ʿAbd al-Rāziqs, Umm Kulthūm and her family moved to Cairo to stay. She brought widely shared views of *aṣāla,* certain skills, and a common background *min al-mashāyikh* with her to the stages of Cairo. Her aim was fame and fortune; most likely, she did not intend to become anyone's standard-bearer. Yet her musical and cultural background prompted her audiences to confer a certain value on her. Ultimately, this assured her success there.

Three

Beginning in Cairo

> I met Muḥammad Taymūr near the post office. He asked me whether I had heard the Bedouin girl sing. "Who is the Bedouin girl?" I asked. "She is called Umm Kulthūm." "Is she really Bedouin?" "You will know when you see her and hear her," he replied.[1]

Between 1922 and about 1928, Umm Kulthūm moved from the position of the intriguing but virtually unknown singer recalled by poet ʿAbbās al-ʿAqqād above to that of a major star. At first she was variously characterized as a *shaykha,* or religious singer, a "country girl" or even "Bedouin," probably because of the incongruous headgear she wore. She made great improvements in her musical skills and altered her performance style and her public appearance and demeanor, as she sought a repertory and professional identity that would yield continued employment and the fame and fortune for which she had moved to Cairo in the first place. A talented singer with some experience, Umm Kulthūm entered the mainstream of musical performance and negotiated a course for herself.

Music in Cairo

The Egyptian economy was relatively strong during the 1920s, a factor of great importance to entertainers. Middle- and upper middle-class Egyptians patronized entertainment through their purchases of tickets or recordings. Over a dozen new magazines appeared that dealt with music and theater or featured prominent columns for news and criticism of entertainment. Patronage shifted from individuals and families to institutions such as theaters and recording companies.

Public commercial entertainment establishments began to proliferate in urban areas of Egypt during the nineteenth century. The center of commercial music in Cairo was the theater district near Azbakiyya Garden (see map 2). The area had long been a gathering place for entertainment for such traditional occasions as the celebration of the Prophet's birthday. After the arrival of the French in 1798, "local Christians and Europeans . . . started taverns, restaurants, and cafes in the European style" in the vicinity. The development of the Garden by Khedive Ismāʿīl brought with it public restaurants and open-air music halls. The Garden itself housed entertainment "kiosks" and outdoor music halls such as Ṣālat Santī, a favorite venue for aspiring young singers.[2] It offered working space for fortune-tellers, clowns, snake charmers, sorcerers, and other freelance entertainers. In addition, according to historian Ḥusayn Fawzī's description, one could hear marches by John Philip Sousa, renditions of "Way Down upon the Swanee River," operettas by Gilbert and Sullivan, and whatever was considered the latest fashion from abroad.[3] The theater district, centered on ʿImād al-Dīn Street, featured European productions at the Opera House, Arabic adaptations of European plays, and original Arabic productions, some of which included music. Many young singers began their careers performing during the intermissions of these productions.[4]

An entertainment district of secondary importance was Rawḍ al-Faraj, located along the river north of the city center. This area had its own collection of music halls and theaters, some outdoors on the banks of the river. Young singers started in the music halls there and older ones retired to them. Small theaters also grew up in the working-class districts of Cairo, for instance in the area near the Ḥusayn mosque. Both Umm Kulthūm and the young ʿAbd al-Wahhāb performed at these establishments in the early years of their careers.

Arabic theatrical productions had gained increasing popularity since their beginnings in the mid-nineteenth century. The Arabic play was an adaptation of European, usually French, models. One of the pioneers of Arabic theater, the Syrian Mārūn al-Naqqāsh (1817–55), "enlivened the play by inserting several airs and tunes, of Oriental character; these were performed by an orchestra and choir and were often, but not always, related to the subject of the play."[5] Aḥmad Abū Khalīl al-Qabbānī was commonly regarded as the founder of musical theater in Egypt (ca. 1884), and singer Salāma Ḥijāzī its most successful exponent in the first two decades of the twentieth century.

The musical plays drew upon a wide variety of melodic materials, and songs from plays were usually considered to be new genres. Racy wrote that

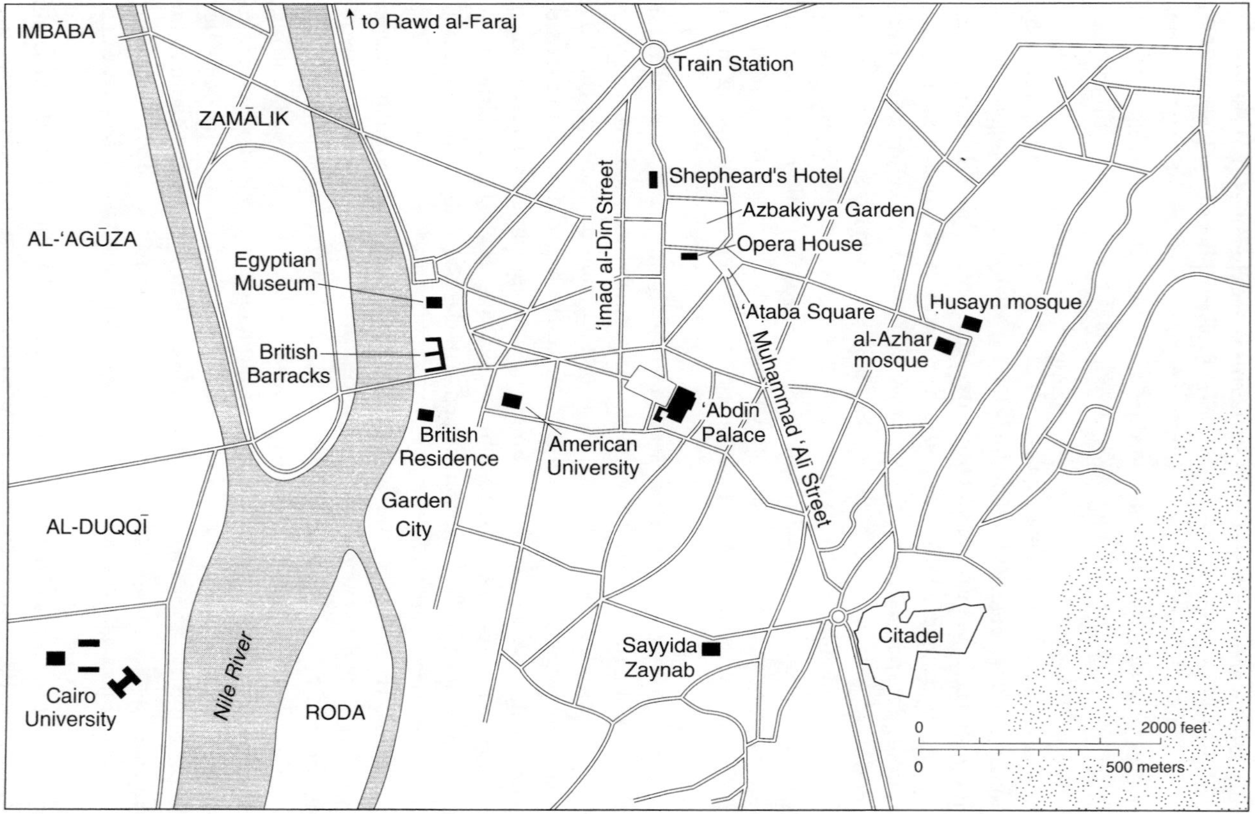

Map 2. Cairo in the 1920s

> Because theatrical music was composed to express a variety of textual contents, it was natural for it to appear in a wide spectrum of styles ranging from the martial and nationalistic to the lyric and folk. It is not surprising that throughout this departure from established norms, the standard theatrical song was generally referred to not by a regular generic name but as *laḥn masraḥī* (literally, "a theatrical tune").[6]

As musical plays increased in popularity, particularly during the 1910s with the rise of Salāma Ḥijāzī's theatrical troupe, music designed expressly for theater affected other musical styles as well. Typically, musical plays included familiar genres such as the *qaṣīda* and the *ṭaqṭūqa* alongside genres adapted from European models especially for the plays such as the instrumental introduction (*muqaddima* or *iftitāḥ*) and the monologue, dialogue, and trialogue. Accompanying ensembles were relatively large, modeled on their European counterparts and, overall, theater music was commonly considered to be the most Westernized of repertories.[7]

The theater attracted the attention of some of the elite young men of Cairo, both as patrons and participants. The neoclassical poets Aḥmad Shawqī and Ḥāfiẓ Ibrāhīm and the playwrights Maḥmūd Taymūr and Muḥammad Taymūr wrote works for the stage. Shawqī was involved in the production of the first Egyptian talking picture, *Awlād al-Dhawāt.*[8] The critics for newspapers and journals were often noted writers and intellectuals such as Ibrāhīm al-Māzinī and ʿAbbās al-ʿAqqād.[9] This engagement continued into the 1930s as the educated elite assumed positions of authority on boards of directors of radio and film companies. Dr. ʿAlī Pāshā Ibrāhīm, head of the medical college of the Egyptian University, was the Egyptian chairman of the supervisory board for radio. Medhat Assem, the son of one of the lawyers for the Egyptian side of the Dinshawai trial, was director of music programming. Ṭalʿat Ḥarb, who had established the first Egyptian owned and operated bank, also invested in theater and film, sent film technicians to Europe for training, and took a personal interest in the general operation of both enterprises. The involvement of moneyed and educated elites with the higher echelons of commercial entertainment (the biggest theaters, the national radio, etc.) colored these venues by carrying the interests, influence, and tastes of wealthy private patrons into the commercial and institutional domain.

At the same time this engagement brought performers, most of whom originated among the lower classes, with their *azjāl* (colloquial verses), their religious *inshād,* and their localized characters, into the domains of elites. In this way the "popular" became difficult to distinguish from what, in another time and place, would be called "art," "classical," "folk," or "religious." One result was the gradual emergence of the category "al-mūsīqá 'l-ʿarabiyya" discussed by El-Shawan, an unbounded place to which music from a variety of sources might be admitted through a process of indefinite consensus dependent on what the listeners of adult generations chose to accept as their heritage.

Audiences tended to be drawn from the professional and merchant classes. Patrons of theaters and music halls were usually middle- and upper middle-class men.

Music halls (*ṣālāt,* s. *ṣāla*) proliferated, especially in and around the Azbakiyya Garden.[10] The programs varied. For instance, Casino Shahrazād during the 1910s featured European female dancers. When the actor Najīb al-Rīḥānī became enamored of one of them, he applied for work and presented short Arabic sketches and plays there. Ultimately, in the environment of Casino Shahrazād, he developed his famous character Kishkish Bey.[11]

Upon entering these venues Umm Kulthūm juxtaposed herself with numerous well-established and successful female entertainers working in a variety of styles.[12] Tawḥīda (d. 1932) represented the older generation of women at the time. An immigrant of Syrian extraction, she had been the featured singer at the club Alf Layla wa-Layla since 1897. Before that she had been a singer and dancer in the Azbakiyya area. She married an Egyptian Greek who opened Alf Layla especially for her and, when he died, she inherited the club and continued to manage it herself. Like most other successful singers in this environment, Tawḥīda performed new songs written for her by well-known composers. She made few if any commercial recordings, which was unusual, but she retained a loyal, if relatively small, audience.

Tawḥīda's younger colleague, Munīra al-Mahdiyya (d. 1965), pioneered women's roles in musical theater. Munīra began her career singing in clubs during the early 1910s, notably Nuzhat al-Nufūs which was frequently closed by British authorities for the anti-imperialist character of performances there. She was one of relatively few women making commercial recordings before World War I. After Nuzhat al-Nufūs closed permanently, she was recruited by director ʿAzīz ʿĪd to perform in his musical theatrical productions. In about 1915 she joined the troupe headed by Salāma Ḥijāzī and, after the onset of his last illness, she sang the roles that had been written for him. She formed her own company and managed it for over ten years and performed new roles written especially for her, including Arabic adaptations of *Tosca, Carmen,* and *Madame Butterfly.* Her company frequently performed nationalistic songs that were summarily censored by the British, giving rise to the slogan, "Hawá 'l-ḥurriyya fī Masraḥ Munīra al-Mahdiyya" (There is love of freedom in the theater of Munīra al-Mahdiyya).[13]

Munīra managed her troupe and her business largely by herself. Occasionally she hired an artistic director to help but eventually rejected his advice and made her own decisions. Her theater and home became gathering places for many notable politicians and journalists: nationalist leader Saʿd Zaghlūl and Prime Minister Ḥusayn Rushdī were among her admirers. She was a strong personality and a great entertainer, on stage and off.

Fatḥiyya Aḥmad, a talented young singer and quiet personality, began her career in musical theater as a young girl in about 1910. She appeared with the well-known companies of Najīb al-Rīḥānī and Amīn Ṣidqī until 1925 when she decided to focus her energies on public concerts, saying she wanted greater control over her repertory. She became an important *muṭriba ʿalá takht* in the tradition of Almaẓ and others, a solo singer of precomposed Arabic songs with accompaniment by a small ensemble of two or more instruments called a *takht.* The *takht* usually included an *ʿūd, qānūn,* violin, and sometimes *riqq* and *nāy.*[14] During the nineteenth century such singers performed for private patrons by contract for specific events, *ālātiyya* (male singers) for gatherings of men and *ʿawālim* (female singers) for women, or, singing from behind a screen, for men. Performances typically featured groups of pieces, vocal and instrumental. Al-Khulaʿī described a proper performance by *ālātiyya* as follows: the performance should begin with a *bashraf* (a metrical instrumental piece of Turkish origin), then a series of metrical and nonmetrical songs that would include instrumental improvisation at some point. This suite, called a *waṣla* (pl., *waṣalāt*), was concluded by a lengthy and impressive vocal piece, often a *qaṣīda.*[15] Fatḥiyya was one of the singers who carried this practice into the twentieth century. She also made numerous commercial recordings and toured Syria and Palestine annually where she developed a large following.

She married a well-to-do landowner in the early 1920s and retired from the stage in 1929 to have children. When she returned several years later it was to appear regularly as the star singer in Badīʿa Maṣabnī's by-then famous music hall; Fatḥiyya also managed the hall when Badīʿa toured. Fatḥiyya performed regularly and well until the late 1940s when she began to suffer from a lengthy illness.

Badīʿa Maṣabnī's music hall was a model of its genre. Established in 1926 with cash accumulated from her career as an actress and dancer and with gifts from her male admirers, Ṣālat Badīʿa, as it was called, featured a variety program centered around a female singer. Badīʿa hired performers, trained her own dancers, and would argue, it was said, with anyone over a single piaster. She became an important patron of young singers and afforded first opportunities to such well-known stars as Ibrāhīm Ḥamūda, Farīd al-Aṭrash, Najāt ʿAlī, Layla Murād, and Nādira. Badīʿa established a weekly matinee for women only.[16] The success of her enterprise prompted many imitations, most of which closed after a year or two. Ṣālat Badīʿa remained a prominent feature of the entertainment world in Cairo until she retired from the business after World War II.[17]

Other singers, including Faṭma Qadrī, Faṭma Sirrī, Sayyid Darwīsh's favorite ingenue Ḥayāt Ṣabrī, the Syrian Mary Jubrān (also known as Mary Jamīla), and religious singer Sakīna Ḥasan worked regularly in Cairo. The theater district supported actresses such as ʿAzīza Amīr, Zaynab Ṣidqī, Faṭma Rushdī, and Rūz al-Yūsuf (who later founded the literary and political magazine of the same name), to name only a few. The city constantly attracted new performers including singers Malak Muḥammad in 1926, Layla Murād in 1927, Nādira in 1928 and the Aṭrash family with Asmahān and her brother Farīd al-Aṭrash in the late 1920s. Most of them were talented individuals from the lower classes for whom performance brought necessary income. Like Umm Kulthūm, they came to Cairo seeking opportunities for fame and fortune.[18]

The young Muḥammad ʿAbd al-Wahhāb was emerging as a gifted singer, composer, and handsome actor in the early 1920s. He was at once an accomplished exponent of historic practice and an advocate for the development of "modern" music. Extemporaneous invention over the text of a *qaṣīda* was still regarded as a fine art, but few performers were capable of it.[19] ʿAbd al-Wahhāb himself was one of the last masters of this art in Egypt. However, his compositions often juxtaposed disparate European and Arab styles.[20] Largely at his inspiration, precomposed pieces, instrumental and vocal, took on greater importance in the musical culture. Borrowing from

Western models, he introduced exact replication of a notated composition as an important standard in musical performance. He challenged the performance-generated practice central to Arab music, with its varied repetitions and audience involvement. Umm Kulthūm entered a musical world in which the composed piece occupied an increasingly important place.

Munīra al-Mahdiyya's nationalistic songs of the 1920s and the anti-British performances earlier at Nuzhat al-Nufūs formed part of the widespread public attitude of resistance to foreign rule that permeated city and countryside throughout the first quarter of the century. The attitude of resistance in turn informed much of the most highly regarded expressive culture. Whereas "unrestricted Westernisation" had reached a high point at the turn of the century among the middle and upper classes, afterward, "in days of mounting national pride the glorification of a foreign culture scarcely commended itself to the public. . . . Although the trend towards Westernisation was by no means reversed, too ostentatious an admiration for the ways of the West was out of fashion."[21]

A widely held view advocated the combination of essential features of Arab music with innovations learned from the West, along the lines espoused generally by writer Ṭāhā Ḥusayn: "not innovation but Renovation, the revitalisation of a great cultural heritage by bringing the best modes of Western thinking to bear on it, and this in emulation of forefathers who in the heyday of Islam, had drawn freely on the resources of Greek civilisation."[22] Musician Aḥmad Ṣidqī remarked that he saw no objection to the introduction of European musical instruments and "tactics" (*taktīk*), as long as the essential Eastern character (*ṭābiʿ*) of Arabic music was preserved, and his view was common.[23] In the opinion of a leading Egyptian music historian, the Egyptian people had been seeking a truly Egyptian musical art since the nineteenth century. The popularity of Turkish genres diminished while style perceived to be essentially Egyptian in character increased in demand.[24] One critic wrote in 1924, "Every leader in Egyptian creativity would like to free one hour of production and creation from the foreign stamp."[25]

The 1919 Revolution, the second nationalist uprising in Egypt within forty years, won support from people from many walks of life.[26] In the words of critic Kamāl al-Najmī, it "awakened the personality of the Egyptian people," and its impact, like that of the ʿUrabī Revolt and the Dinshawai Incident, reverberated for years after. For expressive culture, the 1919

Revolution and the attitudes that supported it advanced the growing pride in local Egyptian heritage. "The Egyptian people," al-Najmī wrote, "have their own way of singing. . . . Singers have overlooked this way for hundreds of years. The people lived, singing for themselves, while professional singers would sing for the sultans, princes and Mamlūks, then for the Ottoman Pāshās."[27]

Audiences enthusiastically supported work such as that of Munīra al-Mahdiyya. They appreciated Sayyid Darwīsh, whose songs and musical plays were often modeled on melodies and tales of working-class people, cast in local dialects, and aimed toward both resistance to the British in particular and an affirmation of the viability of local cultural and political precedents in general.[28]

Equally popular were *azjāl* (s., *zajal*), colloquial verse by such poets as ʿAbd Allāh al-Nadīm, Badīʿ Khayrī, and Bayram al-Tūnisī who relied heavily on Egyptian idioms, and the humor of comedian Najīb al-Rīḥānī's plays, all of which retained great popularity for many years. *Azjāl,* often dealing with current events, were published in newspapers and recited during entr'actes of plays.[29] The poetry, plays, and songs were rarely prescriptive of solutions nor did they usually advocate any particular action. They were not works of protest in this way. Rather, in sound and sentiment, they fostered Egyptians' value of their own culture and society, even as the performances used the devices of the West—the sound recording, the theater, and, later, the radio and the saxophone.

For example, in a simple tune with colloquial words, Sayyid Darwīsh's and Badīʿ Khayrī's characters sang

> The foreigner always blocks the way, and [then] the Egyptian next to him turns out to be a flop.

and

> Forget America, forget Europe, there is no [country] better than my country [Egypt].[30]

These characters linked musical theater with working-class Egyptians, for the characters were usually workers who spoke in realistic idioms—here, a skilled craftsman in the first instance and a sailor in the second. The melodies linked performers with the music familiar to lower-class Egyptians, in this case music that almost anyone could sing. They spread quickly throughout the Middle East. "My grandfather," a Lebanese-American friend recounted, "said these songs were sung in Jerusalem, in Tripoli, in Beirut within days of their release on records."

Al-Rīḥānī developed an overwhelmingly popular theatrical character from a stereotype of rural Egyptian life: Kishkish Bey, a village mayor and seemingly dull-witted peasant who consistently had the better of his urban counterparts. As Cachia described him, "at first sight naive and easily imposed upon, Kishkish Bey ultimately reveals himself as the mouthpiece of the people's sound and earthy sense," and "the genuine voice of Egypt's conscience."[31] Sayyid Darwīsh with his work songs and social criticism, Najīb al-Rīḥānī with his character Kishkish Bey, Zakariyyā Aḥmad and the *mashāyikh* with their familiar religious song all brought expressions viewed as authentically Egyptian quite literally to center stage and so constituted a musical expression of "Egypt for Egyptians." Notices in the press about these men rarely failed to mention their "essential Egyptianness" (*aṣāla*).[32] Their work with indigenous materials cut a path that others later followed.

The "Bedouin" Singer

When Umm Kulthūm arrived in Cairo, Zakariyyā Aḥmad and Ṣiddīq Aḥmad, the theatrical agent, arranged for her to sing during the intermissions of plays, initially those of ʿAlī al-Kassār for whom Zakariyyā was working at the time. Her performances moved from establishments in working-class quarters to the main theater district, where Ṣiddīq Aḥmad and Abū Zayd booked her into music halls such as Ṣālat Santī in Azbakiyya Garden and the smaller theaters.[33]

Composer Muḥammad al-Qaṣabjī first heard her at a music hall; he later recalled that "she sang old *adwār* [a genre of song] in the style of the *mūlid* [saint's day], accompanied by her father and a chorus made up of turbaned *mashāyikh*. She also sang new *ṭaqāṭīq* [light-hearted, strophic songs]."[34] Al-Qaṣabjī, like many others who saw her, was impressed by the fact that she wore a *kūfiyya* and *iqbāl,* a head cloth and circular cord holding it in place, associated (at least by Cairene concertgoers of the time) with Arab or "Bedouin" boys and men:

> She wears a black men's robe [*ʿabāʾa*] and wraps her head with a scarf held in place by a cord as the Arabs of the desert do. She appears in all her beauty on the stage surrounded by four *mashāyikh*, for Umm Kul-

> thūm is not accompanied in her singing by instrumentalists nor by the lamenting of the lute. . . . She sings standing with no instruments, trusting in the music of her matchless voice, the like of which no one has ever heard, whose tones from the highest to the lowest, have a resonance that move one.[35]

Historian and writer Ḥusayn Fawzī remembered her as

> a beautiful country girl, an exemplar of Islamic modesty. She stood among her family in the clothes of a Bedouin man; she sang vintage Egyptian music, consisting of religious songs. She raised her angelic voice calling forth in it the voices of the authentic religious Egyptian people.[36]

Her repertory was characterized by listeners as principally the religious songs of the *mashāyikh*.[37] But, as al-Qaṣabjī recalled, she also integrated light, currently popular new songs into her repertory, sometimes grudgingly, in response to the demands of audiences. These songs included some sophisticated *qaṣā'id* and *adwār* but relied increasingly upon light *ṭaqāṭīq*, strophic songs in colloquial Arabic, quickly composed and learned and suited to the six-minute sound recording.

The *ṭaqṭūqa* (pl. *ṭaqāṭīq*) was usually amorous, and both text and music were viewed as simple and straightforward. At the turn of the century, the *ṭaqṭūqa* was associated with female professional singers. The easy-to-sing strophes on light-hearted topics became widely popular and, after World War I, men took up the genre as well; the *ṭaqṭūqa* remained a vehicle for composition for decades.[38] Its simplicity rendered it declassé in the view of sophisticated listeners who complained of the proliferation of vapid, meaningless texts such as "Oh moonlight, oh moonlight, oh cutie, oh putter of henna on the bird's tail." More than other genres of song, *ṭaqāṭīq* became vehicles for expressions viewed as suggestive or even obscene.[39] Famous examples include "Close the curtains so the neighbors won't see" and "Who among you is my father?" Such texts were seen as signs of the declining quality of public entertainment.

While Umm Kulthūm's repertory at the time excluded obscenity, it was eclectic. In its inaugural review of her performances, the weekly magazine *al-Kashkūl* described and commented on one of her 1922 concerts:

> She devoted her first set to *qaṣā'id* in praise of the Prophet, God bless him and grant him peace! Then, in the second part, she appeared sing-

> ing various amatory *qaṣā'id* and other types of love songs. In the third segment, she embarked on singing "Kishkish-type" ditties called *ṭaqāṭīq*. Perhaps the reason for this mixture and lack of unity, this jumping from the Prophet's life to "The man I love, his whims make me crazy," and "Apples sweet and fine," is the desire to satisfy the people, to stoop to all of their passions and whims![40]

She acceded to audience requests and sought means to increase her own popularity. An appearance of grasping at straws resulted.

Early reviews of Umm Kulthūm stressed the power and raw talent of her voice, the closeness of her style of rendition to that of religious song as well as her "countrified" appearance. *Al-Masraḥ* praised

> the melodiousness of her voice, purity and clarity of articulation, excellence of delivery as well as the deep feeling for what she sings, for the most beautiful singing is that which moves the singer herself. And above all that she excels in her choice of poetry, ancient and modern, which is unparalleled in beauty of style and loftiness of imagery. Umm Kulthūm is a strong character who pours forth singing . . .[41]

However these talents were not enough by themselves:

> We do not deny Umm Kulthūm the strength of her voice and the unique resonance of its intonations, but in this I have come to consider her to be only a tradition-bound imitator. Beyond beauty of voice and melodiousness there is something called art. And Umm Kulthūm proceeds on the strength of natural ability only. This is really not sufficient.[42]

"Where are her innovations??" *Rūz al-Yūsuf* asked. "She is a religious singer, and this style of song has been present in Egypt for decades."[43]

Her appearance, to her critics, was too somber, her manners unsophisticated, her companions "crude peasants [*fallāḥīn*]." Reporters laughed over her countrified expressions. In one instance, Umm Kulthūm told a visiting friend from the Delta that her new apartment, could he imagine, cost 24 £E ($120) per month in rent, "and that's without meat!" The writer chuckled that she used the metaphor of meat, a valued commodity among the poor, for living expenses in general.[44] Another time, an angry "friend" repeated a story involving Umm Kulthūm's mother, who was so unaccustomed to electricity that she interrupted one of her daughter's gatherings to ask her loudly what kind of fools electricians were: How could she be expected to turn off the light when she could not reach the bulb in the ceiling?[45]

Umm Kulthūm's greatest success during these years came with commercial recording. She was recruited by Odeon Records in 1923 and introduced to Aḥmad Ṣabrī al-Najrīdī, a dentist from Ṭanṭa who composed songs as a hobby. He wrote most of the songs for her initial recordings. The company director, Albert Levi, also introduced her to Muḥammad al-Qaṣabjī, another composer on retainer to Odeon, who had written a song intended for Naʿīma al-Maṣriyya. Levi decided to give it to Umm Kulthūm instead, and the song became one of her first recordings.[46]

Odeon released fourteen of Umm Kulthūm's recordings between 1924 and 1926, all newly composed and none religious in theme. There were virtuosic *qaṣāʾid* on amatory themes such as "Mā lī Futint" (Oh why have I been charmed by your fatal glance) as well as simpler *ṭaqāṭīq* intended as light entertainment, for instance "Ana ʿala Keefak" (I am at your pleasure) and "il-Khalaaʿa" (Frivolity). The latter included the refrain, "Frivolity and coquetry are my creed, By God, I have always loved them." This text was perceived as inappropriate to Umm Kulthūm's apparent persona, insufficient to her vocal potential, and exemplary of the worst traits of the popular song of the day: hastily written, lacking in imagery and artistry, and morally reprehensible.[47]

A small issue of recordings was offered at a low price, which was the customary way of introducing a new singer to the commercial market. To the surprise of all concerned and despite criticism of some of the repertory, the first records sold extremely well and the company made a large profit. As Umm Kulthūm later explained, "Everyone from the countryside in whose home or at whose wedding I sang, bought my records in order to be able to say to his friends, 'Come and listen to the girl who sang at my daughter's wedding.'"[48]

> Compared to the Cairo singers, I was more well-known to the rural audience. When someone from the country came to Cairo it was natural that he would buy the recording of a singer whom he had heard and seen before. Of course, this was before the time of broadcasting; and many of the famous female singers from Cairo did not travel much to the country.[49]

Whereas singers and theatrical troupes appeared in provincial capitals or at the country estates of the wealthy, they rarely traveled to working-class and peasant weddings and community festivities as Umm Kulthūm did. Thus the recording stars of Cairo lacked the popular base outside the city that Umm Kulthūm had developed during her youth.[50]

Because of this success, Umm Kulthūm was able to obtain increasingly lucrative recording contracts. She released an average of four or five new recordings per year.[51] They sold so well that, with each batch, she was able to raise her fee. Her high fees attracted attention and a telling explanation from Albert Levi:

> In 1926 Odeon Records paid Umm Kulthūm 50 £E [$250] per recording. This is an exorbitant amount. No one has ever been paid so much. Salāma Ḥijāzī himself got no more than 20 £E [$100] per record and neither ʿAbd al-Ḥayy Ḥilmī nor Yūsuf al-Manyalāwī was paid such a high fee. In our day, Muḥammad ʿAbd al-Wahhāb takes 10 £E [$50] per record and Ṣāliḥ ʿAbd al-Ḥayy takes 12 £E [$60]. How is a company such as Odeon able to do this? Its director, M. Albert Levi, says that the number of Umm Kulthūm's records sold exceeded 15,000 in three months.[52]

Umm Kulthūm's recordings also helped her maintain a large audience outside the realm of middle-class concertgoing Egyptians.

The same year, Umm Kulthūm left Odeon for an even more lucrative offer from Gramophone Records, the Egyptian director of which was Manṣūr ʿAwaḍ. The recording contract Umm Kulthūm signed had important ramifications. It provided 80 £E ($400) per disc in 1926, rising to 100 £E ($500) in 1927, and an annual retainer of 2,000 £E ($10,000).[53] The retainer was unprecedented and extremely important, for it secured her income in a volatile economic market and allowed her to choose carefully among other opportunities. Like most artists, however, she continued to decline a contract based on percentage of sales until 1959 by which time she had suffered repeated losses under contracts for fixed fees. "No," she answered when offered a percentage of sales in 1926. "That would be a lot of trouble. Do I have time to run around inspecting your company's account books?"[54]

Her early recordings reflected the widening scope of her repertory as she sought to enlarge her audience and accommodate the tastes of the ticket-buying public. Although she later said that she always wanted to champion religious songs, she was clearly not content with the marginal position available to religious singers. Working in prestigious theaters was a priority. She sought "a combination that [would] work."[55]

She began to solicit lyrics and musical settings composed especially for her and, with help from poet Aḥmad Rāmī, to choose sections of older poems to be set to music. The texts of her old religious songs and *qaṣā'id* were usually in literary Arabic, removed from the language and sometimes from the understanding of most people. The texts of the popular *ṭaqāṭīq,* written quickly and usually intended for fast sale as commercial recordings, were often of low caliber. Umm Kulthūm requested that Rāmī write colloquial poetry of high quality for her to sing. She asked the young al-Qaṣabjī to set ten of Rāmī's texts to music; these were released as commercial recordings in late 1926. One of these, entitled "Akhadt Ṣootak min Ruuḥi," quickly became one of Umm Kulthūm's most popular songs.[56]

An Education in Music and Performance

It was clear to Umm Kulthūm almost immediately upon her arrival in Cairo that she would require some sort of help to develop her artistic skills and public presentation on stage. She began music lessons and related efforts to improve her career in the city. Although the Oriental Music Club offered lessons, women were not admitted in the mid-1920s, and Umm Kulthūm's father hired her teachers privately. As was the case for many of her colleagues, her teachers came from the ranks of her mentors.

Shortly after hearing her sing at Ṣālat Santī in 1924, the poet Aḥmad Rāmī began visiting her and bringing her books to read for pleasure. With Rāmī, Umm Kulthūm memorized poetry and learned some of the principles of its construction.[57]

Working with al-Najrīdī, the composer of her first songs for Odeon Records, Umm Kulthūm developed greater vocal flexibility and lightness of tone. Her father hired Maḥmūd Raḥmī of the Oriental Music Club to teach her to play the *'ūd* and to sing *muwashshaḥāt,* complex songs, command of which was supposed to hone one's skills in sophisticated Arabic melodic practice. Composers Ibrāhīm al-Qabbānī, Dāwūd Ḥusnī, and Muḥammad al-Qaṣabjī also instructed her on the *'ūd* and in composition.[58]

But her principal teacher was al-Shaykh Abū 'l-'Ilā Muḥammad. Abū 'l-'Ilā was well versed in the musical heritage of the *mashāyikh;* his repertory consisted of Arabic songs viewed as "classical," nineteenth-century *adwār,* especially those of 'Abduh al-Ḥāmūlī, and *muwashshaḥāt:*

> Al-Shaykh Abū 'l-'Ilā and other authentic Arab singers all drank from one spout: the book of al-Sayyid Muḥammad Shihāb al-Dīn (d. 1857) called *Safīnat Shihāb,* a collection of about 350 *muwashshaḥāt* in various modes and rhythms, representing an important segment of the musical art of the Arabs.[59]

Abū 'l-'Ilā taught Umm Kulthūm *qaṣā'id* and *adwār,* principles of composition and performance. He helped her improve her control over her powerful voice, increase its flexibility, and develop virtuosic skills with the particular goal of attaining "agreement" [*tawāfuq*] between the vocal sound and meaning of the text and the tune: he emphasized *taṣwīr al-ma'ná,* the heightening of the meaning of the text in the rendition of a song.

The "placement of words and melody in a single vessel" was the essence of his style and the central component of the style of the *mashāyikh* generally. This aesthetic marked "truly Arabic rendition." Using it, "al-Shaykh Abū 'l-'Ilā and a group of his contemporaries . . . freed [Egyptian song] from the jangle of Turkish and gypsy songs."[60]

In Umm Kulthūm he found a willing student. To illustrate the nature of his influence, she remarked that once while performing a *qaṣīda* she omitted a phrase when she realized that she did not understand its meaning and therefore could not sing it properly. "Al-Shaykh Abū 'l-'Ilā changed me," she said. "He taught me to understand the words before I learned the song and sang it."[61] He continued coaching her until his death in 1927.

By all accounts she was quick to learn. Observing her listening to music on a social occasion during the early 1920s, Muḥammad 'Abd al-Wahhāb remarked, "As was her custom, Umm Kulthūm memorized the first section simply by hearing it once." Dāwūd Ḥusnī's son recalled that "she learned very fast, having had all sorts of practice from learning the Qur'ān." During the early years in Cairo she said she practiced daily. Part of her training involved a daily regimen of sleep, diet, and exercise devised by her father who believed it would keep her in good health and maintain her voice. Her considerable willpower was trained to self-discipline and self-improvement which had great impact on her later success. A common view was that "among the most important components of the genius of Umm Kulthūm is her education, which she herself brought about through effort and perseverance."[62] The extent to which she pursued musical training distinguished her from most of her peers.

Her efforts extended into the realm of dress, manners, and language. As a promising young performer, Umm Kulthūm was invited into elite circles. In the ʿAbd al-Rāziq house, she had opportunities to observe the costume and bearing of wealthy and cosmopolitan Egyptian ladies. She became friendly with a few women from these families: Rūḥiyya al-Mahdī, the wife of the head of the Oriental Music Club, and, later, Samīra Abāẓa and her immediate family as well as the sister of Ḥijāzī Pāshā, governor of Cairo. She copied their manners in an attempt to avoid ridicule of her social origins. In matters of everyday living, many of the women of these families provided models of elegance and sophistication at home with Egyptian Muslim practice.[63]

She also broadened her horizons. At the ʿAbd al-Rāziq house in Cairo,

> you would see in one corner former ministers of state and political leaders discussing political issues and in their midst His Grace Maḥmūd Pāshā ʿAbd al-Rāziq. . . . A few steps away from them, another group convenes and in it are Dr. Ṭāhā Ḥusayn, Manṣūr Fahmī and others talking to al-Shaykh Muṣṭafá ʿAbd al-Rāziq arguing about a scholarly matter. . . . In another corner sits al-Ustādh ʿAlī ʿAbd al-Rāziq, around his scholars of religion. . . . In another al-Ustādh Ismāʿīl ʿAbd al-Rāziq with specialists in the arts of agriculture.[64]

These "informal networks or cliques of particular families" formed the basis for the political parties of the time and were hotbeds of nationalist discussion."[65] From one socioeconomic end to the other, Umm Kulthūm's world was colored by a wash of concern with local control and with resistance to domination by the foreign.

Along with ʿAbd al-Wahhāb and others she was invited to the musical salons of the Khayrat family and of Amīn al-Mahdī, the scion of a prestigious and wealthy family who was also an amateur *ʿūd* player of good reputation. All these elite families facilitated upward mobility for Umm Kulthūm, for Ṭāhā Ḥusayn, and other aspiring and promising young people. Their homes offered access to learning, influence, and power, and their invitations to perform opened doors to other homes and put the names of performers into circulation among wealthy and elite patrons.[66]

A Turning Point

Umm Kulthūm and her biographers refer to the season of 1926 as a turning point in her career—a time at which, in retrospect, her success was assured and failure or marginality avoided. Of course the "turn" did not simply happen but was effected by actions begun months and years earlier.

Choices that Umm Kulthūm made in musical and personal style took on consistent patterns by 1926. For a number of years she had been seeking attire that was both modest and appropriate to successful public performance in a cosmopolitan environment. Her style, apparently developed from models offered by the elite Muslim women of Cairo, involved fashionable dresses with sleeves, usually with a covered bodice, extending below her knees to whatever length was in vogue at the time. She sang increasing numbers of new love songs written and composed specifically for her by Aḥmad Rāmī and Muḥammad al-Qaṣabjī. By 1926 she was prepared to constitute a season completely with new songs and a few *qaṣā'id* of Abū 'l-ʿIlā. Gone were the cheap dresses, men's head coverings, and songs from celebrations of saints' days.

In the beginning of the fall season she made a single dramatic change that drew attention to the other shifts as though they had just occurred. She replaced her family of singers with a prestigious instrumental *takht.*[67]

Owing to her developing vocal and social abilities, Umm Kulthūm had reached the upper echelons of singers and was routinely compared with established stars Fatḥiyya Aḥmad and Munīra al-Mahdiyya.[68] One critic wrote that she was admired by artists and musicians and careful listeners, and that she never gave a concert but that the hall was filled. For those who valued Egyptian Arab tradition, Umm Kulthūm was a potentially great singer: "If, one day, Egypt was to be proud of its musical achievements, it would only take pride in two singers: Ṣāliḥ ʿAbd al-Ḥayy and Umm Kulthūm."[69]

But to others she remained an anachronism. Negative criticism reached its height in the spring of 1926, and the worst of it was directed toward her male accompanists. By this time, her vocal ability had overrun theirs, and their role in her performance was minimal. *Rūz al-Yūsuf* appraised the result as follows:

> I recently read the letter of an anonymous writer asking about the secret of the presence of [Umm Kulthūm's] turbaned orchestra and imploring the young singer to replace it with a *takht,* or, at least, if their presence is inevitable—to set them behind the curtain.
>
> People's talk about Umm Kulthūm's orchestra is not new. Ever since she appeared, surrounded by the honorable Shaykh Ibrāhīm and

> Khālid, and I don't know whom else also, people have asked what the secret is of their appearance with her on stage when they are not (and praise God who is the only One praised for what is unpleasant) a bit good looking or elegant so that we could count them as part of the scenery or decor. What need does the lady have for them when they have nothing to do except to yawn from one minute to another or for one of them to nod off not to waken until the clapping?[70]

The editor of *al-Masraḥ* wrote:

> As for her presentation on stage, the weakness there is our gentlemen "the shaykhs" who surround her, sometimes sitting like stone idols, sometimes stirring about. What is the use of their sitting around her so? Do you know anyone who does not complain about their presence around her in this contemptible manner which invites only disgust, especially when they raise their ugly voices roaring like the sound of a camel screaming in distress!!
>
> This appearance detracts half from Umm Kulthūm's success in a situation where these stone idols are unnecessary. What is even more ridiculous is that, when people clap for Umm Kulthūm, one of them stands up, in all his repulsiveness, smiling and saluting the audience. Have you ever seen anything so tasteless? Art is light of spirit, lively and fun. Such dull baseness spoils it.[71]

The few religious *qaṣā'id* and *tawāshīḥ* still sung by the family were viewed as inappropriate to the cosmopolitan audience, and she was seen as too serious in general:[72] "They say that she does not drink . . . smoke or indulge herself in any way, but the first requirement of a singer is that she be light-hearted and witty. These she may be, but she is also conceited and haughty."[73]

Audiences expected a female singer to be good-looking, possibly glamorous, and that she would attempt to beguile them with her wit, charm, or coquetry in one way or another. This view was affected to some extent by the stars of silent films and visiting performers from Europe and the United States. However, local social values played a role in standards of dress, styles of performance, and hospitality. Precedents set by Munīra, Fatḥiyya, and others informed public opinion, and Egyptian entertainers were not merely copies of their Western counterparts. Umm Kulthūm's stern artistry seemed out of place, and the uncompromising statement of moral righteousness made by the constant presence of the male members of her family began to be a liability more than an asset.

This spate of criticism may also have resulted from Umm Kulthūm's material success: she became a worthy target for Fatḥiyya and Munīra who could muster support among their journalistic friends. But Umm Kulthūm, despite her own inexperience and naïveté with regard to the press, by that time had her own partisans who could have rebutted the attacks (as they did on other occasions) had she been determined to persist in her course as a singer of religious *qaṣā'id*. It is possible that she was ready to hire a *takht* and allowed, even encouraged, the criticism in order to facilitate the move she wanted to make.[74] She in fact experienced a slackening of interest in her concerts. In June of 1926, *Rūz al-Yūsuf* noted that, "to induce people to come to her concerts, promoters have also billed 'the astonishing man who eats three hundred eggs, fifty pieces of bread, and ten jars of pickles,'" adding, "For shame! The name of Umm Kulthūm used to be enough."[75]

The effect of the new *takht* was dramatic. The musicians were impressive in themselves. They were among the most accomplished in Cairo, and their reputations at the time exceeded that of Umm Kulthūm herself. The *qānūn* player, Muḥammad al-ʿAqqād, was called the "shaykh" of instrumentalists. He had accompanied the famous singer ʿAbduh al-Ḥāmūlī in the nineteenth century and had made many successful recordings. He was a musician "of the old school," who had never accompanied a female singer before.[76]

Sāmī al-Shawwā, the violinist, was considered to be among the best in the Middle East and had long been a featured soloist. He had written books on teaching Arab music and, with Manṣūr ʿAwaḍ, established a music school in Cairo in 1906 that remained in existence until 1925. He toured extensively in the Middle East, and his engagements extended to Europe and North and South America. Like al-ʿAqqād, he was considered a classically trained musician.

The *ʿūd* player was Muḥammad al-Qaṣabjī. Although much younger than his colleagues, by 1926 he had composed songs for most of the famous singers in Cairo. He was viewed as a good composer and accomplished performer, noted for his interest in innovation. One of Umm Kulthūm's coaches, Maḥmūd Raḥmī, played *riqq* with the *takht*, and Umm Kulthūm's brother Khālid (newly outfitted in a European suit) remained in the new ensemble as an accompanimental singer (*mazhabgi*).[77]

More than their musical competence, these men signaled an important shift in style: the use of instrumentalists represented artistic sophistication, modernity and, to a lesser extent, secularity. By appearing on stages in Cairo with a *takht* Umm Kulthūm became a *muṭriba ʿalá takht* (a singer with a *takht*) rather than a *shaykha* or a *munshida*. This was an important distinction at the time, noted by virtually all of her critics.

It was important for her not only symbolically but artistically. On the one hand she moved herself from the ranks of community performers to the realm of professional artists associated with courts, theaters, and "classical Arabic tradition" populated in contemporary discourse by such luminaries as ʿAbduh al-Ḥāmūlī and Almaẓ, virtuosic singers of the nineteenth century. At the same time, the historical role of the *takht* allowed and in fact encouraged the manner of rendition familiar to Umm Kulthūm and her larger audience: the solo rendition of sophisticated texts shaped in relation to audience response calling for varied repetition of lines and supported by creative but unintrusive heterophonic accompaniment.

She searched the theater district for a music hall appropriate to her first public concert of the 1926–27 season, inquiring at first about Masraḥ Azbakiyya, the largest theater in Cairo, and finally settling on Dār al-Tamthīl al-ʿArabī where, not incidentally, Munīra al-Mahdiyya often performed.[78] From the beginning, the new *takht* was viewed by all except her most dedicated enemies as an overwhelming success:

> Umm Kulthūm, who gave her concerts of religious song . . . , who rolled up her sleeves and ate with her hands, today sings *ṭaqāṭīq* and *adwār* of love and passion, eats with a knife and fork, asks you "Comment ça va?" and answers "Bien, merci."
>
> She used to wear a yellow cloak over a *jallābiyya* made of cheap material without an element of taste in color or design. Now she dresses elegantly in good taste in crêpe de chine, designed in the latest style such that one is unable to distinguish between her and wealthy girls brought up wearing silk.
>
> Only one thing she was not able to change until recently and with difficulty: her orchestra of *mashāyikh,* although this change was written about by friends and enemies alike . . .[79]

An audience member who had seen Umm Kulthūm as a girl in al-Manṣūra wrote,

> The simple girl has been transformed into a graceful, elegant girl, flirtatious and charming. I saw her and I sat with her and I was astonished by her quick wit, her nice engaging conversation, and her female wickedness which fills the soul with bewilderment and surprise.[80]

By mid-season it was apparent that she had attained resounding acclaim. One reviewer wrote, "If we except Munīra al-Mahdiyya, Umm Kulthūm is without doubt the premiere singer in Egypt, male or female. Her voice has a perfect sound, especially after she advanced these new developments this season."[81]

How did she manage to fire her father? According to her later account, the *takht* was his idea and he simply retired. Even if this were so, the matter remained of finances and positions for himself and his son, and the solution was not as simple as she later made it seem.[82] Umm Kulthūm negotiated a contract with her father, Khālid, and Ṣabr, the terms of which provided that she keep half her income and the men divide the other half. Al-Shaykh Ibrāhīm was to pay the rent and the living expenses of the family. Together, she and her father bought 126 *faddān*s of land with their savings which, eventually, Khālid managed. Umm Kulthūm's father retired from performing but not from overseeing her business affairs, nor did he relinquish his position of general authority as the head of the family.[83]

1926 and Beyond

In the fall of 1926, *Rūz al-Yūsuf* wrote that Fatḥiyya Aḥmad and Umm Kulthūm would be competitors now that Umm Kulthūm had hired a *takht*,[84] and so they were. Fatḥiyya left Cairo for an extended trip to Syria almost immediately after Umm Kulthūm's season premiere. Her adversaries said that she would not come back until Umm Kulthūm failed. However, by February of 1927 she was planning her return, possessed of a new recording contract with Odeon (which firm Umm Kulthūm had left the year before), a new contract with the agent Ṣiddīq Aḥmad (with whom Umm Kulthūm had recently argued), and a contract to perform at Badīʿa Maṣabnī's *ṣāla*. She worked several nights a week for Badīʿa for the next six years, often advertising herself as a singer in the Turkish style. At this time she added the *mawwāl* to her repertory, a genre that Umm Kulthūm did not sing.[85] Fatḥiyya defined a new place for herself. At the end of the 1920s, when she retired from singing temporarily to have children, her audience eagerly awaited her return.

Following the success of Umm Kulthūm's new songs, Munīra al-Mahdiyya began to include them in her own concerts. In so doing she departed from her previous attitudes of ignoring Umm Kulthūm or regarding her with detached amusement. She essentially acknowledged that her young competitor could create musical fashion.[86]

In 1926, after Umm Kulthūm had experienced significant success, Munīra al-Mahdiyya used her friends in journalism to attack Umm Kulthūm's vulnerabilities. Her principal vehicle was ʿAbd al-Majīd Ḥilmī, editor of *al-Masraḥ*. He called into question Umm Kulthūm's image of pristine morality, and this attack hit its mark. He used the frequent presence of her clique of supporters in her home to assert that Umm Kulthūm must have married one of them, so often was he present and acting as a head of the household might. He persisted in developing this theme for several weeks, precipitating a major crisis when Umm Kulthūm's outraged father decided to take his family back to the village and end his daughter's career. Only the personal intervention of Amīn al-Mahdī stopped al-Shaykh Ibrāhīm, and Umm Kulthūm then announced publicly that she would receive no visitors at all in her home.[87] She also became profoundly wary of the press.

Munīra's fortunes declined in the late 1920s and she never recovered. The factors involved illuminate the world of entertainment of the time and influenced the decisions of performers, including Umm Kulthūm, for decades to come.

Unlike both Umm Kulthūm and Fatḥiyya, Munīra made little effort to learn new songs, skills, or styles. Beginning in about 1927, she was criticized as one who "has a beautiful voice, but [whose] songs are ordinary" and who "has a beautiful voice . . . but . . . does not know how to use it." Criticism gained momentum quickly and was augmented by reviewers from Syria and Palestine who compared her unfavorably to Fatḥiyya and Umm Kulthūm.[88]

This problem was viewed as soluble. Another of Munīra's afflictions was not. Theatrical productions were more expensive to stage than concerts. In the late 1920s, as the economy worsened, Munīra was left with a larger payroll than Fatḥiyya or Umm Kulthūm, the same or greater expenses for clothing, jewelry, and entertainment, and a dwindling audience of theatergoers. Managers of theatrical troupes were compelled to search far and wide for solutions.

One of Munīra's efforts ultimately became the most dramatic reason for her decline. She decided to stage the opera *Cleopatra* conceived by the always popular Sayyid Darwīsh, who had left it unfinished at his death. It had never been performed.[89] Munīra hired Muḥammad ʿAbd al-Wahhāb to finish the music and to appear opposite her in the leading role. It must have seemed a good idea at the time, for everyone loved Sayyid Darwīsh and ʿAbd al-Wahhāb was a rising young star.

Cleopatra opened on January 20, 1927. According to almost every critic, ʿAbd al-Wahhāb had written excellent songs, well suited to his voice, for himself, and short, simple, unimpressive pieces for Munīra. Despite her greater experience and more impressive presence, Munīra was upstaged and her weaknesses as a singer underlined. Some critics even accused ʿAbd al-Wahhāb of rewriting Sayyid Darwīsh's songs to his own advantage.[90] The first performance was fraught with technical difficulties, such as power failures that caused actors to be singing to the wrong character when the light returned. During the death scene, ʿAbd al-Wahhāb claimed that Munīra threw herself into his arms suddenly, her considerable weight knocking them both to the floor at the finale of the tragedy.[91] Afterward, either Munīra fired ʿAbd al-Wahhāb or he left in anger.

Apparently recalling her successes singing Salāma Ḥijāzī's roles, she decided to sing the male role herself and hired Fatḥiyya Aḥmad to sing Cleopatra. This production was not successful. She then returned to the female role and hired Ṣāliḥ ʿAbd al-Ḥayy to play Mark Antony, believing this accomplished but unassuming singer would draw an audience and not upstage her. He sang well, but as one observer remarked, he was not especially handsome and "looked funny" to the audience. The play in its third version failed as well.[92] Munīra contracted with Baidaphon Records to produce commercial recordings of the songs from *Cleopatra,* singing all of them herself. ʿAbd al-Wahhāb objected and said he would have them recorded by someone else, preferably Umm Kulthūm.[93] It is hard to imagine what else could have gone wrong.

After this, Munīra became ill time and again from vague complaints. Many believed she had been worn down by the humiliation and had become demoralized and depressed. She continued to perform; however, after 1928, the woman beloved of the entire theater district, whose popularity had been unassailable in the early 1920s, whom most writers viewed as much more beautiful and congenial than Umm Kulthūm, and who had shown herself to be an aggressive competitor, was no longer a potent force in commercial entertainment.

Journalists discussed *Cleopatra* for years, giving expression to the widely accepted notion that ʿAbd al-Wahhāb only wrote good music for himself.[94] Munīra's disaster was clearly one reason Umm Kulthūm did not agree to work with ʿAbd al-Wahhāb until 1964, and she was not alone. It is noteworthy that the females in his song films during the 1930s were usually aspiring young singers or actresses who rarely sang rather than established singing stars. ʿAbd al-Wahhāb later claimed there was a dearth of photogenic singers at the time but this history hardly supports his position.[95]

New singers continued to come to Cairo despite declining opportunities, and Umm Kulthūm began to be confronted with purposeful imitators.[96] Saniyya Ḥasanayn, brought to Cairo by Munīra and dressed in a "Bedouin" costume, imitated Umm Kulthūm's singing style and became known as the "new Souma," adopting Umm Kulthūm's nickname.[97] Najāt ʿAlī, known in 1930 for her "voice, preferred by many over her colleagues among the other young singers, for its strength and sweetness," moved about accompanied everywhere by her father, as had Umm Kulthūm. Like Umm Kulthūm, Najāt had a poet who wrote lyrics for her. She was observed to defer to her father with a gesture "exactly like Umm Kulthūm's."[98] Other singers, such as the very accomplished Laure Daccache, did not adopt Umm Kulthūm's demeanor but acknowledged that they had learned to sing by imitating her.

Pretty, photogenic Malak Muḥammad appeared in the theaters of Cairo in 1926 and sang concerts with a *takht.* She had a light voice described as "very expressive," indicating "an excellent future in the world of song."[99] When the Gramophone record company contracted to record Malak's songs with the company's *takht,* including Umm Kulthūm's famous *qānūn* player Muḥammad al-ʿAqqād, Umm Kulthūm insisted at the last minute that she required al-ʿAqqād in another city, and Malak had to settle for another player of less skill and reputation.[100]

Whether they desired it or not, the newcomers were subjected to comparison, usually unfavorable, with Umm Kulthūm, Fatḥiyya Aḥmad, and, occasionally, Munīra al-Mahdiyya. "The new singers and composers use only one range of the voice and produce short-lived songs," complained *Rūz al-Yūsuf* in 1932. Compared to Umm Kulthūm, whose stage presence was described as "elegant," "there is Khayriyya, Sihām, Najāt and even Nādira, [new singers] of whom the earth produces hundreds every day . . . who close their mouths or open them wide, whether appropriate to the singing or not," and who resembled, on the whole, "exhibits in the windows of shops in the Muskī and in dentists' offices."[101]

Commercial entertainment rode the wave of the cotton economy, and when it worsened in the late 1920s, so did the opportunities and income of entertainers. The season following the fiasco of *Cleopatra,* 1927–28, was bad for performers in all venues, and the economy continued to decline into the Great Depression of the 1930s. What began with depressed sales of tickets and recordings progressed to permanent closings of theaters, a dramatic decrease in the number of solo concerts, suspension of publication of theatrical magazines, and a major crisis in the recording industry to which the development of radio eventually contributed. A writer for *Rūz al-Yūsuf* noted that, of five major troupes to begin the season, only two were working steadily one month later.[102]

Umm Kulthūm had learned to protect herself financially by taking her fee "off the top," and, with continuing good record sales, her financial position was not at all bad. But the problem of poor attendance again threatened her reputation.[103] Touring, in the provincial cities of Egypt, North Africa, Syria, Palestine, or even the Americas was one strategy to find work and income. Umm Kulthūm was slow to do this, accepting an invitation to perform in Syria for the first time only in 1931. She did not always refuse earlier invitations but demanded very high fees, a tactic she often used when she did not want to accept an invitation. Her response prompted *Rūz al-Yūsuf* to opine that "the agent certainly cannot agree to that fee, especially not with the current drop in the value of Syrian currency these days. . . . We did not think Umm Kulthūm would refuse this offer after the past unlucky season when she did not earn 500 £E altogether!"[104]

Music halls, modeled on Badīʿa Maṣabnī's very successful example, proliferated, perhaps because of the character of the program. The *ṣāla* typically featured variety shows that included the singing or dancing of the owner-manager, two or three other dancers, a comedian or a "folk singer," (apparently someone who sang songs such as *mawāwīl* associated with working-class gatherings), occasionally a European troupe or a short Egyptian play, and a singing star. Such variety programs probably appealed to a larger audience than would any single star; the principal singer earned less money but also assumed less financial risk than in solo concerts.

Aspiring stars began careers in music halls. Nādira, a Syrian, began in the *ṣālāt* in early 1928 and became well established in the 1930s. She sang *qaṣā'id,* played the *ʿūd,* and composed. She attracted an impressive array of admirers and patrons including ʿAbbās Maḥmūd al-ʿAqqād who wrote poetry for her to sing, Dr. ʿAlī Pāshā Ibrāhīm (the head of the medical college), and violinist Sāmī al-Shawwā who, she said, "discovered her."[105] Layla Murād made her debut at Ṣālat Badīʿa in 1927 and later became a leading film star.[106]

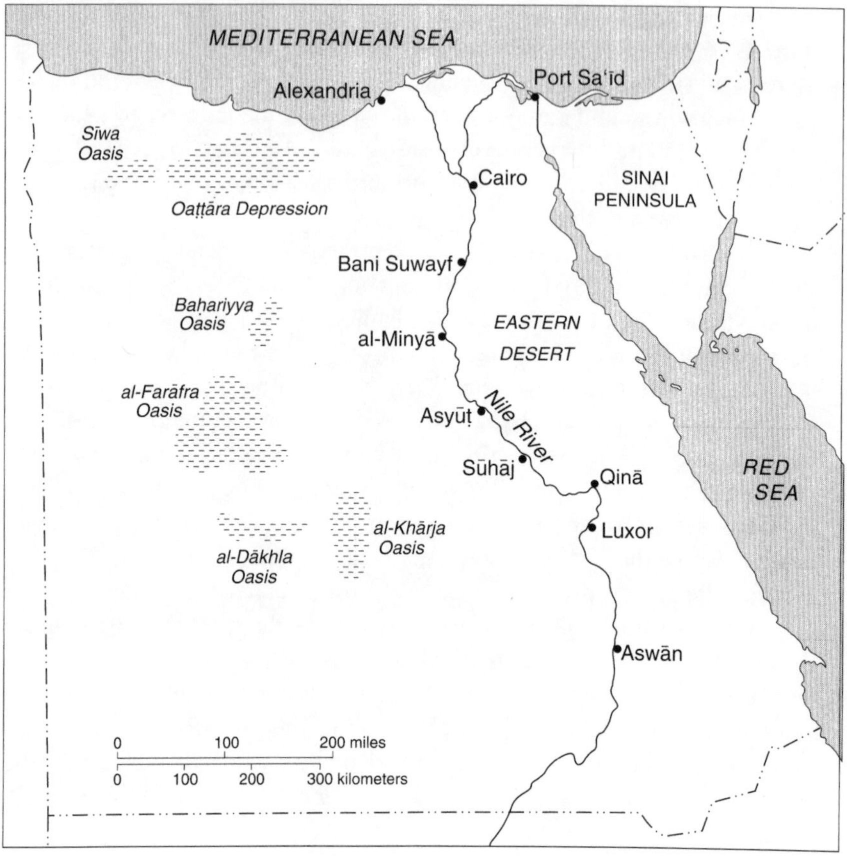

Map 3. Main cities of Egypt

Having struggled with Fatḥiyya's and Munīra's firm grip on popular musical styles, public presentation, ways of dealing with agents, theater owners, journalists, and record companies, Umm Kulthūm attained power such that newcomers had to deal with her own increasingly formidable presence in these institutions. Although her opportunities and income were limited by the worsening economy, she could still exercise choice in artistic direction and venues, owing largely to the financial arrangements she had made with her recording company and her increasing artistic authority. In the 1930s she went on to establish relationships with the new institutions of the entertainment business that would work to her advantage. She continued to work on developing a distinctive idiom. She sought to enlarge her audience. And she began to assert her strong will and newfound authority to arrange business in a manner that suited herself.

1. Umm Kulthūm as a young girl, dressed in her boy's coat and "Arab" head covering, with her brother Khālid (origin uncertain; copy in the archives of *Akhbār al-Yawm*).

2. The actress Rūz al-Yūsuf, 1926. (publicity picture).

3. Singer Fatḥiyya Aḥmad, 1927 (publicity picture, courtesy of Dār al-Hilāl).

4. Singer and music hall owner, Tawḥīda (publicity picture).

5. Munīra al-Mahdiyya, star of musical theater, costumed for a play, 1925 (publicity picture).

6. Dancer, comedienne, and music hall owner, Badīʿa Maṣabnī, 1925 (publicity picture).

7. Umm Kulthūm, ca. 1924 (publicity picture).

8. Muḥammad ʿAbd al-Wahhāb, ca. 1925 (publicity picture).

9. The singer and composer Zakariyya Aḥmad and actor Ḥāmīd Mursī, 1925 (publicity picture).

10. Religious singer ʿAlī al-Qaṣabjī, father of Muḥammad al-Qaṣabji (publicity picture).

11. Virtuoso violinist, Sāmī al-Shawwā (publicity picture).

12. Egyptian Director of Gramophone Records, Manṣūr ʿAwaḍ (publicity picture).

13. Composer Muḥammad al-Qaṣabjī (publicity picture).

14. Religious singer ʿAlī Maḥmūd (publicity picture, courtesy of Dār al-Hilāl).

Four

Media, Style, and Idiom

Her Majesty the Queen expressed her admiration for Miss Umm Kulthūm's choice of her dress which combined modesty and elegance in flawless taste and good selection. And what circulated in the discussion about the concert included the remark of His Excellence the great Shaykh al-Marāghī that he noticed that Miss Umm Kulthūm is the only one of all the singers who does not speak ungrammatical Arabic in her delivery and meticulously respects what is set down . . . in fundamentals of grammar, pronunciation and declension. His Grace Ḥāfiẓ ʿAfīfī Pāshā, our ambassador in London, responded saying that goes back to the fact that she memorized the *Qurʾān* . . .[1]

Taking a Direction in Style

As Umm Kulthūm's musical decisions infused an internal consistency into her new repertory, the direction it took fed the romantic current of expressive culture. The song texts she chose, the plots of the new films she made, tended to be individualistic, removed from the circumstances of daily life and elevated in tone. Lyrics were focused upon the self and often expressed exaggerated emotions, notably extreme desolation at the departure of the beloved.

The romantic style she helped to build was founded on past practices. Her songs were typically sophisticated vocal genres such as the *dawr* or highly virtuosic monologues. Based on a love poem, usually in colloquial Arabic and cast in one of the poetic meters, the *dawr* consisted of two principal sections, the *madhhab* or opening section sung by a chorus and the *dawr,* a longer solo section. Muḥammad ʿUthmān, al-Shaykh al-Maslūb, and ʿAbduh al-Ḥāmūlī developed the genre in Egypt during the nineteenth century from a musically simple song, both sections having the same melody, into a virtuosic piece. The solo singer reiterated the lines of the *dawr* section in many different ways and improvised, sometimes on the syllable "ah" in alternation with the *madhhab.*[2] The result was a new piece based on historic principles of musical composition and performed almost exclusively by professional singers owing to its technical difficulty and the requirements of virtuosic display. Its lifespan extended from the mid-nineteenth century through the 1930s.

Originally a theater piece, the monologue was conceived as a lengthy, solo expression of the thoughts and emotions of a single character, somewhat like the aria of European opera to which Egyptians occasionally compared it. Musical phrases were typically extended and virtuosic. The language was usually colloquial Arabic. Neither text nor music had a predetermined form, and the piece was through-composed.[3] Muḥammad al-Qaṣabjī was its chief exponent during the 1920s and 1930s.

Al-Qaṣabjī and Aḥmad Rāmī dominated Umm Kulthūm's repertory during the late 1920s and 1930s. Her musical romanticism was collectively fashioned by al-Qaṣabjī's syncretic compositions for Aḥmad Rāmī's distinctly romantic texts and her own virtuosic renditions. The monologue "In Kunt Asaamiḥ" by al-Qaṣabjī and Rāmī typified Umm Kulthūm's new style: it was virtuosic, dramatic, romantic, and innovative in genre and melodic line.

Fundamental to historically Arabic compositional practice was the establishment of music in a certain melodic mode, or *maqām*. Following the classical model, a performer would begin on any tone of the *maqām* but usually in the lower range, ascend gradually in stepwise motion, emphasize one or more intervals characteristic of the *maqām*, modulate to compatible *maqāmāt*, and end on the *darajat al-rukūz* or "final" of the original *maqām*. While popular exceptions existed, in general this description reflected early-twentieth-century creative practice.

Al-Qaṣabjī's opening in "In Kunt Asaamiḥ" immediately bespeaks its innovation. The instrumental introduction, leaps in the melodic line occurring near the beginning of the song, and triadic arpeggio-like passages in vocal lines and accompaniment conveyed the "new" character to the listener. Whereas older performance practice utilized short and familiar instrumental pieces (*dūlāb*, pl. *dawālīb*) or *taqāsīm* to orient the listener (and the singer) to the mode, "In Kunt Asaamiḥ" featured a newly composed introduction. By the mid-1930s, these almost completely replaced the *dawālīb* as well as introductory vocal improvisations (*layālī*) (see example 1). Al-Qaṣabjī began the vocal line with leaps and triads that spanned the ambitus of the piece quickly, within a single phrase. The difference between this opening and older practice may be seen by comparing the beginning

Example 1. Introduction and first line from "In Kunt Asaamiḥ"

of "In Kunt Asaamiḥ" with that of the *qaṣīda* "Afdīhi in Ḥafiẓ al-Hawá," performed during the same period but which followed older models (see example 2).[4] These features of "In Kunt Asaamiḥ" were heard as "modern" (*ḥadīth*) or "advanced" (*mutaṭawwir*), and as "operatic" (*ūbirālī*) by those familiar with European classical music. The song aptly illustrates the creativity common in Umm Kulthūm's repertory. Specific melodic gestures were borrowed from European music and from Arab genres such as the *dawr* which the monologue resembled in its virtuosity. The result was at once musically new and familiar.

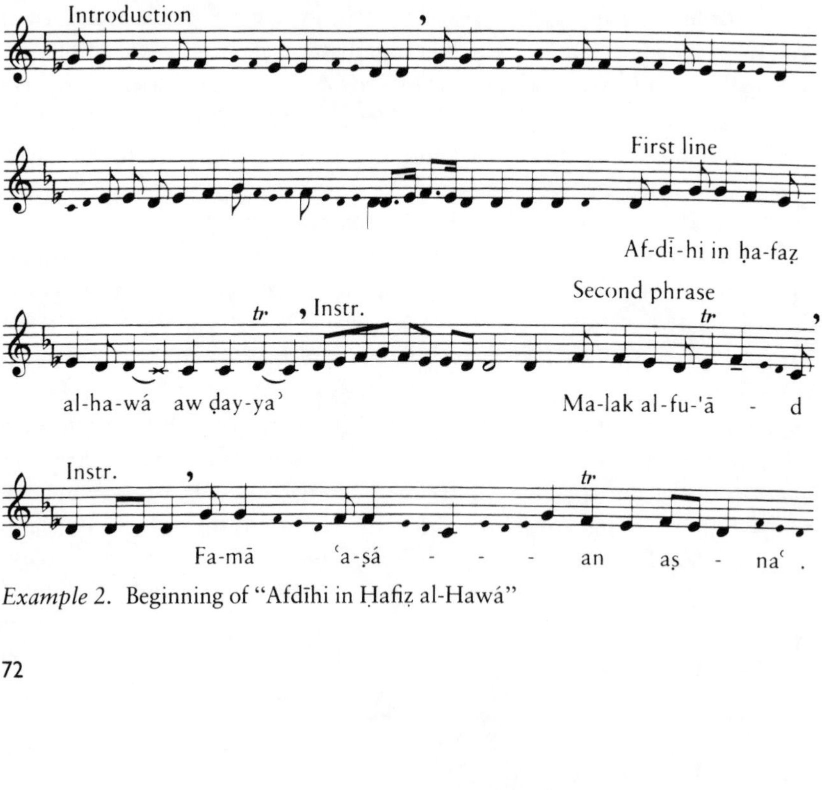

Example 2. Beginning of "Afdīhi in Ḥafiẓ al-Hawá"

Upon its release the recording sold unprecedented numbers of copies.[5] With "In Kunt Asaamiḥ," Umm Kulthūm adopted the monologue as her own. The texts were usually serious, dramatic, and sad, themes that pervaded her repertory long after the monologue had given way to other genres. Her love texts resembled torch songs, speaking of love lost, love denied, and a woman left alone. The theme of love lost remained constant in Umm Kulthūm's songs even as the tone, language, and genre of the songs changed. It became a metaphor for other losses and anticipation of events that did not occur. Lyrics expressed the anguish of the struggling individual (later understood as the struggling society) but, as critics were quick to point out, offered no solutions, urged no action.

Rāmī's text for "In Kunt Asaamiḥ" manifests his romantic character. Its vocabulary was familiar, but its syntax lay closer to romantic poetry than to colloquial expression, as the first three lines illustrate:

In kunt asaamiḥ w-ansa 'l-asiyya,
ma-akhlaṣṣ ʿumri min loom ʿenayya.

Dabbil gufunha kutr il-nuwaaḥ,
faaḍit shu'unha wi-nomha raaḥ.

Tiqul-li insa wa-shfaq ʿalayya,
w-aahii ansa yiṣʿab ʿalayya.

(If I were to forgive and forget my grief,
all my life I would not finish with the reproach of my eyes.

Their eyelids withered from much weeping,
their tears flowed, their sleep is gone.

They tell me "Forget, and have pity on me,"
but I cannot do that at all.)

These lines depend on an image from classical Arabic literature, that of love entering the body through the eye, hence the "reproach" of the long-suffering eye if its grief were to be forgiven or forgotten. The focal point of the text is the individual tormented by the emotions of love lost.

Whereas most poetry and even its often poorer relation, the song lyric, differ by definition from ordinary speech, the style exemplified in "In Kunt Asaamiḥ" contrasts markedly with the colloquial texts (*azjāl*) popular at approximately the same time.[6] Umm Kulthūm sang a few of these in the 1920s and 1930s, and they were widely circulated, published in newspapers, and sung by many performers. The contemporary *zajal,* terse and colloquial, put down roots in conversational speech and local imagery. For example, Badīʿ Khayrī wrote the following *zajal* recorded by Umm Kulthūm in 1930:

Huwwa da yikhallaṣ min Allah,
Il-qawi yidill il-ḍaʿiif
Ḥatta yibkhal bil-miṭalla
Shiʾ wi-law duun il-ṭafiif.
Lee da kullu, miin yiquul lu
Ithidi w-khalliik laṭiif.

Qalbi kullima tiqwa naaru
W-inta fiih, yitkhaaf ʿalayk
Ḥadd yiḥraq bass daaru,
Iwʿa tigniiha b-iideek
Liin shwayya, mush ʿalayya
Kun ʿala ruuḥak raʾiif
Ṣuun ḥalawtak min shaqawtak
Ithidi w-khalliik laṭiif.

(Does this make you exempt from the judgment of God?
The strong humbles the weak?!
And is even stingy with the slightest visit?!
Why all of this? Who will say
Behave yourself and be nice!

As the fire in my heart grows stronger,
with you in it, I fear for you.
Does anyone light a fire in his own house?
Don't do it with your own hands!
Be a little gentler, not only to me,
Be kind to yourself.
Save your sweetness from your naughtiness!
Behave yourself, and be nice!)

Words and expressions such as "lee da kullu" (why all of this?), "iwʿa" (don't [you dare]), and "khalliik laṭiif" (be nice) pepper everyday speech. The rhyme created by "ḥalawtak" and "shaqawtak" used in close succession is a much-loved feature of colloquial poetry and song as well as jokes and conversation.

The language of "In Kunt Asaamiḥ," unlike that of "Huwwa da Yikhallaṣ min Allah," emphasized the distance between artist and audience while at the same time engaging listeners with commonly felt emotions. The compositional style reinforced this distance. The monologue was a solo that focused attention on the emotional outpouring and musical artistry of the virtuosic singer.

The heavy reliance on virtuosic display manifest in Umm Kulthūm's repertory suggests a means by which she may have developed the unassailable stage presence that came to characterize her persona. Provided a song was interesting to the listeners, the virtuosity of the piece itself and, in the case of the monologue, the absence of the responding chorus would have virtually precluded one potential for audience rowdiness known to Umm Kulthūm in the 1920s: singing along. The emotional impact of the monologue text and its theatrical aim emphasized the solo singer's role as the center of attention. By-products of the through-composed structure, virtuosic display and absence of chorus were to rivet respectful and appreciative attention on the singer. This was the position Umm Kulthūm cultivated.

Al-Qaṣabjī's leaps and triadic figures updated song style without necessarily removing it from the realm of *maqāmāt*. In "Khaaṣamatni," he used leaps to fashion an innovative introductory line and an arpeggio as a virtuosic flourish late in the song. Much of the remainder of the composition proceeded in stepwise motion. Similarly, "Ya Nigm" (1935) included triadic phrases in the *maqām nahāwand,* which can be made to resemble the Western minor mode, alongside substantial sections in *ṣabā* that were largely stepwise in motion and less susceptible to the addition of triadic motives. He added harmonic accompaniments to some of the monologues, and this too was viewed as an innovation. Few songs were thoroughly harmonized; chords appeared as one of a variety of new musical gestures incorporated in songs. These techniques developed primarily in the musical thinking of al-Qaṣabjī and Muḥammad ʿAbd al-Wahhāb and had great impact on Arab music.[7]

Al-Qaṣabjī's experimental style for Umm Kulthūm culminated in his songs for the film *Nashīd al-Amal,* many of which included harmonized passages and heavy orchestration. At about the same time he wrote "Ya-lli Gafeet, Irḥam Ḥaali" for her—a song that was uncharacteristic of her repertory, especially in the domination of the voice by the instruments. Al-Qaṣabjī on several occasions grounded pieces in the Western modalities of major and minor. He became increasingly interested in European models. He wrote some operatic songs for Asmahān and offered to write a song for Umm Kulthūm that would be completely based on European compositional principles.[8] She declined and, after *Nashīd al-Amal,* sang fewer of al-

Qaṣabjī's songs and turned to the neoclassical works of al-Sunbāṭī and the Egyptian colloquial style of Zakariyyā Aḥmad.

Musical experimentation yielded the *ughniyya,* literally "song," a new genre in the 1930s. It probably emerged as a consequence of continued work with the *dawr, ṭaqṭūqa,* and monologue.[9] Eventually distinctions blurred and listeners resorted to *ughniyya* to designate the unique structures, often featuring some sort of internal repetition such as a refrain, virtuosity, colloquial language, and musical invention. These formed an increasingly important part of Umm Kulthūm's repertory during the rest of her career.

Triadic passages, melodic leaps, occasional harmonization, and a few new instruments such as the violoncello were virtually the only Western features of Umm Kulthūm's repertory in a musical world where Muḥammad ʿAbd al-Wahhāb, with his extensive borrowings from Western musics, was a potent force. Both Riyāḍ al-Sunbāṭī and Zakariyyā Aḥmad updated Arab compositional principles with rhythmic, instrumental, or melodic innovations. "Maa lak ya Qalbi," for instance, allowed a traditional style of rendition (including responses by men's chorus in the second half of the *dawr*) alongside an innovative instrumental section that featured a pizzicato bass line accompanying the nāy.[10]

Virtuosic display, as a marker of individuality, was a musical constituent of the romantic expressive culture that characterized the late 1920s and 1930s. Individualism, escapism, exoticism, and romanticization of the past distinguished songs, plays, poetry, novels, and films. This romantic spirit pervaded literary works and commercial popular culture. Poet M. M. Badawi offered the dedication from ʿAlī Maḥmūd Ṭāhā's first volume of verse, published in 1934, as an example: "To those enamoured of longing for the unknown, those lost on the sea of life, those who haunt the deserted shore."[11] The denouements in fiction and in the new commercial films that attracted great attention typically depended on sudden good fortune or divine intervention. The romantic poetry of Ibrāhīm Nājī, Aḥmad Rāmī, and ʿAbbās al-ʿAqqād, published in newspapers as well as in books, became very popular. The vast majority of texts sung by Umm Kulthūm during the 1930s were written by Rāmī.[12]

Sentimental stories in ornate language, such as the work of Muṣṭafá Luṭfī al-Manfalūṭī, became well known, and Umm Kulthūm spoke of al-Manfalūṭī as one of her favorite authors. Salma Jayyusi explained al-Manfalūṭī's work as offering "what was needed in literature at that time, namely reading material of a kind that could satisfy the emotional promptings of a society newly awakened to its own handicaps and disappointments, which would forge a link with the West and, at the same time, keep a firm grasp of the best in the old traditions both in style and ideas."[13]

The disappointments in Egypt were economic and political, resulting from the Great Depression, colonial governance, and the failure of local initiatives to gain, retain, and effectively use power. As they had in the past, these problems pervaded the society. As the 1930s wore on, the developing crisis in Palestine fueled debates over the issue of national sovereignty. The question of Palestine brought to the fore the need to assert or defend Islam as a socioreligious alternative and the matter of the proper role of the West in the Middle East. Charles Smith characterized intellectual attitudes during the 1930s as infused with a longing for what was perceived as the stability and order of the past, for village life and the authority provided by Islam in light of the uncertainty of the present.[14] This attitude itself was, of course, not without romantic overtones.

Discussions of political issues took place in newspapers and magazines. Political lectures were suggested as programs for the national radio station established in 1934 alongside songs and plays performed over the airwaves. The broader issue of independence from foreign authority remained a topic of concern, and the attendant evaluation of culture found its way into many venues.

"Modernization" persisted as an important problematic. The motivations encapsulated by the motto "Egypt for Egyptians" and the indigenous expression associated with it met at every turn the desire to make use of the tools of the powerful "other." The manifestations of the contradiction marked Egyptian culture and continually redefined what was Egyptian.

These issues engaged every committee at the international Conference on Arab Music held in Cairo in 1932, in the form of such questions as "Should Arab ensembles adopt the violoncello and string bass?" "Can the *maqāmāt* be harmonized?" and "Should Arab music abolish quarter-tones?" The willingness of some Egyptian delegates to adopt European musical practices alarmed a number of Europeans who advocated "preservation" of the indigenous heritage, which attitude, in turn, outraged those Egyptians who saw Westernization as the path to cultural accomplishment or who believed themselves, not European scholars, to be the appropriate judges of what constituted their musical heritage and how it might best be perpetuated.[15]

Answers to these questions were being formulated on the ground daily by musicians themselves performing in Egyptian society. ʿAbd al-Wahhāb's and al-Qaṣabjī's work offer examples, and many others were produced. Some of Dāwūd Ḥusnī's *ṭaqāṭīq* lay so close to the style of Egyptian folk song that they entered that repertory and lost their association with the great composer. His innovative *adwār,* like al-Qaṣabjī's monologues, drew from Arabic, Turkish, and European sources.

Muḥammad al-Qaṣabjī was and still is regarded as the teacher of a generation of composers and musicians. A number of the musical inventions popularized in the monologues remained as permanent features of Umm Kulthūm's repertory and those of other singers as well. Nor were pieces with these features always viewed as Westernized. They were more commonly characterized as imaginative, sophisticated, or "intercultural," different from both Western and Arab music. An elderly engineer eloquently clarified the difference:

> Muḥammad al-Qaṣabjī is more Westernized from *your* point of view. . . . I beg to differ. . . . He is trying to apply *methods* of Western music. He tried to apply harmony and counterpoint. . . . [al-Sunbāṭī] was more influenced by Western *feeling* in music, though not applying the methods. That's why *you* think he's more Oriental.[16]

Many of al-Qaṣabjī's compositions have passed into the *turāth* or heritage of Arab music.

Serious musicians, those who engaged most of their time and energy in the production of musical culture, used many materials. They grasped symbols of cultural accomplishment from the West—instruments, chords, melodic passages, and visual trappings such as evening gowns, tuxedos, and bowing to acknowledge the applause that displaced the compliments traditionally called out to the performer—and introduced these into compositions and performances that also bore traces of past Egyptian-Arab practice. The lives of the artistic products of this process varied greatly in length; some existed for only a single performance while others lived on for decades and, by the 1990s, had passed into the *turāth.*

Producing Concerts

In the 1930s, Umm Kulthūm launched seasons of public concerts that were also broadcast on the first Thursday night of each month.[17] These were undoubtedly her best-known venture, and she continued them almost every season of her career until 1973. They became important and distinctive social events.

The experience of listening to her concerts when she initiated them in the 1930s seems not to have carried the impact recalled by listeners in later years. They began as more ordinary entertainment events enjoyed (or not) by ticket buyers. A writer complaining in 1927 about Umm Kulthūm's lateness wrote one of the most complete contemporary descriptions of her early concerts available:

> Al-Sayyida Umm Kulthūm, on the evening of the first day of the feast, was singing with her *takht* at Buffet Luna Park in Miṣr Jadīda. She was supposed to start singing at 9:30, but at 10:30 al-Sayyida had just arrived. Finally, after clapping of protest from the audience and after the organizer of the concert invited Aḥmad Fatḥī al-Fār to appear on the stage to make the audience laugh until Umm Kulthūm arrived—after all of that, she arrived with her entourage and her *takht*. Then the members of the *takht* insisted on readying their instruments and setting them up until 11:15. Then Umm Kulthūm began singing. At 12:45 she announced the conclusion after having sung two *qaṣā'id* only. Al-Sayyida Umm Kulthūm takes 30 £E [$150] for each concert. Does she think that she entertained the audience at the Luna Park concert 30 £E worth? And does she think that, if she continues to arrive at concerts at 10:30 and then sings for an hour and rests half an hour and then sings for another hour and then goes home with her entourage and friends and friends of friends—does she think that she will find people in the future who will pay 20 piasters [$1.00] for the sake of listening to her sing for two hours? [18]

The writer's complaint resonates with other, less colorful descriptions of Umm Kulthūm's practices. She along with her accompanists were characteristically meticulous musicians and accomplished performers who took whatever time they deemed necessary to prepare to perform. Sometimes she appeared at more than one place in the same evening and was late arriving at the second place. Throughout her public life Umm Kulthūm manifested a strength of character, sometimes read as arrogance, that helped enable her to do what she wanted. In fact it is likely that she cultivated this attitude for the same reason that she demanded high fees: it helped her assert her primacy over other entertainers. It was an occasionally annoying, but recognizable and effective, means of establishing status.

She typically devoted most of an evening to two or three *qaṣā'id,* singing shorter pieces later, if time permitted.[19] Each song occupied thirty to sixty minutes and was followed by a lengthy break. The program was rarely announced in advance. This format remained constant until the late 1960s.

The following schedule of concerts, for September of 1928, was not unusual:

Tuesday	September 6	Masraḥ Ramsīs	Cairo
Thursday	September 8	Masraḥ Ramsīs	Cairo
Friday	September 9	Casino Zinziniyyā	Alexandria
Saturday	September 10	Casino Bātīnāj	Cairo
Sunday	September 11	Buffet Luna Park	Cairo
Tuesday	September 13	Masraḥ Ramsīs	Cairo
Sunday	September 18	Casino Ḥadā'iq al-Qubba	Cairo
Tuesday	September 20	Masraḥ Ramsīs	Cairo

Singers whose main enterprise was public concerts worked three to five nights per week. Five appearances a week were a great many, and singers whose financial situation permitted a choice opted for fewer.[20] Umm Kulthūm's pattern of appearances stabilized in the late 1920s and early 1930s. She usually arranged a series of concerts at the same theater on the same two days a week, usually Thursday and Saturday, and her contracts for these performances eventually covered an entire season. At some point during the mid-1930s, she began to offer season tickets for her regular concerts.[21]

She started producing her own concerts in the early 1930s without an intermediary agent. She negotiated theater rental and presumably arranged for advertisements as well. This was not an unusual task for a female star. It involved greater risks, but, for a popular performer, resulted in greater profits and more control over all aspects of the performance. Extraordinary expenses for such ventures were occasionally underwritten by silent investors interested in sharing the profits. Assuming responsibility for her own productions was regarded as yet another sign of Umm Kulthūm's accomplishment. *Rūz al-Yūsuf* described her partnership for a concert season in terms that highlighted her social identity and background: "It is a long way between a plain singer and a singer who is the owner of a music hall . . . and then a female partner of a Christian who the *mashāyikh* of al-Sinbillawayn . . . would say drinks wine and eats pork!"[22]

Reports of a performance in the provincial city of al-Minyā, to which dozens of performers had traveled following the entourage of King Fu'ād, illustrate the sometimes calamitous nature of commercial entertainment that prompted Umm Kulthūm and others to assume as much control as possible over the conditions of their appearances. In al-Minyā, Badīʿa Maṣabnī obtained the prime location which was the Palace Theater, then the only one in town. Sharing the stage with Samḥa al-Baghdādī, she filled the hall.[23] Umm Kulthūm, performing in a nearby tent, fared worse. An early report claimed that

> No one bought Umm Kulthūm's tickets, so the agent had to reduce the price to 5 piasters ($0.25). When Umm Kulthūm saw the small number of people and the dirtiness of the place, she refused to sing. The audience complained of the loss of 5 piasters, and one man took his chair home with him . . . she went home cursing al-Minyā and its people.
>
> So it was said. But we received the following letter from Tawfīq Fatḥ Allāh who was present. He said the audience was large and waited two hours for Umm Kulthūm. She had scarcely arrived with her *takht* when two men came and attempted to take her away forcibly. It was said that a man of high position wanted to hear her . . .[24]

Private parties, weddings, and holidays augmented seasons of public concerts for most singers. Umm Kulthūm, ʿAbd al-Wahhāb, and most of the others sang for royal birthdays, benefit parties, religious celebrations, and parties in honor of such people as Egypt's first pilot. A program for the second night of the Muslim holiday of ʿĪd al-Fiṭr in 1932, for instance, brought together Umm Kulthūm, Najīb al-Rīḥānī playing Kishkish Bey, and thirty Parisian dancers.[25] Umm Kulthūm, among others, appeared on the program of the final concert of the 1932 Cairo Conference on Arab Music, singing Abū ʾl-ʿIlā's *qaṣīda,* "Afdīhi in Ḥafiẓ al-Hawá." Al-ʿAqqād's *takht* also appeared, Sāmī al-Shawwā played violin *taqāsīm,* and the theatrical troupes of Faṭma Rushdī and Yūsuf Wahbī performed excerpts from two of Aḥmad Shawqī's plays in a program clearly intended to exhibit neoclassical Arab art.

While performers usually accepted invitations from diverse patrons and sometimes opposing interest groups, some performers were sought by particular groups. Egyptian feminist Hudá Shaʿrāwī, for instance, hired masters of distinctively Arab arts for her benefits. Such patrons identified Umm Kulthūm, the young ʿAbd al-Wahhāb when he sang neoclassical *qaṣāʾid,* al-Riḥānī, and Zakariyyā Aḥmad as suitable choices.

Umm Kulthūm was approached with offers of roles in theatrical productions at least twice. Playwright Ḥamīd al-Ṣaʿīdī, who had heard her sing at a village wedding, recommended her for the leading role in a new play. The offer was met with flat refusal, apparently because her father believed theater to be of little value. In the second instance, negotiations proceeded for a time with Umm Kulthūm making difficult demands: she wanted the high fee of 300 £E ($1,500) per month and the right to choose the composer and the leading man. Agreement was never reached.[26]

Negotiating the Public

The commercial environment presented many more problems for entertainers than did private homes or community gatherings: audiences were larger, usually unknown to the performer, alcoholic beverages were frequently sold in music halls, and patrons were occasionally rowdy. In some cases, singers employed by the music halls were required to socialize or drink alcohol with patrons.[27] The public venue presented difficulties that Umm Kulthūm experienced even in villages, where as a young girl she had to confront a drunken man wielding a gun.[28] Such incidents were occasional but afflicted virtually every singer, and each was compelled to find a way to deal with them.

For a time, Umm Kulthūm's family retained a comedian whose role was to tell jokes in order to assuage a difficult audience. A more common tactic, and one that Umm Kulthūm adopted, was to bring along one's own supporters who would loudly voice approval of the singer and contend with problematic patrons themselves. Journalists sarcastically referred to these groups, whose behavior was sometimes ostentatious in the extreme, as the singer's "court" or *balāṭ*.

A *balāṭ* usually comprised middle- or upper middle-class men, disposed to frequent the theater district, who took a special interest in a particular singer.[29] A critic described Umm Kulthūm's *balāṭ* as "the obvious troupe who walk behind her wherever she goes and sit in front of her or at her feet wherever she sits. . . . Whoever wants to may attend a concert of hers and count the people yelling and making a display of their admiration or simply count those sitting in the first row."[30] The *balāṭ* became a minor institution in the theaters and music halls of Cairo, and entertainers' contracts sometimes included clauses providing for the accommodation of this group free of charge. Occasionally, they formed part of the entertainment: "When each musical *waṣla* ended, al-Muʿallim Dabsha would blow loud kisses to each of his table companions, and then to everyone else he recognized in the room."[31]

The *balāṭ* offered moral and material support. Manṣūr ʿAwaḍ promoted Umm Kulthūm's records. ʿAlī Bey al-Barūdī taught her to use bank accounts. When *al-Masraḥ* alleged an illicit relationship between Umm Kulthūm and Ḥifnī al-Darīnī, three of the men sued on her behalf for slander.[32] No one, asserted *Rūz al-Yūsuf,* not even Cleopatra, got more adoration or service from her clique than Umm Kulthūm.[33]

Sometimes their assertive good will caused problems. Having signed an agreement with an agent to perform exclusively for him in Alexandria, Umm Kulthūm found that three of her supporters had made other arrangements on their own authority, which almost cost her the money involved in the penalty clause of the first contract.[34] If they annoyed other patrons and occasionally Umm Kulthūm herself, these men outraged her father who found their behavior well outside reasonable bounds. He objected when their advice and decisions took precedence over his own. However, both father and daughter tolerated and even encouraged the *balāṭ* most of the time, as did other entertainers, for the support they could offer, the occasional favor, the influence that some could wield, and the impressively large presence a singer could manage when accompanied by such a group to performances.

Most entertainers' careers also depended on less obvious connections with influential Egyptians who supplied prestige of association, entrée into elite circles, and the occasional accommodation for a problem. Umm Kulthūm cultivated relationships with such people.[35] These friends and admirers met her at home under the watchful eyes of her brother and father. Her salon eventually attracted artists, musicians, literati, and journalists.[36] Through her connections she met public figures including Ṭalʿat Ḥarb, poets Aḥmad Shawqī and ʿAbbās Maḥmūd al-ʿAqqād, politicians Makram ʿUbayd, Fatḥ Allāh Barakāt, Ḥasan ʿAfīfī and Fikrī Abāẓa, who served as her lawyer in one instance.[37] Umm Kulthūm benefited from her associations with these people in material ways through favors and invitations. From them she also learned to speak intelligently about politics and literature and to emulate the manners of elite society.

Her public interactions in the 1920s had shown Umm Kulthūm to be unsophisticated and naïve, qualities that were duly noted. She also appeared to be imperious, demanding, and hard to please. *Rūz al-Yūsuf* reported that, after singing at a benefit concert sponsored by the Egyptian feminist leader Hudá Shaʿrāwī, both Umm Kulthūm and ʿAbd al-Wahhāb were invited to select a gift from the bazaar of handmade goods available for sale. ʿAbd al-Wahhāb chose something, thanked his employer and went home. Umm Kulthūm, after much deliberation, said there was nothing she liked.[38] She remembered grievances and carried grudges. A set of cartoons entitled "How to Win Her Heart" depicted ways to gain the favor of Umm Kulthūm and other entertainers, which included giving gifts of money and jewelry, exhibiting strength of character, playing hard-to-get, writing poetry and passionate expressions, and, for Umm Kulthūm, demonstrating "admiration and servitude."[39]

Wary of the press and mindful of the need to control her public image, Umm Kulthūm developed a corpus of statements about herself that reflected the way in which she wanted to be regarded and remembered. Like many other public figures, she developed answers for questions she was commonly asked. There were topics, usually relating to her personal life, about which she simply refused to speak. For years she declined to give broadcast interviews, saying that stars of singing were not necessarily stars of speaking; when she finally permitted such an interview, after hearing the tape she asked that the interview be redone, which it was. The first one, she said, was just a rehearsal.[40] She exerted herself to control her public image and carefully chose the persons who had access to her. She cultivated friendships with selected journalists and, by 1931, she had "begun to understand the role of journalists" who earlier had "attacked her as no singer or actress was attacked before."[41]

Recordings and Radio

Commercial media provided the means for dissemination of an increasingly large portion of Umm Kulthūm's performances. During the 1920s and 1930s she established relationships with the available media—commercial recording, film, and, most important, radio—that would serve her well for decades.

Her contract with Gramophone in 1926 helped establish her position at the top of the commercial market, for she argued successfully that since she was paid the most she was also the best singer and should continue to be paid the most and to obtain various other benefits and privileges. Attracted by another lucrative offer, Umm Kulthūm returned to Odeon Records in 1930 and, shortly thereafter, the market for sound recordings declined precipitously.[42] The new radio stations made it possible for listeners to request records to be played without buying the recordings, and film captured the imagination of the classes with money to spend on entertainment. As a result Umm Kulthūm was able to record only small numbers of specified songs, already proven to be popular in live broadcasts or films. This situation persisted throughout the 1940s when she recorded for Cairophon Records: scarcity of shellac and complications in shipping and communications caused by World War II severely limited the number of recordings made.[43] Commercial recording as a medium was on the decline.

After a relatively inconspicuous beginning, radio became extremely popular throughout the Arab world, easily replacing the phonograph as the predominant medium of popular culture. Although less glamorous than the new films, radio ultimately assumed a role of vast importance in the society.

During the 1920s, entrepreneurs and other interested individuals opened a number of private radio stations in Cairo. Artists including ʿAliyya Ḥusayn and her children, Farīd and Āmāl al-Aṭrash (later known as Asmahān), classical pianist Medhat Assem, and others performed over the airwaves of these stations, said to number over one hundred. The stations fought for survival, many disappeared, and, in the early 1930s, the Egyptian government itself decided to harness this resource and established Egyptian Radio.[44]

Egyptian Radio was administered by Englishmen.[45] An Egyptian advisory board was headed by Dr. ʿAlī Pāshā Ibrāhīm of the medical college and included ʿAbd al-Ḥamīd Pāshā Badawī, Dr. Ḥāfiẓ Pāshā ʿAfīfī, and Sayyid Bey Luṭfī. They hired Medhat Assem to plan music programming.[46]

Its first program was broadcast on May 31, 1934. The popularity of radio grew quickly. The costs of equipment and licensing posed little problem for many listeners for, like the gramophone player and, later, the cassette tape player, radios were shared and appeared in public places such as groceries and coffeehouses.[47] By the late 1930s Medhat Assem's music programming built Egyptian Radio into what El-Shawan described as a "central institution in Egypt's musical life": "It was one of the main sources of patronage for solo vocalists, composers, song-text writers and performance groups. In addition, [it] was the major vehicle for the dissemination of music, superseding the record and film industries, as well as live performances."[48]

Whereas the local radio stations that had come and gone in Cairo during the 1920s had very little impact on the society, the new, stronger national station with its live performances by major stars became widely popular. This precipitated a crisis for the recording companies, as the radio replaced the phonograph in public places, and would-be record buyers began to request their favorites from the radio station. Recording companies such as Odeon sought compensation from broadcasting for the use of the company's records.[49]

When Medhat Assem recruited Umm Kulthūm for Egyptian Radio in 1934, she hesitated as she did not like performing without an audience. He overcame her objections by pointing out that Muḥammad ʿAbd al-Wahhāb had already signed a contract. Not to allow advantage to her competitor, she signed one too. Both artists insisted on singing only on Thursday nights, and Assem divided the programs between them. They were each paid 25 £E (about $130) per broadcast consisting of two songs. Both contracts stipulated that if any other singer were paid more, their pay would be raised immediately to the same level. Assem generally treated Umm Kulthūm and ʿAbd al-Wahhāb equally and better than any other singers "because they were very good and more popular than the others."[50] Assem and Egyptian Radio contributed to increasing their reach throughout Egyptian culture.

In 1937, Umm Kulthūm contracted to have some of her concerts broadcast live. The first took place on January 7, at the Opera House.[51] With these, she garnered three or four hours of prime time once every month during the season. The financial arrangements for the broadcasts illustrate the tenacity and assurance she had learned to bring to business dealings. Umm Kulthūm received half of the proceeds of each concert in addition to her 50 £E ($253) fixed fee from broadcasting; Egyptian Radio got the remaining proceeds, amounting to 50 £E per broadcast in 1937. Thus Umm Kulthūm made 100 £E ($506) and the radio station, after paying the singer's fee, made no money at all. From the performer's standpoint this arrangement was, artistically and commercially, excellent. Unsurprisingly the station wanted to cancel the agreement for the following season. Umm Kulthūm countered by raising her fee. Broadcasting authorities refused. She offered to "compromise" by accepting her old fee and half of the concert receipts provided that amount was not less than 40 £E. At this point the negotiators for broadcasting wanted to return to the conditions of the previous contract, but she was adamant and managed to improve what was already a good bargain.

Live broadcasts were ultimately of much more value to Umm Kulthūm's place in Egyptian culture than to her purse: they institutionalized the first Thursday of every month as "Umm Kulthūm Night" for the vast majority of Egyptians. They were the activity for which she was probably most famous and which had the greatest impact on musical and social life in the Middle East. Like commercial recordings but with much greater effect, radio broadcasting enabled Umm Kulthūm to reach the large audience of Egyptians who either could not afford or did not choose to attend public concerts. The broadcasts became occasions for invitations and gatherings around the nearest radio to listen to the evening's program and socialize with friends and relatives. People who did not like Umm Kulthūm found themselves listening anyway because, for the many who did, these concerts were paramount. The "first Thursday" broadcasts became major events in Egyptian popular culture until Umm Kulthūm's final illness brought them to a halt thirty-six years later.[52] Radio became the principal medium through which Umm Kulthūm reached her audience.

Making Films

In the early 1930s, a main event in entertainment was the development of talking films: "The fashion today is cinema and its future in Egypt . . . and the roles of singers," wrote *Rūz al-Yūsuf.*[53] Attempts at local filmmaking began in 1917, but floundered until 1925 when banker Ṭalʿat Ḥarb established his film company along the same organizational lines as his bank: utilizing exclusively Egyptian personnel, some of whom he sent to Europe for specialized training. The first Egyptian-made film appeared in 1926. In 1929, there were fifty cinema halls in Cairo and the provincial capitals.[54] The first Egyptian song film, *Unshūdat al-Fu'ād* starring Nādira, was released in 1932, and others soon followed. Muḥammad ʿAbd al-Wahhāb's first film, *Al-Ward al-Bayḍā'*, was released in 1933 with veteran actress Dawlat Abyaḍ as the costar. Munīra al-Mahdiyya's *Ghandūra* opened in October of 1935. Faṭma Sirrī and Fatḥiyya Aḥmad began planning films, as did Badīʿa Maṣabnī who eventually produced a song and dance revue on film.[55] Although production costs were generally high, if financing could be arranged, the profits and fees were much greater than those from any other source. New stars vied for roles, many coming from Syria and Palestine as they had in years past for parts in musical theater. Recollecting the early 1930s, singer Najāt ʿAlī later remarked that "real fame and money came from films."[56]

Umm Kulthūm became interested in film shortly after ʿAbd al-Wahhāb's *Al-Ward al-Bayḍā'* and, in 1935, began work on *Widād,* the first of her six films. At the outset she said that she wanted a historical plot about Arabs or Bedouin. Fikrī Abāẓa was her choice to write the script and ʿAbd al-Wahhāb to be her costar. A longtime audience member and admirer, Būlus Ḥannā Pāshā, offered to underwrite the costs.[57]

Widād was produced by Studio Miṣr, Ṭalʿat Ḥarb's company; in the end Aḥmad Rāmī wrote the script based on a story invented by Umm Kulthūm about the loyalty of a singing slave girl to her master, set in thirteenth-century Egypt. The male leading roles were played by Aḥmad ʿAllām and Munassá Fahmī, veteran stars of Arabic theater in Cairo, as were most of the other actors and actresses with whom she worked.[58] The film was well received and became the first Egyptian entry in an international film festival in London.[59]

Immediately upon the completion of *Widād,* Umm Kulthūm began *Nashīd al-Amal* (Song of hope), a film about an aspiring singer in modern Cairo. One of the songs, an anthem entitled "The University Song," appealed to students to rouse themselves for the sake of progress and country. At the time student demonstrations for responsible local government and independence from Britain occurred regularly and forcefully.[60] Appearing as it did at the height of student involvement in national politics, this song became immediately popular. Her third film, *Danānīr,* opened in September of 1940.

The films bore many of the same characteristics as her other repertory of the time. The subjects of the film plots were romantic, featuring glamorous characters, exotic settings from Arab history, clearly drawn lines of good and evil, and resolutions in favor of goodness and justice. In each film Umm Kulthūm cultivated sophistication and respectability in her public image and styled herself as an elegant exponent of Egyptian romanticism. The style of cinematography and direction followed the models provided by contemporary Hollywood studios. As film critic Samīr Farīd wrote, the words of some of the songs, for example "The University Song," were the only distinctively Egyptian features of the films.[61] The music was, for the most part, virtuosic, provided by the same composers who wrote her concert and recording repertory.

The film songs tended to take unique shapes, *ughniyyāt,* rather than *qaṣāʾid* or *adwār,* although these were heard in films as well. Most of the songs were short; the timing of the films offered little if any opportunity for the sort of musical elaboration that was an essential characteristic of Umm Kulthūm's live performances. The short song itself was nothing new to the singer or to the audience, as both were already accustomed to commercial recordings and broadcast performances constrained by time limitations. Some of the film songs passed into Umm Kulthūm's concert repertory, and a few became very popular. Transferred to the concert setting, Umm Kulthūm elaborated on the short compositions in a manner similar to her other renditions.

In other regions of the world, short film songs often accompanied by Western orchestras exerted a strong influence on popular musical styles generally, replacing lengthy improvisatory performances with three to four minute precomposed songs and introducing new instruments and ensembles. This impact was felt in Egypt as well. But, in Umm Kulthūm's case, the effect of film songs was mitigated by her monthly broadcast concerts featuring the older style of improvisatory performance. These reached more listeners than the films and balanced the style of film song.

In imitation of their Western counterparts, composers for many Egyptian song films utilized relatively large orchestras that included European instruments. Virtually every composer experimented with new instruments and ensembles in music for films. Such invention was hardly new, for Muḥammad ʿAbd al-Wahhāb tried the accordion, slide guitar, violoncello, string bass, clarinet, saxophone, and various percussion instruments in the 1920s, and orchestras for musical theater followed European models. However, the film orchestras effectively lodged large ensembles in Egyptian musical ears. Using a stage orchestra became almost unavoidable.

Background music for the films might be newly composed or borrowed, often from Western popular and classical repertories. While, in other films, nineteenth-century European symphonic themes were juxtaposed with both tango music from recent Hollywood productions and new Arabic songs in what was heard as jarring succession, Umm Kulthūm's films featured a minimum of borrowed background music, and the worst problems of blending and transition seem to have been successfully solved.

Umm Kulthūm demanded and received great control over the films, regardless of her lack of acting experience. Her contract for *Widād* gave her final approval of the music and the right to participate in all aspects of the production. She stipulated that the plot must remain within the bounds of "*al-taqālīd al-sharqiyya,*" or "Eastern traditions."[62] She received guaranteed compensation in the amount of 1,000 £E ($5,050) plus 40 percent of the profits of the film after expenses provided that they not exceed 7,000 £E ($35,385). Considering her inexperience, the contract granted her astounding authority and constituted additional evidence that, by 1935, Umm Kulthūm had attained a position of considerable influence in the entertainment world of Egypt.

She was completely frank about her inexperience, saying in a promotional interview that she had been totally unaware of the requirements of filming: "I have never in my life been an actress nor do I have knowledge of the fundamentals of acting and its various forms. My concern was simply to understand my role and the feelings required in various circumstances—to imagine myself 'Widād.'"[63] Her speech made use of and also reinforced the higher status of the singer compared to the actress.

In five of the six films she ultimately made, Umm Kulthūm portrayed singers, which relieved some of the difficulty for one who had never acted. In *Widād, Danānīr,* and, later, *Sallāma,* she played virtuous and heroic singing slave girls from various periods in Arab history. In *ʿĀyida,* she played a village girl who grew up to star in an Arabic version of the opera *Aida,* and she portrayed an aspiring modern singer in *Nashīd al-Amal.* Umm Kulthūm believed that songs fit more easily and appropriately into stories about singers, and she was partial to settings from Arab history: "There is sincerity in the character of the slave girl and modesty is a mark of historical heroines," she said. "I value sincerity and I incline to modesty."[64] Her roles typically featured virtuous women who overcame trouble.

Film was the preferred medium of the singer believed to be Umm Kulthūm's most formidable competitor at the time, Asmahān. Asmahān was a beautiful woman with a well-controlled voice, flexible over a wide range of pitch. Victor Saḥḥāb credits her with creating a vocal style that integrated Arab and European aesthetics in virtuosic performances.[65] However, her talent and capabilities were offset by her determination not to sing in concerts or in music halls, nor for money under any circumstances other than filmmaking. Unlike Umm Kulthūm, who practically required an audience, Asmahān, by her own admission, hated the demands and feared the criticism of the live audience.[66] This attitude placed her at a disadvantage: Asmahān's professional visibility was not maintained in the manner that Umm Kulthūm's was.

On the other hand, Asmahān's private life may have been entirely too visible for the Egyptian public. Having returned to her homeland, Jabal Druze, for a marriage to her cousin, the Druze Prince Ḥasan, she returned to Egypt and involved herself with well-known journalist Muḥammad al-Tābiʿī, banker Ṭalʿat Ḥarb, the powerful head of the king's administrative council Aḥmad Ḥasanayn, film director Aḥmad Badr Khān, and her best friend's exhusband Aḥmad Sālim, all in a period of less than four years.[67] During World War II, she was allegedly involved with a British intelligence operation in Jabal Druze. All of these activities and the attendant jealousies and offenses led to various legal and professional problems, including revocation of her Egyptian residence visa, a battle for custody of her daughter, and declining interest in her as an entertainer. She suffered from the comparison to Umm Kulthūm's by then well-cultivated image of respectability.

From her varied enterprises Umm Kulthūm, as well as other successful commercial musicians, made enormous amounts of money.[68] In the 1920s, a singer's income usually derived from public concerts, private parties, and recordings. Fees for public concerts and recordings were agreed upon in written contracts and remained more or less constant over a season. Payment for private parties, on the other hand, fluctuated dramatically.

On the evening of her first concert with a *takht* in October of 1926, Umm Kulthūm made 50 £E ($250), which she considered a huge sum. Subsequent concerts that fall, arranged by the same agent in the same theater, brought 35 £E ($175) each.[69] Umm Kulthūm paid her accompanists. The agent paid theater rent and advertising costs and took whatever remained as profit.[70] Umm Kulthūm paid her *takht* about 9 £E ($45) per night, leaving 26 £E ($130) for her own fee. She sang at least twice a week regularly, yielding a monthly income of over 200 £E ($1,000) from this single source.

This was an amount sought by peers and attained by few. Fatḥiyya Aḥmad, regarded as a well-paid star in theater, reportedly received 60 £E ($300) per month in 1924–25 and 120 £E ($600) per month the following season. For that, she probably worked three to five nights per week. Thus, even if her pay doubled for the 1926–27 season, she would have made less for each performance than Umm Kulthūm. The other well-known singers in Cairo made less than Fatḥiyya, Umm Kulthūm, and Munīra al-Mahdiyya.[71]

Umm Kulthūm consistently used money, fees, and contracts to constitute herself as "the best" singer in her domain. By the end of the 1930s, she was very wealthy and a well-established star of film and radio as well as concerts and commercial recordings. She and ʿAbd al-Wahhāb, referred to as the "high priests" of the business in 1935,[72] claimed more money and attention than did anyone else.

Her purchase of land in 1926, however, indicated that she wanted not only wealth but the upward mobility and "solid worth" afforded by landownership.[73] By acquiring land, she improved the position of her family, at least locally, in a way that wealth alone would not have done.

Developing an Idiom

Where had Umm Kulthūm's extensive vocal training brought her? She worked successfully in the virtuosic, romantic style developed by al-Qaṣabjī, ʿAbd al-Wahhāb, and, to a lesser extent, Zakariyyā Aḥmad in his innovative *ṭaqāṭīq* and *adwār*, often on texts by Rāmī. However, other singers mastered the style as well—certainly Asmahān, and also Layla Murād, Najāt ʿAlī, Laure Daccache, and Nādira, for instance.[74]

Umm Kulthūm's background, training, and inclinations led to a distinctive idiom of rendition that localized her as an Egyptian singer competent in classical Arabic song. Using her native abilities as a foundation, she cultivated what the cognoscenti of Cairo taught as historically Arab aesthetics of singing and joined them to the style of the *mashāyikh*. She applied that sound to new compositions, and it became one of her signal accomplishments.

The basis of her idiom was meticulously controlled vocal power. Volume, as Jihad Racy wrote, was an indispensable attribute for a successful singer in early twentieth-century performances.[75] The circumstances of performance, often without microphones and sometimes outdoors before relatively large audiences who expected to be able to hear the songs, simply required power. But in addition listeners greatly appreciated a strong voice; this was distinguished from the voice that was simply "too loud," a quality considered crude.

The concept of vocal strength also involved the ability to sing well over long periods of time, throughout evenings of entertainment that would extend for hours. Singers who were unable to project good renditions throughout an evening were criticized as weak.[76]

Umm Kulthūm's voice was equally strong and its quality uniform from the lower to the upper ends of its register, without noticeable shifts or breaks. A typical appreciation of this characteristic was written by Muḥammad ʿAbd al-Wahhāb: "Her voice did not change to the ear as a result of the change of range in any composition. The low [pitches] were like the middle [and] like the high in control, and she sustained the color which characterized her voice."[77] Clarity of pitch and tone was important throughout the range.[78] Coloristic change between head or chest resonance or into falsetto was used for ornamentation, to draw attention to a particular point in the text or melodic line. To shift from chest resonance to head resonance in the course of the simple delivery of a phrase was a weakness or fault.

While voices were acknowledged to have different characters, the concepts of soprano, alto, tenor, and bass were not relevant to Arabic song. Especially during the early years of the century, when repertories formerly associated with either male or female singers came to be performed by men and women alike, the upper range of a man's voice and the lower of a woman's often overlapped by as much as ten or eleven pitches.

Umm Kulthūm's voice extended over two octaves in the 1930s. Although her precise range is hard to ascertain owing in part to the poor technical quality of some of her early recordings, her voice was always strong in its lower register, descending approximately to G below middle C and, until about 1955, she could easily reach a high g.

She developed breath control. Listeners appreciated the long phrase, whether extensive textually, musically, or both. Singers were admonished to develop capability for long phrases and advised on postures to avoid that hampered good breathing and clear pronunciation.[79]

Coloristic change served as a decorative device and a manifestation of virtuosity as well; in Umm Kulthūm's idiom, it effected *taṣwīr al-maʿnâ* for, unlike the addition of ornaments or melodic invention, coloristic shifts could often be accomplished without disrupting the articulation of the text. Indeed, vocal colors could be closely linked to the sound and meaning of the text where melodic invention was viewed as devoid of meaning or textual connection. For Egyptian listeners this distinction separated text oriented Egyptian singing from the more melodically motivated Turkish style or European bel canto, and linked Umm Kulthūm's singing to that of the *mashāyikh*.

Among the colors recognized by Egyptian listeners as beautiful and important in good performances was *baḥḥa,* literally "hoarseness." According to al-Khulaʿī, *baḥḥa* was at once a quality of the weak or tired voice, and a natural color in the strong and healthy voice, in which case it was beautiful.[80] In the best examples, *baḥḥa* involved allowing the voice to break on a high pitch, usually to enhance emotional climaxes in the text.

Good singers also commanded a wide range of frontal resonances, from relatively open resonance off facial bones to more close nasality produced by resonating simultaneously in the mouth and nose. Nasal resonance needed to be properly placed: critics distinguished the sweet nasality (variously referred to as *ghunna,* or, in colloquial Egyptian, *khanaafa*) from "singing through the nose" (*khunna*) which was viewed as unpleasant and musically uncultivated.[81] *Ghunna* was a quality of beauty that could be a permanent property of a voice or a coloristic variation used from time to time in the course of a rendition. It was mandated in some vocal contexts, for instance in Qur'anic recitation,[82] and it was frequent in religious song. It linked performances to historically Arabic singing. Al-Fārābī (whose treatises on music are characterized by an interest in practice as well as theoretical abstraction) described *ghunna* as a desirable quality.[83]

Voices described as "weak," "soft," "tired," "thin," "unclear," or "muddy" were bad voices.[84] One that seemed to be clogged, constricted, or obstructed was undesirable. Hoarseness in combination with weakness or softness was also bad. Voices that were "too loud," "clamorous," "thin and sharp," or "excessive" were not admired, and criticism also attached itself to the singer who changed uncontrollably from one tone color to another.

Falsetto, vibrato, and trilling served coloristic purposes. Falsetto was often used in conjunction with a trill or turn on the highest pitch of a climactic phrase. The singer would typically utilize these, as well as huskiness in upper or lower registers, frontal resonance, *baḥḥa* and *ghunna* in the service of *taṣwīr al-ma'ná* and to create varied repetitions of lines. Tone color might change frequently within the rendition of a song or even a single line; more rarely, it would remain the same throughout if that color were perceived to be particularly appropriate to the style of the song overall.

"Wa-Ḥaqqika Anta" illustrates Umm Kulthūm's treatment. The first line is marked by clear articulation. In the second half of the line she introduced coloristic variation with a falsetto trill and in the fourth, she enlarged her palette to include *ghunna* and *baḥḥa.*

Beyond the development of vocal capacity, virtuosity was linked with vocal flexibility, command of *maqāmāt, zakhārif* (ornaments), and tone colors. Umm Kulthūm displayed these skills by improvising *layālī* in performances of technically difficult pieces and, most important, in the varied repetition and improvisation she embedded within the composition. The ideal *layālī* manifested the singer's understanding and creativity by establishing the principal *maqām* of the performance in a recognizable but original manner. In a song the first task was the clear and skillful delivery of the initial segment (line, stanza, or section otherwise understood) of the composition. Depending on audience response, the singer would then repeat that section, introducing variations, or go on to the next section of the piece. In the ideal performance the singer would vary one or more lines upon encouragement from the audience and thus extend a five-minute song to twenty or thirty minutes or more.

The song performance was shaped in this way by singer and audience responding to each other. In the context discussed by al-Khulaʿī, performances were largely private or semiprivate gatherings of family and friends, usually men. Such concerts, widespread in the Arab world, were

> more a mingling of refined sensibilities than a confrontation between the artist and the audience. There was no stage, no platform, but, better, there existed a direct and permanent contact, a respectful understanding, an exchange of comments, even the possibility of assuming the role of performer for a while.[85]

Al-Khulaʿī clearly had this kind of setting in mind when he prescribed correct behavior for singers and listeners. While such events belonged principally to upper-class social life, a similar relationship between performer and audience obtained in more popular contexts and even in commercial concerts. Direct contact, relatively polite if somewhat louder exchanges, and mutual responsiveness were expectations in many performance contexts. The result, as El-Shawan remarked, was that

> The "final" form and meaning of a musical composition were not predictable or subsequently replicable in another performance. Rather, it depended on the muṭrib's manipulations of the laḥn, primarily through repetition and the addition of zakhārif, ḳaflāt and ḥarakāt. It must be noted that although these manipulations depended on the muṭrib's skill and talent, they were largely induced by audience response.[86]

The performer was expected to take the tastes of the audience into account at all times: to select texts appropriate in theme and literary sophistication to the listeners, to shape the song in response to audience reaction, and to accommodate requests. Certain behavior was incumbent upon the audience as well. In general, the audience was expected to show approval of the singer, to "let him know they want to hear him, to encourage him with cries of 'Allāh' or 'Ya Ḥayya.'"[87] The audience must be "smiling of face and welcoming to the singer." Requests should be made before the tuning of the instruments, according to al-Khulaʿī, and, while singers should make every effort, audience members should not insist that each request be fulfilled, for, "if he wanted to sing to each person what he wanted, it would be ten days at least before he pleased everyone."[88]

Acclamations or requests must be properly timed. Interruptions of lines of poetry were considered rude, intrusive and ignorant: if one could not hear the line how could one appreciate what the singing meant? Listeners not well versed in music should refrain from interrupting the singer with specific requests, for the *maqām* of the desired selection might not be compatible with that of the song currently being sung or appropriate to the tuning of the instruments. Furthermore, "nothing is more difficult for a singer than when an audience member cries, 'Once again, that phrase in *jihār kāh,*' when the phrase was actually in '*'irāq.*'" All such behavior was "undignified." Listeners must not "drink too much, [then] stand up, grasping the singer's *'ūd* or his hand" to fulfill a request or repeat a song. Whistling and clapping were viewed as crude and noisy and "incompatible with Eastern customs," although both became common in later twentieth-century performances.[89] Verbal acclamations at the ends of phrases were appropriate, as was clapping at the end of a performance.

The roles of singer and audience and the attendant implications for the structure of performance resonated historically, documented as early as the tenth century in *Kitāb al-Aghānī.* Shared by instrumental performance, dance, and Qur'anic recitation, this relationship was central to the aesthetics of much expressive culture.[90]

Umm Kulthūm based her musical competence on this aesthetic system; her performances—including demeanor and gesture as well as musical sound—were informed by her personal history as a singer for community celebrations, public concerts in and out of Cairo, and in elite homes. The version of the historic model she advanced combined the performance aesthetic known principally to elite men with those familiar to working people who appreciated the *mashāyikh*'s formulation of the historic aesthetic. Her practical experience equipped her to respond to the less elegant rowdiness of the large and differentiated public concert audience.[91]

Umm Kulthūm's personal idiom developed during the 1920s and 1930s. Her clarity of diction was among the first qualities of her performance noted by critics. In 1922, *al-Kashkūl*'s critic wrote of her "splendid voice, skilled artistry, and beautiful diction" (kānit ḥasanat al-ilqā').[92] It was manifest in one of her very first commercial recordings, "Mā lī Futint." Each word was clearly articulated and phrases broken for breaths only at places appropriate to the syntax. She delivered the opening phrase in its complete form as "Mā lī futintu bi-laḥẓiki 'l-fattāk." When she repeated only the first three words, she correctly dropped the last vowel before the pause: "Mā lī futint."[93]

By contrast, her colleague and competitor, the relatively skilled Fatḥiyya Aḥmad, incorrectly broke phrases repeatedly in her recording of "Kam Baʿathnā." Two instances of her incorrect breaks are marked with slashes below:

Kam baʿathnā maʿa ʾl-nasīmi salāman
Lil-ḥabī // bil-jamīl ḥaythu aqāma.
Kam baʿathnā maʿa ʾl-nasī // misalāman . . .

In both cases, Fatḥiyya detached the final consonant of a noun and its declension and attached them to the succeeding word. Correct delivery would have been "lil-ḥabībi ʾl-jamīl" and "al-nasīmi salāman," respectively. Listeners, especially educated ones, noticed such mistakes and remarked that Umm Kulthūm rarely made them. As Muḥammad ʿAbd al-Wahhāb remarked, even in her early years "Umm Kulthūm had perfect command of language. . . . Never would you listen to her and ask 'What did she say?' She had perfect pronunciation." This was, he said, "a product of studying the Qurʾān."[94]

Before he died in 1932, the poet Aḥmad Shawqī observed that Umm Kulthūm's great value, in addition to her beautiful voice, was that she was educated (*adība*) and understood what she sang. In 1935 the magazine *al-Mūsīqá* devoted an entire article to criticism of the ways in which various popular singers delivered texts. Umm Kulthūm was found to be the best: "She pronounces the *qaṣāʾid* and monologues and all the songs in literary Arabic and she is almost the only one who penetrates the meaning and understands the secrets [of the poetry]."[95]

Her vocal skills were manifest in the performance of long phrases extending over a wide range of pitch, subtle and rapid changes of tone color, and a wide variety of other vocal ornaments, usually linked with delivery of a text. She could move quickly and easily throughout her range and alternate among resonances and tone colors with facility. In "Mā lī Futint," she descended to an A below middle C to end a phrase and ascended moments later to a high f in the same strong vocal tone.[96] The closing line of "Zarni Ṭeefik" includes an exemplary melisma (which may be viewed as an instance of *taṣwīr al-maʿná*) on the words "songs of the birds" (alḥaan ʾl-ṭuyuur) (see example 3).[97]

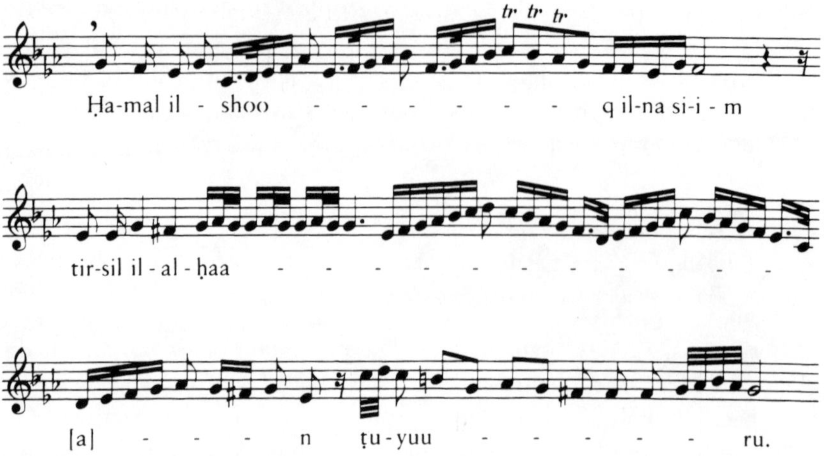

Example 3. Excerpt from "Zarni Ṭeefik"

In some of her early recordings, her nasal resonance was brash and dominated the entire performance. It remained in her nose almost from start to finish of "Ṭalaʿ ʾl-Fajr," matched or exceeded by nasal responses from her male accompanists (which might account for the criticism of them as "like the sound of a camel shrieking in distress").[98] Poor recording quality may have exacerbated the problem.

Umm Kulthūm quickly became adept at *ghunna* and the manipulation of tone colors generally. She frequently introduced it in melismatic passages, to drive home the impact of a word or phrase. Similarly, she used *ghunna* to shift attention from one part of the phrase to another and to create an affective cadence. *Ghunna* also served as a purely coloristic device during *layālī.*[99]

Umm Kulthūm's early performances featured accompaniment by a *takht* consisting of violin, *ʿūd, qānūn, riqq,* or combinations of these, playing in a heterophonic manner that did not interfere or obscure the singer's line. This was a practice with precedents that extended back at least to the mid-nineteenth century.[100] Opportunities for instrumental virtuosity came in *taqāsīm* before or between songs, in elaborations of *lāzimāt,* or interludes within songs, and in creative accompaniment. A member of a *takht* might undertake his own elaboration of a line at an appropriate range and time. This practice, known as *tarjama,* generally decreased as the number of musicians in the ensemble increased.[101]

During the 1930s the *takht* gave way to a bulkier ensemble especially noticeable during instrumental introductions and interludes.[102] Musicians often attributed this change to the popularity of the larger ensembles used in musical plays and films. Some instruments, for instance the piano, had serious limitations in the tuning of pitches necessary to Arabic *maqāmāt*, and such instruments never became favorites. Musicians most used instruments on which the pitch could be varied, especially string instruments but also, later, electronic keyboard instruments, the tuning of which could be more easily adjusted than that of the piano. Instruments such as the clarinet and saxophone appeared occasionally for coloristic purposes. Borrowed instruments signaled innovation. Conversely, small or small-sounding ensembles and particular instruments (notably the *nāy* and the *duff*) commonly served as markers of local practice.

The first new instruments Umm Kulthūm used were the violoncello and string bass along with multiple violins. The violins simply doubled the melody line while the cello and bass usually reinforced the significant pitches of the lines.[103] Pizzicato became a popular playing technique. Suggestions of triadic harmony recurred in her repertory, but, like the occasional pizzicato bass line, these passages served a decorative and incidental purpose.

Most elements of Umm Kulthūm's style were emphatically Egyptian. As the potency of Turkey and things Turkish waned in Egypt—for instance, as the wealthy began to vacation in Europe rather than on the Bosphorus, and as economic and political power began to pass from the hands of the Turkish elite into those of native Egyptians—the attraction of Turkish culture receded. Because her singing held elements of familiarity to most Egyptians, Umm Kulthūm was able to increase her audience of nonconcertgoers and of non-Cairenes, using mass media as these became available. By contrast, Fatḥiyya Aḥmad, who announced herself as a singer in the "Turkish style," apparently had no trouble maintaining her audience in Cairo and the cities of Syria and Palestine as well as an acceptable level of record sales, but her appeal never became as widespread in Egypt as Umm Kulthūm's. With the political and economic events of the 1940s in Egypt and throughout the Arab world, the later Egyptian Revolution of 1952, and President ʿAbd al-Nāṣir's dramatic expansion of radio, this local authenticity helped to increase Umm Kulthūm's importance as a singer.

Five

"The Golden Age of Umm Kulthūm" and Two Cultural Formations

Zakariyyā Aḥmad's style in composition was distinguished by his attention to genuine Arabic character. He did not borrow nor did he bring into his music any other color because his music sprang from his spirit and his Egyptianness.[1]

Qaṣā'id are the foundation of Arabic song.[2]

The 1940s were the Golden Age of Umm Kulthūm.[3]

The 1940s

The Egyptian economy recovered from the Depression with painful slowness, and indeed improvements were sometimes barely noticeable. The struggle against British occupation dragged on. The Anglo-Egyptian Treaty of 1936 granted a measure of independence to Egypt but within such severe constraints that it was a pyrrhic victory. Among other provisions, it allowed the continued presence of the hated British troops in Egypt.

In 1939, Egyptians were once again subjected to the hardships of what many viewed as a European war. Wages for most Egyptians were still low. During the war cotton acreage was restricted. Prices rose sharply as "the war caused inflation and a dislocation of food supply so that in 1942 there were famine riots, labor disputes and strikes for higher wages." Between 1946 and 1948, Cairo and Alexandria witnessed strikes of textile workers, transportation workers, police, hospital workers, and others.[4] The increased presence of foreign troops on Egyptian soil further aggravated the situation. A malaria epidemic in 1944 that wiped out entire villages multiplied the Egyptian burdens.

To an already bad situation "a new explosive element was added with the partition of Palestine. The Palestine war proved to be disastrous, and the disappointing performance of the Egyptian army was only partly redeemed by such gallant acts as the defence of Faluja."[5] Public outrage was heightened at the news that military losses were due in large measure to unscrupulous dealings in munitions at high levels of the army and ruling elite, which effectively left the Egyptian soldier without the means to defend himself.

Exasperation with the British grew, the result of long years of fruitless negotiations. Miles Lampson's ultimatum to King Fārūq to appoint a pro-British prime minister or be deposed, delivered in 1942, was viewed by all and sundry as a great insult. Egyptians became increasingly disenchanted with their own government's ability to deal effectively with the British and with domestic problems such as the malaria epidemic.

Economic and political strains reached deeply into Egyptian society. Social and economic problems acquired an immediacy and fostered a fundamental change in attitude characterized by growing dissatisfaction and lack of patience with the dominant powers: Europeans and Egyptian governors who capitulated to them.

Their relative wealth protected many commercial musicians personally from the worst effects of these disasters; but as working performers, their careers were strongly affected by the bad economy. Moreover the shared radios and record players, tours of the countryside and, to a lesser extent, local movie theaters, integrated commercial performers into the daily life of the society. The well-known involvement of artists such as Sayyid Darwīsh and Badīʿ Khayrī in the articulation of local causes lived in the minds of listeners. Performers and audiences alike remembered Sayyid Darwīsh's powerful model of engagement with the community of Egyptians. As patriotic Egyptians, as performers desirous of patronage and as heirs to Sayyid Darwīsh, musicians turned their attention, to varying degrees, to the plight of the society.

In this context, the romantic escapism of the 1920s and 1930s failed as an expressive formulation. Badawi's description of the turn away from romanticism in poetry applies to expressive culture generally:

> There were obvious signs that [romantic poetry] was on the wane immediately after the Second World War. This is not at all surprising, for the war was an important landmark in the literary no less than in the political, social and economic history of the Arab world: the traumatic changes it had brought about, both directly and indirectly, had a powerful impact on the poetry of the time. Despite its distinguished contribution romanticism had by that time developed its own conventional diction, imagery, irrelevant to an Arab world that was growing painfully aware of its harsh political and social realities. It was criticized on

> the grounds of being escapist, immature, wanting in reality, as devoid of a hard core of sense, as too vague and lacking in precision, as sentimental, false, sugary, facile and verbose.[6]

Egyptian audiences applauded works that dealt with tangible reality. The romantic themes of the 1930s seemed remote from the deteriorating conditions of everyday life. Viewed in the past as dreamily romantic, Aḥmad Rāmī's lyrics were now criticized as "inane."[7] Bayram al-Tūnisī's poetry "spoke to the vast majority of people, unlike Rāmī's work, absorbed in romanticism and love which appealed only to a certain temperament."[8]

Rather suddenly in the early 1940s, Umm Kulthūm began to cultivate a repertory designed to speak in musical and linguistic terms closer to most Egyptians than Rāmī's romantic lines and al-Qaṣabjī's experimental songs. In place of the remote and solitary heroine of the 1930s, the working population of Egypt, represented by Umm Kulthūm, played a collective protagonist in her songs and films. Colloquial songs by Zakariyyā Aḥmad and Bayram al-Tūnisī dominated her repertory during World War II and its aftermath. Her successful films gave expression to the everyday sensibilities of many Egyptians. The change was dramatic: whereas Rāmī wrote roughly 90 percent of her song lyrics in the 1930s, he wrote fewer than half of her new texts in the 1940s. Al-Qaṣabjī's share of her new compositions dropped from almost 50 percent to less than 20 percent.

Musical Populism

Bayram al-Tūnisī, a well-known colloquial poet and political satirist, wrote texts for Umm Kulthūm that resembled bits of conversation, artistically constructed. They included common expressions and displayed a profound identification with working-class Egyptians, as did most of Bayram's poetry.[9]

His imagery depended on short phrases of three or four words and familiar gestures: the waiting woman "put her hand on her cheek" as a sign of distress rather than sitting alone in her room gazing at the moon, an image familiar to Rāmī and the romantics. The more fanciful concepts of sitting awake at night contemplating the loved one or the isolation of the lonely lover were replaced by expression of the pain and passion of simply "waiting." Bayram's speaker expressed herself in the strong and direct terms of the Egyptian working woman rather than the sheltered daughter of aristocracy.[10]

The text of Bayram's "il-Awwila fil-Gharaam" (The first thing, passion) was cast in one of the shapes common to the Egyptian *mawwāl*. Bayram utilized the formulaic *il-awwila* (the first thing), *il-tanya* (the second thing), and *il-talta* (the third thing) to introduce phrases which were then augmented in successive appearances: "The first thing, passion and love entangled me," became "The first thing, passion and love entangled me in the glance of an eye," and so forth.[11] The word *awwila* was particular to the Egyptian *mawwāl*.

Zakariyyā Aḥmad prided himself on taking musical inspiration from working-class people. He retained his many contacts with the musicians and audiences of the middle- and lower-class quarters of Cairo. He began his career *min al-mashāyikh,* learning to read the Qur'ān and learning religious song and *muwashshaḥāt* from al-Shaykh Darwīsh al-Ḥarīrī and al-Shaykh Ismā'īl Sukkar. He wrote religious songs for al-Shaykh 'Alī Maḥmūd as well as *ṭaqāṭīq* and pieces for musical theater.[12] Those who knew him described him as one who would just as readily perform for a saint's day in the traditional quarters of Cairo as for an elite wedding or in a downtown theater.

Dress was an important marker of social identity in Egypt. For instance, in his youth, writer Ṭāhā Ḥusayn distinguished those who, like himself at the time, were pursuing traditional Islamic professions from other Egyptians according to headgear: "turban-wearers" for the former and "tarboosh-wearers" for the latter. Similarly, Zakariyyā Aḥmad wrote in a memoir that it was his older friend, Badī' Khayrī, who was the principal agent in his change from "a turbaned *shaykh* to an *afandī* [wearing a] tarboosh."[13] The man's robe or *jallābiyya* indicated attachment to values thought to be indigenously Egyptian by contrast to the Western suit and was worn by members of the upper classes as well as working classes, exemplified by the patriarch of the 'Abd al-Rāziq family in the 1920s. Like many Egyptians, Zakariyyā used clothing to signify cultural affinity, appearing frequently in a *jallābiyya* rather than the European clothing that was more common in the theater district.

His music drew on the styles of performance associated with the *mashāyikh,* the *mawwāl,* and other styles considered to be distinctively Egyptian. As the poet Ṣāliḥ Jūda wrote, "There is in all of his songs a special quality that no one can imitate. It is the quality of Egyptianness, of being permeated with what is really Egyptian, permeated with what is Cairene."[14]

The melodies themselves were often deceptively simple. Phrases were short, narrow in range, and free of intricate melodic motives. Zakariyyā wrote in all of the genres current in his day, and his songs relied upon *maqāmāt* especially popular in Egypt: *rāst, bayātī, huzām,* and *ṣabā.* The artistry of his songs for Umm Kulthūm lay in the initial clear delivery of a clever or appealing text and the subsequent variation of its melody using rhythmic and melodic alterations, with changes in vocal tone color to heighten its meaning. Few were in fact easy to sing, for, in their entireties, his songs typically utilized a wide vocal range, and effective rendition of the simple melodies demanded a high degree of musical creativity and command of style.

Despite the current trend toward large ensembles, Zakariyyā wrote sparse accompaniment intended to follow the vocal line. His introductions and interludes were newly composed but short. The accompaniment was almost always heterophonic with little suggestion of harmony. The modes Zakariyyā often chose for his songs, *ṣaba, huzām,* and *bayātī,* did not lend themselves easily to triadic harmonization or to the conventions of Western major or minor melodic lines (see example 4).

Zakariyyā highlighted the singer's leading role. His rhythmic structures accommodated extra time for clear articulation of a consonant, addition or omission of melodic embellishment, and prolongation of the cadence, all important practices in historically Arabic song. Viewed as proceeding directly from indigenous tradition, Zakariyyā Aḥmad's songs were also considered to be new owing to his rhythmic innovations and new combinations of familiar styles. Almost all of the songs were *ughniyyāt,* taking

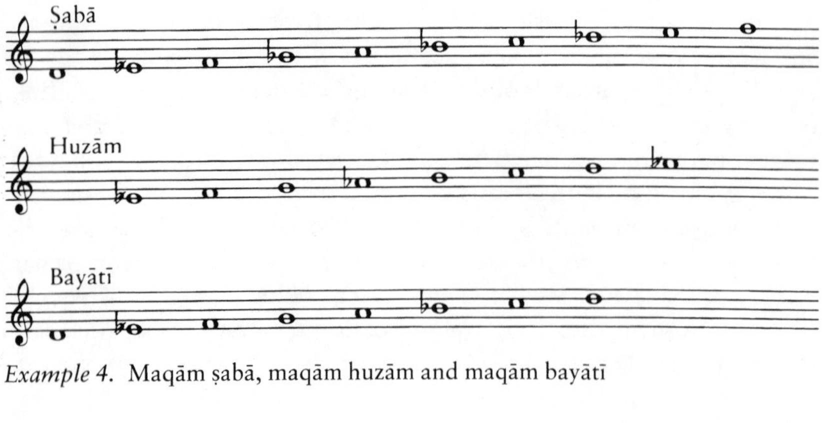

Example 4. Maqām ṣabā, maqām huzām and maqām bayātī

shapes that varied from song to song, but all drawing on well-known Egyptian Arabic practices.

Umm Kulthūm applied her now well-honed musical and interpretive skills to these pieces, and they constituted roughly half of the performances that formed her "Golden Age." She was at the height of her vocal powers, a mature musician who commanded many skills brought to bear on expressing the meaning and mood of poems. She applied herself to the widely familiar styles of song where melodic virtuosity took a distant second place to emotive renditions and inventions around words. In "Ana Fi-ntiẓaarak" (see example 5), the female speaker, distressed at waiting for a lover, says simply, "I want to know that you're not angry, that your heart does not belong to someone else." The composed melody is relatively plain but offers opportunities for variation on two important words, "angry" (*ghaḍbaan*) and "someone else" (*insaan*). Umm Kulthūm gives *insaan* relatively elaborate musical treatment, although nothing inherent in the word would necessarily require this particular handling. Her extension of the words brought out the broader meanings and emotions of the line, drawing out the anguish of the sensation that one's beloved might turn attention to someone else.

She often treated expressions of longing such as "If only" in a similar way, as in "Ya retni maʿaak" ("If only I were with you," from "Faakir lamma Kunt Ganbi"), "Ya retni" ("If only," from "Ana Fi-ntiẓaarak"), and the more elevated literary equivalent "Yā laytanī" ("If only," from "Aghāru min Nasmati 'l-Janūbi").

Listeners also remember "Ḥulm," "il-Ahaat," and "Bi-riḍaak" as powerful examples of sung colloquial verse, *zajal*. Her performances lay close in style to the music ordinary people heard at weddings and holidays and used to hear in coffeehouses where local singers plied their trade. But Zakariyyā Aḥmad did not simply stylize folk song.[15] He wrote the innovative, new songs that Egyptian listeners demanded.

The fruitful collaboration of Bayram al-Tūnisī, Zakariyyā Aḥmad, and Umm Kulthūm was short-lived. Zakariyyā protested the low pay given to a popular and experienced composer such as himself compared to the earnings of a singer or of a record company. He sued for 4 percent of the profits of record sales from Cairophon Records and for timely and accurate payment of composers' fees from Egyptian Radio and from Umm Kulthūm. Although she said she supported him in principle, she did little publicly to

Example 5. Excerpt from "Ana Fi-ntiẓaarak"

ameliorate his situation, and Zakariyyā's cases remained in court for over ten years.[16] The problem was exacerbated by the fact that Bayram and Zakariyyā found Umm Kulthūm to be imperious and demanding. Like others, they appreciated her great vocal abilities, but the clash of their personalities made solutions to problems hard to find. Bayram continued to provide a few texts for Umm Kulthūm in later years, and Zakariyyā wrote a final song for her in 1960. However, after 1947, the collaboration of these artists was lost.

New Films

Two of Umm Kulthūm's most popular films, *Sallāma* and *Faṭma,* largely the work of Zakariyyā and Bayram, fell in line with the populist direction of the rest of her repertory of the 1940s. Released in 1945, *Sallāma,* like *Widād* and *Danānīr,* featured a singing slave girl; but this time Bayram attempted a realism new to Umm Kulthūm's films in the song texts and dialogue. They were cast in a dialect suggestive of Bedouin.

Sallāma offered a tour de force of Arabic song. In addition to several *ughniyyāt* that became very popular such as "Ghanni li Shwayya Shwayya," Sallāma sang a *muwashshaḥ,* a *qaṣīda,* a religious *mawwāl,* a riddle song, and a lament similar in style to the songs of caravan drivers. She also read several lines from the Qur'ān. Umm Kulthūm was able to display her wide-ranging skills in all of these genres, while portraying an entertaining but virtuous daughter of the Arabs.

Like *Nashīd al-Amal* (1937), the film *Faṭma* (1947) was set in contemporary Cairo; but where *Nashīd* dealt with the tension between an aspiring singer and her criminal husband resolved by stardom and remarriage to a wealthy doctor, *Faṭma* concerned the ill-treatment of a poor nurse by the son of a wealthy Pāshā, resolved in courts of law and through the collective action of the common people of the nurse's neighborhood. Faṭma, the nurse, lived in an urban neighborhood and was beloved of the people there because of her help whenever one of them was sick.[17] She was the sole provider for her widowed mother and her orphaned cousin. While nursing a wealthy Pāshā, Faṭma attracted the favor of one of his brothers, Fatḥī, who tried to seduce her. Encountering rejection, he married her to attain his objective. This prosperous union was initially viewed as great luck by Faṭma's family and neighbors. However, her new husband abhorred the manners and customs of her working-class relatives and friends and soon left Faṭma and her neighborhood. He then married an aristocratic young lady and took steps to divorce Faṭma.

Meanwhile Faṭma bore a son of which Fatḥī had no knowledge. Embarrassed by his brother's marriage to one of such low estate, the old Pāshā bargained with Faṭma to keep the news from Fatḥī. The people of the neighborhood, who had stood by Faṭma's side throughout the entire painful episode, brought suit against the faithless husband on her behalf. In the end sentence was pronounced against Fatḥī, and all of the neighborhood celebrated the success with Faṭma.

The important themes of the film illustrate current sensibilities in Egyptian society: the flagrant misbehavior and perfidy of the wealthy (here punished by the state at the behest of ordinary people); the importance of solidarity of friends and neighbors; and the value of the virtuous woman who successfully resists temptation. The denouement of the plot depends on activating fundamental values of Egyptian society rather than the sudden good luck seen in earlier films and stories.

The remaining film of the 1940s, *ʿĀyida,* first released in 1942, was one of Umm Kulthūm's few failures, and may be viewed, in part, as further evidence of contemporary preference for essentially Egyptian productions. *ʿĀyida* revolved around the life of a young Egyptian girl who aspired to sing in the opera, the daughter of a poor man who worked on the estate of a wealthy landowner. The rich man's son fell in love with ʿĀyida, but there were many obstacles to their marriage. ʿĀyida received a scholarship to the Institute for Arab Music and starred in its production of an Arabic version of the opera *Aida.* She won acclaim at the institute for her excellent performance and her first well-wisher was the rich man.

In its first version, the film ended at this point, immediately after the performance of the second act of the Arabic *Aida.* The sudden ending, without resolution of the romantic problem, was cited as one of the reasons for the failure of the film. Others included the long operatic portion, which relied upon alternations of recitatives with duets and aria-like passages in the European style, criticized as unappealing to Egyptian audiences. Finally, Umm Kulthūm, as the Ethiopian princess ʿĀyida, wore black makeup which so startled the audience, many of whom had come to the film simply to see the main singing star, that they were distracted from the other aspects of the production. A second version was released nine months later with these problems corrected. New songs were solicited from Zakariyyā Aḥmad and Bayram al-Tūnisī to make the film more attractive. The improvements were lauded and the new songs well received, but the production as a whole failed to gain the acclaim that Umm Kulthūm's other films did.[18]

Faṭma was Umm Kulthūm's last film. Her eyes, adversely affected by strong lights, may have been a factor that contributed to her departure from the film industry. Additionally, despite experience, she was not professionally an actress, and she may have felt she was coming to the end of the roles she could convincingly portray. In 1947, she was in her mid-forties. Most of the other female film stars who took leading roles were at least ten years younger. Although they may not have been able to compete successfully with Umm Kulthūm vocally, visually they could, certainly in the ingenue roles that Umm Kulthūm played.

Her departure was probably not a decision deliberately and finally taken. She later considered other film projects, including a few with Muḥammad ʿAbd al-Wahhāb, but these never came to fruition, lost in the gradual process of choosing repertory and considering projects that characterized her career.

Umm Kulthūm's populist repertory retained popularity for decades. "Il-Ahaat" (1943), "il-Awwila fil-Gharaam" (1944), "il-Ward Jamiil" (1947), "Ghanni li Shwayya Shwayya" (1945), "Ana Fi-ntizaarak" (1943), "Ahl il-Hawa" (1944), and "il-Amal" (1946) enjoyed singularly long lives. The same could not be said for Umm Kulthūm's earlier repertory. The songs of the 1930s were not frequently performed or sold (although they were broadcast over the radio) after their immediate period of popularity. Many were reissued after Umm Kulthūm's death as interesting artifacts of an earlier time.

Umm Kulthūm's repertory for this period was not exclusive of other styles. Riyāḍ al-Sunbāṭī and al-Qaṣabjī wrote new songs for her, several of which enjoyed long lives, notably al-Qaṣabjī's "Raqq al-Ḥabiib." The roles played by al-Sunbāṭi and al-Qaṣabjī in Umm Kulthūm's repertory changed during the 1940s. Al-Sunbāṭī gradually wrote more songs for her, contributing to all of her films. He began to develop what would be his specialty, the *qaṣīda*. Al-Qaṣabjī's position as Umm Kulthūm's composer diminished, and after 1946 she never sang another of his compositions. He continued to offer her new songs which she consistently declined to sing, sometimes after having encouraged him to compose them.[19] He continued to compose for other singers, to handle administrative affairs for Umm Kulthūm's instrumental ensemble, and to play in it, and he remained a close personal friend until his death in 1966.

Neoclassicism

In 1946 Umm Kulthūm introduced a group of new *qaṣā'id,* most by Aḥmad Shawqī set to music by Riyāḍ al-Sunbāṭī. These ten neoclassical *qaṣā'id* carried Umm Kulthūm into the mid-1950s; she sang only seven other songs during this period. On the one hand, the new repertory grew naturally out of her experience and preference for the genre. She had performed new *qaṣā'id* during almost every year of her career. Every feature film included at least one. At the same time that Umm Kulthūm focused her attention primarily on Zakariyyā's populist songs, she included some of her old *qaṣā'id* by Abū 'l-'Ilā Muḥammad in her concert repertory.

On the other hand, there was a great contrast between the songs of Bayram and Zakariyyā, on which she had recently concentrated, and the difficult poetry of Shawqī and Rāmī with complicated musical settings by al-Sunbāṭī, to which she rather suddenly turned. One factor in the change was certainly her legal difficulty with Zakariyyā. Umm Kulthūm's choice may be viewed, however, as part of a strong, deep social and political current toward reaffirmation of Islam and classical Arab civilization as the bases for social order. This particular group of *qaṣā'id,* performed at the time it was, focused attention on the genre: her audience defined her henceforward as an important contributor to the rendition of *qaṣā'id* and to the major cultural formation of neoclassicism. The poetic texts and Umm Kulthūm's idiom forged strong links with Muslim religious expression. This neoclassicism reaffirmed the value of old Arabic and Muslim forms and practices as a basis for cultural development.

For several decades, Egyptian responses to Westernization, whether in opposition or in favor, frequently had recourse to some aspect of Islam. The teaching of religious leaders Jamāl al-Dīn al-Afghānī and Muḥammad 'Abduh at the turn of the century—that modernization of Arab society should properly proceed from the tenets of Islam—and the related debates greatly influenced the leaders of the next generation. As Pierre Cachia observed in his discussion of Ṭāhā Ḥusayn and his contemporaries during the 1920s,

> Broadly . . . it may be said that the Conservatives regarded the aping of the West by their benighted contemporaries as tantamount to the triumph of materialism and immorality over Islam and the supposedly innate spirituality of the East; they held that all new problems had to be solved in accordance with the Qur'ān and the *sunnah* as interpreted

> by early Muslim authorities; in connection with literature, they linked Arabic with the Qur'ān, considering it the "mother" of all languages and a sacred heritage which the moderns have no right to alter in any way, and they favored the perpetuation of the "elegant," ornate style of writing which had prevailed in Arabic literature after the tenth century.[20]

When battle was joined, a number of "modernists" found it necessary to justify their views in religious terms, and to explain their positions on such matters as "the character of Quranic inspiration and the relevance of its message to a Muslim country to-day."[21] Islam often provided the terms for argumentation where it was not the point of the matter at all, as Charles Smith argued with reference to the career of author Muḥammad Ḥusayn Haykal:

> Once the Wafd-Liberal coalition split in 1928, [Haykal] and his party were faced with charges of atheism from the Wafd as well as from the 'ulamā' [religious leaders], which had to be answered. The result was that for the next ten years Islam and the claim to be its true defender was to be a major issue in Egyptian politics.[22]

As in the past, in the 1940s Islam offered terms for discussion of options and a widely accepted philosophical basis for protests against injustice, local and international. It was seen by some as an important source of alternatives to submission to foreign authority, whether political, economic, or cultural, and to local manifestations of bad government; since the mid-nineteenth century "Egyptian national consciousness" was "fused with Muslim consciousness," in the words of Mounah Khouri:

> Throughout the occupation period, a strong Islamic current, fed by the great majority of the contemporary Egyptian poets, was running along and flowing into the national current. This Islamic current was charged with religious zeal, national feeling, and a fierce spirit of resistance to the encroachments of Europe on the Muslim world.[23]

Support for such organizations as the Muslim Brotherhood grew rapidly during the latter 1940s, and the membership and activities of the Brotherhood reached a new high level.[24] The appeal of Islamic institutions, behaviors, or forms of cultural expression might be viewed as an aspect of the desire for local control, as another manifestation of the goal of "Egypt for Egyptians." As Marsot wrote,

> we can say that movements of protest in Egypt take on a religious colouring when all channels of discourse are closed to the population; and when autocracy reigns, supported and encouraged by outside forces which are seen to manipulate the local society for their own political and economic ends.[25]

These sensibilities charged the atmosphere in Egypt during the 1940s. Islam became a rallying point for the assertion of indigenous values. In this context, Umm Kulthūm introduced her new *qaṣāʾid.*

The concept of neoclassicism developed in the realm of literature. One of its principal exponents, Aḥmad Shawqī, was a well-known poet who served in the court of Khedive ʿAbbās as the khedive's principal spokesperson during the first decade of the century. A wealthy Egyptian of Turco-Circassian parentage, he was known for loyalty to the Ottomans and his "virulent" attacks on the British. As Khouri described it, the "ugly image of Cromer's administration, however impressionistic or prejudiced it might be, was reproduced with more or less vigor by Shawqī and . . . by Ḥāfiẓ, and served as a model for most of the minor poets of this period."[26]

Both Shawqī and his colleague Ḥāfiẓ Ibrāhīm were among the leading neoclassicists of the twentieth-century Arab world. Whereas others emulated Western poetry and adopted its models, Shawqī and Ḥāfiẓ, although admiring of European literature, believed the problem confronting Arab poets was "insufficient acquaintance with the resources of Arabic and insufficient faith in its possibilities of development."[27] Accordingly, Shawqī took his models from classical Arabic poetry, alluding in his works to Islamic and Arab history while addressing contemporary personages or reflecting on recent events or conditions of contemporary life. Shawqī's poetry, in sophisticated literary Arabic, was "expressive of the deep emotional traits of the Arabs and their kind of inherited wisdom and outlook on life."[28] In Badawi's words, he "used the old idiom to express strictly modern and contemporary social, cultural and political concerns. . . . What Shawqī managed to do, which is no mean service, was to make the traditional Abbasid idiom so relevant to the problems and concerns of modern life that poetry became a force to be reckoned with in the political life of modern Egypt."[29]

The place of the *qaṣīda* in Arabic culture was long-standing. One of the oldest poetic genres, its relatively long texts were cast in hemistiches with a single meter and rhyme scheme throughout. One line typically expressed a single thought while contributing to the broader themes of the poem, which usually involved religious or historical topics or sophisticated descriptions of nature or love. *Qaṣā'id* were frequently commemorative of persons or events. The language was literary and the poems included words, phrases, and allusions well beyond the scope of daily conversation. Ibrahim Boolaky observed its main characteristics to be "its force of expression and compactness of language, its vivid description of the loved one, and its wide appreciation in the Muslim world."[30]

Composers and singers excerpted usually from four to twelve lines of a much longer poem. The musical phrase coincided with the textual phrase and usually a new melody accompanied each new phrase of text. If a musical meter was heard it was often *al-wāḥida.*[31] The overall effect was typically that of a through-composed song, although refrains appeared in some turn-of-the-century examples. Like other genres, the *qaṣīda* admitted innovation as evidenced by the colloquial Arabic refrain occasionally appended, the addition of a variety of accompanying instruments, or the introduction of European waltz and march rhythms as well as indigenous rhythmic patterns not common to the genre.

Umm Kulthūm premiered five *qaṣā'id* by Aḥmad Shawqī and Riyāḍ al-Sunbāṭī in rapid succession during 1946. She sang the first, "Salū Qalbī," a text Shawqī had written in 1914 in commemoration of the Prophet Muḥammad's birthday, in March. In May, she programmed Shawqī's "Salū Ku'ūs al-Ṭilā," a romantic *qaṣīda* written especially for her and given to her as a gift while the poet was still alive.[32] "Wulid al-Hudá" and "Nahj al-Burda" followed, both distinctly religious in theme, and then came "al-Sūdān," expressive of the current political objective of unity with the Sudan. Shawqī's "al-Nīl" and Rāmī's translation of the *Rubā'iyyāt* of 'Umar Khayyām followed in 1949.

The texts ranged widely over historical, political, religious, and amatory subjects, frequently in the same work. Each was unified by a single, overarching theme, such as the commemoration of the Prophet's birthday in the cases of "Salū Qalbī" and "Wulid al-Hudá," and the symbolic taking up of the Prophet's mantle or cloak in "Nahj al-Burda." The hemistiches were designed to be independent units of thought, each contributing to the development of the larger theme.

Shawqī's "Salū Qalbī" opened with an address to the beloved, moved to praise of the Prophet Muḥammad, and included two lines that became a motto for Egyptian nationalist aspirations. As it appeared during a period of increasing nationalist agitation and dissatisfaction with the continuing British presence and the abuses of King Fārūq, audiences were quick to respond to the older lines: "Wa-mā nīla 'l-maṭālibu bil-tamannī wa-lākin tu'khadha 'l-dunyā ghilāban." (Demands are not met by wishing; the world can only be taken by struggle). Shūsha described performances of this poem at the time:

> When the Second World War ended, and the people proceeded to demand the evacuation of the colonialists from the Nile Valley, her concerts resembled political demonstrations in which she ignited nationalist feeling, for she made a point of singing Shawqī's *qaṣīda* "Salū Qalbī" in each concert in which [*qaṣīda*] she would cry out, in a tempest of national ardor, "Demands are not met by wishing; the world can only be taken by struggle."[33]

"Salū Qalbī" came to be considered a nationalistic as well as a religious statement.[34]

"Wulid al-Hudá" contained the following lines: "Al-Ishtirakiyyūn anta imāmuhum" (You [Muḥammad] are the leader of the socialists) and "Anṣafta ahla 'l-faqri min ahli 'l-ghinā" (You [Muḥammad] gave justice to the poor in front of the rich). Songs such as this one and "al-Sūdān," which gave "expression to our national hope for unity with the Sudan," passed in and out of Umm Kulthūm's broadcast repertory depending upon the political positions acceptable to the government at the time and subsequently to the authorities in broadcasting. After its initial performance, "Wulid al-Hudá" was rarely if ever broadcast until after the revolution in 1952; "al-Sūdān," popular in the late 1940s, was infrequently broadcast after President ʿAbd al-Nāṣir's government acknowledged the independence of the Sudan.[35]

Of all the Shawqī texts, "Nahj al-Burda" was perhaps the most difficult to understand. It was effectively a commentary on the "Burda" (literally, cloak [of the Prophet]), a *qaṣīda* by the thirteenth century poet al-Būṣīrī. Shawqī's work took its rhyme scheme and meter from al-Būṣīrī's poem, and knowledge of the older work was often essential to grasp the meaning of Shawqī's poem.

Riyāḍ al-Sunbāṭī created a musical neoclassicism equal to Shawqī's poetic expression. Al-Sunbāṭī's success in casting the classical poetic genre in new molds opened avenues for creativity in Umm Kulthūm's repertory. The

Sunbāṭī *qaṣīda* became the mainstay of Umm Kulthūm's repertory for the rest of her life.

At the time of their first collaboration in the 1930s, al-Sunbāṭī, recently arrived in Cairo from al-Manṣūra, was a young man who had the benefit of a diploma from the Institute for Arab Music. His early songs for Umm Kulthūm are difficult to characterize, and only in the 1940s did his distinctive style assert itself in her repertory.[36]

Riyāḍ al-Sunbāṭī became a neoclassicist par excellence with his *qaṣā'id*. He, following the path of some of his older colleagues, aimed to use historically Arabic raw materials, most notably a range of *maqāmāt*, stepwise melodic motion, and genres such as the *qaṣīda*. The composer Dāwūd Ḥuṣnī had employed historic modes in his *adwār* such as *zinjarān* that had fallen out of use. Kāmil al-Khulaʿī composed new *muwashshaḥāt*. The compositions by these men were best appreciated by the well-educated Egyptian interested in the history of his or her culture. But the works also served to remind others of their heritage and of the potential contemporary value of historically Arab art and custom.

In his musical settings of the Shawqī texts, Riyāḍ al-Sunbāṭī typically retained the arch-shaped structure characteristic of classical composition. The melody usually began with the lower pitches of its mode, developed in that range, and then ascended to higher pitches in the same mode. Modulations into other modes followed, forming the center of the piece. The *qaṣīda* ended with a descent in the original mode. Within this shape, al-Sunbāṭī wrote intricate melodies, difficult for an average singer to perform but well suited to Umm Kulthūm. He introduced innovations such as bass lines and included occasional suggestions of harmony such as outlines of triads in the melody or the accompaniment of a song. He enlarged the accompanimental ensemble to include seven or eight violins in addition to the violoncello, string bass, *ʿūd, qānūn, riqq,* and *nāy*. He utilized some of the new instruments popularized in films and in the experimental songs of ʿAbd al-Wahhāb. This large ensemble, or *firqa,* was viewed in its time as appropriately modern, interesting, and new. However, as in the songs by Zakariyyā Aḥmad, the singer retained the dominant role. The entire enlarged *firqa* played interludes but also functioned as a *takht* when Umm Kulthūm was singing.

Thus al-Sunbāṭī introduced new musical gestures without disturbing the familiar Arab foundation of his compositions. His innovations regenerated

Example 6. Excerpt from "Salū Qalbī"

the older genre, making it suitable for new musical expression. They were musically as well as poetically neoclassical and represented "tradition" in Arab music compared to ʿAbd al-Wahhāb's "modernity," seen as heavily dependent upon Western models.

Umm Kulthūm's rendition linked the classical traditions of recited and sung poetry to the recitation of the Qurʾān. Cast in elevated language with weighty themes, the genre was a natural showcase for the skills learned in recitation of the Qurʾān, as illustrated in "Salū Qalbī" (see example 6). The loosely metrical composition gives way to rhythmically irregular rendition, dependent for the most part upon the relationship of long and short vowels in a manner approximating that of Qurʾanic recitation. Umm Kulthūm sustained pitches on consonants such as the *m* or *lam* and the *l* of *illāhi.* Although the melodic line was relatively plain, she drew attention to the important phrases "judgment of God" (*ḥukmi-llāhi*) and "door of God" (*bābi-llāhi*) using melismas and change of vocal tone color while maintaining clear articulation of the words.

Al-Sunbāṭī's songs for Umm Kulthūm featured frequent modulations to unexpected modes and unusual melodic movements in familiar modes. "Salū Qalbī," for instance, began in *rāst,* moved through several variants of *rāst* to *nakrīz, bayātī, nahāwand, ḥijāz kār, bayātī nawā,* and back to *rāst.* His effective representation of the *maqām,* musically and emotionally, and creative modulations marked his musical accomplishment and complexity and distinguished it from what was viewed as mediocrity and simplicity.[37]

For "Salū Kuʾūs al-Ṭilā" (see example 7), al-Sunbāṭī constructed an introduction that was to be played heterophonically by the new, larger ensemble. The voice entered with the first line of the poem in its entirety. This line was repeated, then followed by the second line of text which closed with a relatively long cadence (*qafla*). The setting was predominantly syllabic. The instrumental writing was heavy during introductions and interludes and light during the vocal rendition. Harmony played a role in al-Sunbāṭī's *qaṣā'id* only occasionally. The second line illustrates his typical treatment of text which allowed extension of the *qafla*. Like most of his songs, this one offered great potential for varied repetition, illustrated in this performance by the phrase "'Ādahā 'l-shawq." Similar features characterized virtually every *qaṣīda* by Riyāḍ al-Sunbāṭī for Umm Kulthūm. What these examples illustrate is artists' work with cultural materials: al-Sunbāṭī's neoclassicism and Umm Kulthūm's idiom were at once distinctive and recognizably constructed from past practices.

During the preparation of the *qaṣā'id* Umm Kulthūm became an active participant, perhaps the dominant force, in the production of a song. She chose the texts and the composer, and made her own emendations in both text and composition. She chose and occasionally rearranged lines and replaced words that were difficult to understand or to sing. In the case of "Salū Qalbī," she selected twenty-one of seventy-one lines in the original poem. Numbering the lines of Shawqī's *qaṣīda* from one to seventy-one, the order in which Umm Kulthūm placed them for her song was as follows: 1–6, 11, 15, 17–18, 25, 48, 51–54, 60–64. Within these lines, she altered two words.[38] Both the *qaṣā'id* themselves and Umm Kulthūm's manner of working on them became hallmarks of her career.

Concurrently with these artistic initiatives, Umm Kulthūm consolidated her authority in the entertainment business particularly in Egyptian Radio. She joined the Listening Committee, which selected the music appropriate for radio broadcasting. Constituted in 1935, the original committee members were Ja'far Wālī Pāshā, Manṣūr 'Awaḍ, Medhat Assem, Muṣṭafá Bey Riḍá, and one Muḥammad Fatḥī. *Rūz al-Yūsuf* wondered who Fatḥī was and complained that none of the composers "people really listen to," such as Zakariyyā Aḥmad, were members.[39] During the 1940s, Zakariyyā became a member as did Muḥammad al-Qaṣabjī, Riyāḍ al-Sunbāṭī, and Ḥāfiẓ 'Abd al-Wahhāb. Umm Kulthūm became the chairman of the committee, and from this vantage point she guarded her own interests and lobbied for the positions she advocated and the people she liked. One of her efforts produced Studio 35, in its time the most modern recording facility in Egypt, built to her specifications. Describing the functioning of this group in 1952, Sāmī al-Laythī wrote that "if anyone is not comfortable with a song, they leave it to Umm Kulthūm to decide."[40]

Example 7. Excerpts from “Salū Ku’ūs al-Ṭila”

Example 7 concluded

Umm Kulthūm's dominance of the airwaves, along with ʿAbd al-Wahhāb, became a commonplace, finding expression, for instance, in a conversation between two characters in a widely read novel by Najīb Maḥfūẓ first published in 1949: "The radio," complained an aspiring singer, "is monopolized by Umm Kulthūm and ʿAbd al-Wahhāb."[41] Her relationship with broadcasting was one of interdependence. A young musician explained:

> They needed her as much as she did them. The heads of broadcasting did more for Umm Kulthūm than for anyone else. But someone always gets ahead. There is a good studio at the radio because Umm Kulthūm wanted it. It is now there for others to use. She did for broadcasting what Farīd al-Aṭrash did for film—the movie industry would not be what it is if he had not helped to build it up.[42]

This fair-minded retrospective was not shared by Umm Kulthūm's contemporaries, to whom her desire for control was becoming plainly manifest during the 1940s. Singer Suʿād Muḥammad, for example, complained for decades about Umm Kulthūm's command, practical and musical, of the radio: "Umm Kulthūm had the entire Egyptian nation which cared more about her than about its political figures, on her side. She had the entire information ministry at her service."[43] Umm Kulthūm's frequent presence on the airwaves attracted the attention and sometimes the disapprobation of some listeners. Especially the younger generation preferred some of the younger singers such as Layla Murād and, during the early 1950s, ʿAbd al-Ḥalīm Ḥāfiẓ. At any rate, many desired variety. The 1940s saw the beginning of a very common, conflicted view of Umm Kulthūm: that she was a gifted, compelling, and learned singer and that her frequent and lengthy presence was tiring.

Umm Kulthūm nominated herself for president of the Musicians' Union for the first time in 1945 and was elected. She encountered opposition in several forms. Khalīl al-Maṣrī, musician, union member, and artistic director of Odeon records, was incredulous: As long as men were available, men should lead, he argued, to which Umm Kulthūm replied, "I also am able to serve as leader. I also have ideas and solutions to problems." "But men come first!" said al-Maṣrī. "A woman can be a president," answered Umm Kulthūm, and so she was.[44]

She became known for the strength of her personality which was manifest in many ways. She was determined that her views be taken seriously and that business proceed in a way that satisfied her. She was known for her sharp wit and barbed humor.[45] It was often said that she was cutting when irritated or taxed. Pointing to her persistent quality of unvanquished pride, Medhat Assem recalled a conversation with her during which he reminded her that he had been present at one of her early performances at the ʿAbd al-Rāziq mansion. He remembered how terrified she had been that night, to which she retorted, "No! *They* were afraid of *me*."[46]

The Impact of the new Qaṣāʾid and the Populist Songs

Umm Kulthūm's choice of these *qaṣāʾid* for her new repertory in 1946 elicited warnings from her friends and colleagues who believed that no one would want to hear old court poetry in elevated language with serious religious and moralistic overtones. The decision to proceed with them seems to have been Umm Kulthūm's alone. "My audience," she said, "is in a Sufi state."[47] She said she felt sure listeners would appreciate and like them. The religious sensibilities of her audience, she said, would prompt them to grasp and enjoy even such a complicated song as "Nahj al-Burda." She believed that her background *min al-mashāyikh* was shared by many Egyptians who would respond positively to religious *qaṣāʾid*.

In fact they met with a good reception. They drew rave reviews from well-educated musicians such as Maḥmūd al-Ḥifnī, who considered "al-Sūdān" a model composition. Al-Ḥifnī called for increased attention to *qaṣāʾid*, new and old, as essential components of the Arabic literary and musical heritage. He praised Umm Kulthūm as being "at the center of artistic leadership in Egypt."[48]

The *qaṣāʾid* received a great deal of airtime on Egyptian Radio through the ten years following their initial performances. In 1955, for instance, "Salū Kuʾūs al-Ṭilā," "al-Sūdān," "Nahj al-Burda," "Salū Qalbī," and "Wulid al-Hudá" were persistently scheduled, occupying the relatively long periods of fifteen to thirty-five minutes each.[49] Umm Kulthūm also programmed these songs in concerts intended simply to entertain people, for instance at King Fayṣal's birthday celebration in Iraq and at a Musicians' Union annual benefit concert featuring a comedian and a dancer as well as Umm Kulthūm.

The songs fared very well with listeners less sophisticated than Dr. al-Ḥifnī. One might not be capable of singing the songs oneself, but the musical phrases and Umm Kulthūm's style of delivery were as familiar to Egyptians as Qur'anic recitation. Musically and textually, the important primary sources for these *qaṣā'id* were Arab, Egyptian, and Islamic. If few Egyptians could read or recite Shawqī's poems, many seemed to know that he was a great Egyptian poet and that his poetry contributed to the commemoration of people and events from Arab history, ancient and contemporary. Anyone who did not know was informed by radio announcers of the history surrounding the new songs.

Umm Kulthūm became the singer who "taught poetry to the masses" through her recordings of Shawqī's texts. As early as 1948, al-Ḥifnī wrote,

> It is as though Shawqī has returned to life [as the result of Umm Kulthūm's singing his *qaṣā'id*]. . . . They are hummed by people in their homes, walking down the street, by the pedestrian in the garden, the student in school. Even the illiterate who have never in their lives heard of Shawqī or his poetry have all memorized his poetry now.[50]

Many writers over the years reiterated the same belief, and Umm Kulthūm became permanently associated with what was thought to be best in Arabic literature; she was viewed as one who carried this heritage to common people.[51] In 1992 an intellectual friend remarked, "When I was in college [in the 1960s], my doorman knew I loved music. 'Have you heard the new [Umm Kulthūm] song?' he would ask, and then recite lines of *shiʿr!* He was illiterate, uneducated, but he could recite great poetry from listening to Umm Kulthūm!"[52] Her performance of these songs deeply colored popular perceptions of her, contributing substantially to her image as an educated, respectable, religious Arab woman.

The *qaṣā'id* established Riyāḍ al-Sunbāṭī as Umm Kulthūm's principal composer and as the most formidable master of the genre in the Arab world.[53] He continued to supply her with *qaṣā'id* throughout her career on texts by Rāmī, Ḥāfiẓ Ibrāhīm, Ibrāhīm Nājī, and many other poets. These became a means by which Umm Kulthūm reinforced her appeal in the Arab world at large, as indicated by the Sudanese poet, Muḥammad al-Mahdī al-Majdhūb: "Umm Kulthūm, in her perfect pronunciation of Arabic, in her choice of excellent Arabic *qaṣā'id* and in her rendition linked in its base with the recitation of the Qur'ān, aroused something deep and basic in the hearts of Sudanese."[54] "I take pride in singing Arabic *qaṣā'id*, especially religious ones," Umm Kulthūm told a group of Arab ambassadors.

"*Qaṣā'id* are the foundation of Arabic song whose history extends over 3,000 years."[55]

The relatively small group of *qaṣā'id* on texts by Shawqī took on extraordinary importance in Umm Kulthūm's career. "The greatest gift Umm Kulthūm gave to Arabic song was the collection of Shawqī *qaṣā'id,*" said ʿAbd al-Wahhāb.[56] "Umm Kulthūm returned us to the *qaṣīda,*" Sāmī al-Shawwā observed, "and with that she preserved for Oriental music a great part of its authenticity."[57] These songs reinforced her association with serious poetry of great literary worth, and their success paved the way for new *qaṣā'id.*

But the greatest importance of these songs as well as the colloquial ones by Zakariyyā Aḥmad is their location within expressive formations. Both the Sunbāṭī *qaṣā'id* and the very different songs written by Zakariyyā Aḥmad and Bayram al-Tūnisī were important expressions of the widely held support for local and historically Arab culture, for that which was *aṣīl* or authentic. The value of indigenous resources and the importance of bringing them to bear on the contemporary political and economic situation constituted a rising tide of feeling in post–World War II Egypt. Umm Kulthūm's new *qaṣā'id* gave musical expression to this complex of nationalistic and religious sentiments of long standing. As Mary Hegland eloquently reminds us, "Religious traditions"—here, expressive forms—"come to us carrying the weight of the past, but they are flexible in taking on nuances and meanings as they are modified by ideas, events and conditions."[58]

Al-Sunbāṭī and Umm Kulthūm fashioned a musical counterpart to literary neoclassicism, to which many artists, predominantly writers but also musicians such as Kāmil al-Khulaʿī, Dāwūd Ḥusnī, and Darwīsh al-Ḥarīrī, had contributed. They drew upon the models of *turāth* offered by instrumentalists such as Umm Kulthūm's former *qanungi* Muḥammad al-ʿAqqād and composers such as Dāwūd Ḥuṣnī who successfully united "heritage" (*al-turāth*) with "modernity." Thus the work of Umm Kulthūm and Riyāḍ al-Sunbāṭī does not stand alone. It flows from and into the cultural formation of Arab neoclassicism.

Similarly, in her populist songs, Umm Kulthūm did not generate a new style; rather she contributed to and advanced a cultural formation of long duration and substantial size that had been in process at least since the time of Sayyid Darwīsh and extended back into the nineteenth century *azjāl* of ʿAbd Allāh al-Nadīm. By 1940 a number of major artists drew inspiration from locally familiar arts for widely popular productions: Badīʿ Khayrī in his colloquial lyrics and plays; Najīb al-Rīḥānī in his character Kishkish Bey; Ismāʿīl Yāsīn in the comic persona he developed in films; Dāwūd Ḥusnī in songs such as "Laḥn al-Marakbiyya" and "Qamar lu Layaali" (which are sometimes perceived as Egyptian folk songs belonging to a heritage predating Ḥusnī), Zakariyyā Aḥmad, and Bayram al-Tūnisī. During the 1940s this movement became stronger and included such new efforts as the realistic films directed by Ṣalāḥ Abū Sayf. Since then this current has been fed by the poets Fu'ād Ḥaddād, Ṣalāḥ Jāhīn, and ʿAbd al-Raḥmān al-Abnūdī, by the voice of Sayyid Makkāwī and the public persona of singer Muḥammad Munīr. These artists gave expression to Egyptian sentiments and affirmed the value of the local.

The songs by al-Tūnisī and Zakariyyā Aḥmad were distinctively Egyptian. While they had a shorter cultural reach and were usually considered less sophisticated than the *qaṣā'id,* they were none the less important. Parts of them are still sung by amateur musicians; they are played by instrumentalists at weddings; in 1992 they existed in settings for electronic synthesizers and appeared in the middle of improvisations on the *mizmār baladī,* a double-reed instrument associated with Upper Egyptian folk music. This repertory helped constitute the second important component of Umm Kulthūm's identity, that of the Egyptian *fallāḥa,* the peasant, the daughter of the countryside.

Both populism and Arab neoclassicism represented a turn away from "Weststruckness" and its significant component, secularism.[59] The depth and longevity of support for these expressive formations indicate the strength of popular sentiments about what John Voll calls the "failure of the West." Seen in the nineteenth century as a positive model, more critically in the early twentieth century as a source of material culture but not moral authority, by the 1940s the West became "associated with materialism and an individualistic perspective on life" that offered "no basis for societal morality."[60] In these times popular attitudes took recourse to local, indigenous, "authentic" values, and these were usually identified with Islam, even by people who were not themselves particularly religiously observant. The process of affirming the value of the local, acknowledging the failure of the foreign, as Mary Hegland suggests,

> freed Muslims from the western beliefs that secularism is a prerequisite of modernization and that modernity is necessarily western, thereby

> strengthening the legitimacy and appeal of a fundamentalist Islam that has remained relatively untainted of the charge of catering to western modernity.[61]

The expressive formations advanced by Umm Kulthūm's repertory of the 1940s allow one to see that Westernism and secularism simply never took root as viable social models.

Six

"The Voice of Egypt": The Artists' Work and Shared Aesthetics

> Umm Kulthūm is a Sufi leader in song. . . . She struts through a melody like a purebred Arabian horse affected by the sound of the *mizmār*. . . . She has her own style in ending musical phrases which she took from the old *tajwīd*, the seven readings [of the Qur'ān] and religious song.[1]

> If you want to know what Arab music is, listen to Umm Kulthūm.[2]

In 1946 Umm Kulthūm was a mature artist at the height of her skills. Her well-developed musical idiom made her sound "full of our everyday life" and helped constitute her as the "voice of Egypt." She had created two substantial repertories—*qaṣā'id* and *zajal*—that would remain in the public ear for another fifty years. In the 1990s these songs would be marketed on compact discs around the world. Although songs she sang later in life also became well known—"al-Aṭlāl" and "Inta 'Umri" leap to mind—and she was not yet the public figure she later would be, by the end of the 1940s her distinctive idiom, her artistic importance, and her musical accomplishment were established. And so the Egyptian audience heard her and affirmed her primacy and the preeminence of her Thursday concerts in their lives. The sound and the performance that marked Umm Kulthūm were lodged in listeners' ears. She was, at this time, the singer and the performer that older listeners of the 1980s and 1990s remember. They later called this her golden age and characterized what came afterward as different. The practices she had established and the styles constituted by Umm Kulthūm, her colleagues, and her audience at this time effectively carried her to the end of her life. And so we pause here to look more closely at how this musical culture was produced. What constituted Umm Kulthūm's artistic power? What tools, what processes, what venues, what work produced these songs?

Poetic assessments, such as the first passage above, entwine several long and strong fibers of perception about Umm Kulthūm: that she is purely

Arab and, via the sound of the Egyptian *mizmār* and image of the dancing horse of popular culture, that she is thoroughly Egyptian; that religious song, Qur'anic recitation, and Sufism are the sources for her sound and demeanor. Her performances depended on a style of rendition that reached deeply felt and widely shared sensibilities. The production of the sound by the artist and the ways in which listeners understood it and located it within their larger frames of reference constituted her idiom and, subsequently, "the voice of Egypt," throughout her life and after it.

Umm Kulthūm's most important public appearances, her monthly "first Thursday" concerts, were the sources of sounds, images, and memories of the singer that provided starting points for local argumentation of who she was and what she did, and answers to the queries of the curious and uninitiated foreigner. Musicians and technicians said that, on the evening of a concert, Umm Kulthūm customarily arrived at the theater at least an hour early. She walked around the stage and listened to *qanungi* Muḥammad ʿAbduh Ṣāliḥ. She watched the audience from behind the curtain, an important moment to her and one to which she frequently referred. Asked what songs she intended to sing at a concert, she often answered, "I will decide when I see the audience from behind the curtain." Describing her own nervousness at performances, she would say that she became nervous when she saw the audience from behind the curtain. Musicians who accompanied her talked about this habit of standing behind the curtain, peering out at the gathering audience, watching, pacing as the ensemble leader improvised on the *qānūn* in the melodic mode in which she was about to sing.

These moments of immediate anticipation followed long preparation. The process of creation, begun in heads and in houses by a few people, was not yet complete. For Arab music "derives its momentum, emotional efficacy and aesthetic consistency from human interplay . . . involving active and direct communication between the artist and the initiated listener." [3] Umm Kulthūm, behind her curtain, watched her listeners and awaited this moment.

Building the Model of the Song

What is the nature of the musicians' work that produced these performances? The point of origin for a new song was almost always the text. Beginning in the 1940s, when Umm Kulthūm assumed increasing control over the process of composition of new songs, she requested texts from poets or located them in literary volumes, edited them herself with assistance from Aḥmad Rāmī, selected a composer, and sent the poem to him to set to music. Usually she sought a particular poet herself and asked him for a text, sometimes for a specific occasion. Her approach was often the result of having heard a lyric she liked sung by another singer. Thus usually she took up a genre or style already present in the public domain. Umm Kulthūm, her composers and accompanists transformed it into a familiar but distinctive product.

She said she looked for the "*kilma ḥilwa,*" the attractive word or turn of phrase, an aesthetic widely shared in the Arab world. Verbal cleverness, in oratory, poetry, song, or ordinary speech separates the witty from the dull neighbor, the effective from the ineffective argument, the artistic from the banal performance. Umm Kulthūm sought new means of expressing common emotions or ideas. She looked for words that allowed the repetition and reiteration essential to her style of rendition.

For her, a good text "should be elevated in meaning, high-minded of purpose and graceful in sound, whether it be love poetry or descriptive poetry or any other kind. That is what I am interested in. I never sing a text unless I am moved by it." Among the lines she liked very well, she frequently mentioned Bayram al-Tūnisī's "Shams il-Aṣiil:" "When I hear the poetic picture, I am greatly moved and affected": "Shams il-aṣiil dahhabit khuuṣ il-nakhiil" (The setting sun has gilded the leaves of the date palms).[4] In addition to Bayram's characteristic economy of language—in Arabic this line uses only five words—the affect depends on the evocation of rural Egypt and the Nile River near which date palms grow. These are powerful symbols of local identity. The combined impact of textual sound, meaning, and wide reference fulfilled Umm Kulthūm's objective.

Not every song did. In her early years and again late in her career she sang texts that were deemed by some trivial in art and thought. Her speech about texts illustrates her determined efforts to emphasize the ideal, to reinforce what she wanted to be remembered and repeated about her work.

Upon receiving a text, she would frequently suggest changes. Bayram al-Tūnisī described the creation of one of his lyrics by saying he spent one day writing the poem and ten days arguing with Umm Kulthūm about it. In this instance, she had also asked for a text for the same occasion from another poet, apparently to give herself a choice.[5]

Once chosen, the song text was passed on to the composer. When he had completed his work, he took his ideas to the singer.[6] Composers experienced with Umm Kulthūm frequently brought two or three beginnings for the same song. She chose among the alternatives or rejected the efforts altogether. After she selected one and offered her comments, he composed the rest of the song.

When she approved a composition in its basic outline she usually suggested her own emendations. "It is not enough," Zakariyyā Aḥmad complained, "that a composer presents her with one melody or two or three. She wants more. And she may demand that a composer write a single section many, many times."[7] Riyāḍ al-Sunbāṭī described his work with her as resembling "the building of the High Dam":

> Sometimes we would sit in her glassed-in room, if it were winter, an entire day without food, water, telephone calls or visits. Umm Kulthūm would spend the entire time rehearsing a single line! For Umm Kulthūm does not sing ordinary songs or ordinary texts. . . . Days spent in this manner became weeks and then months producing a song.[8]

As a result, according to Bayram al-Tūnisī, "she pushed her composers and poets forward,"[9] and her repertory consisted largely of songs heard as excellent, representing the best efforts and utmost polish of Umm Kulthūm and these men. In her last interview she reiterated criticism of music that she voiced many times in her life: "The process of creation is missing. If I take a few high notes and give them a few words, I call it regression, not progress."[10]

Tempers flared on occasion. Her frequent rejections of al-Qaṣabjī's compositions, even after she had initially encouraged him, annoyed the composer and his many friends. During the composition of "Ya Ẓaalimni" (ca. 1951) Riyāḍ al-Sunbāṭī became so aggravated that he stormed out of the house, shouting "Go compose it yourself, then!" Civil court became the venue for settlement of numerous disputes.[11]

She learned new songs by ear from the composers during the process of composition. Al-Qaṣabjī said that she could learn the most difficult piece in two sessions, a rare capability in his estimation. Always interested in modern technology, in her later years she used cassette tapes to study new songs.[12] She then worked with the principal percussionist to establish the tempos. In performance, Umm Kulthūm led the group, setting the pace which was quickly noted by the *riqq* player and conveyed by his playing to the rest of the ensemble. This helped to insure her musical leadership of performances and marked the performances as historically Arab.

When she had learned the song, rehearsal with the ensemble began. She insisted that the players learn by ear and considered this process essential to stylistically correct performance. She said they would thus internalize the piece—they would know it better and understand its musical potential better than they would by reading a notated version.

Many musicians agreed. "Musicians [in her ensemble] never used notes," an old violinist remembered. "This was very important to the oriental style of playing in which notes need not be fixed."[13] "She never used notes. Because of that she forced the musicians to 'live' the song," composer Balīgh Ḥamdī said. "Details that are lost in notation and subsequently lost in a performance based on notation were not lost with Umm Kulthūm."[14]

As a result of the considerable influence wielded by the Institute for Arab Music, already well established by 1932, and its pedagogical practices which utilized notation, formal musical training had become a sine qua non for employment in mid-twentieth-century Cairo. "Formal training" including reading and writing notation. Playing from notes became a common practice.[15] It was commercially desirable because it reduced the number of rehearsals needed and allowed the rapid production of new performances. Umm Kulthūm's view of notation was unusual.

The players learned the new songs from the composer. He usually taught the song using an *ʿūd,* one phrase at a time, over a period of ten or twelve rehearsals lasting two to five hours each. The musicians learned the song during the first three or four. Umm Kulthūm, the composer, and the experienced musicians made emendations during the remainder. She frequently required more rehearsals than other singers. She occasionally supplemented the fee paid the musicians by the recording company for rehearsals. For songs by Muḥammad ʿAbd al-Wahhāb, the number of rehearsals increased dramatically, reaching over fifty for "A-ghadan Alqāk."[16]

The ensemble had three strata: the "core" of older members, al-Qaṣabjī playing *ʿūd,* Muḥammad ʿAbduh Ṣāliḥ, *qānūn,* Sayyid Sālim, *nāy,* Aḥmad al-Ḥifnāwī, Karīm Ḥilmī, and ʿAbd al-Munʿim al-Ḥarīrī, violin, and ʿAbbās Fu'ād, bass. The second layer consisted of eight to ten violinists and two cellists who consistently worked with her but were not members of her inner circle of associates. Finally, there was the layer of people hired for short periods of time, sometimes only for one concert or for one song when more or different instruments were needed. As the ensemble grew, al-Qaṣabjī took on the tasks of its administration. ʿAbduh Ṣāliḥ conducted rehearsals and acted as the head of the group.

Many players remained with Umm Kulthūm for long periods of time. They generally compared her favorably to other singers. They admired her as a musician, and even those who did not like her personally said they valued the opportunity to perform with her. She was unquestionably one of the most demanding performers with whom one might work. However, she valued longevity and attempted to retain good players for long periods of time. Many were replaced only after they died. The musical standards in the group were high, which satisfied experienced performers; young musicians learned useful skills from the older ones and from Umm Kulthūm, and they derived prestige from working for her. As a result, they gained access to other good jobs and were able to command higher fees for their services.

The entire process of production of a single new song lasted as much as twelve months and sometimes more. In her later years, Umm Kulthūm said she preferred this, that she wanted to live with a melody for a year before anyone heard it: "Thus it becomes part of me. And so with the words, for they concern me to the utmost extent."[17]

"She was the first to arrive and the last to leave" these sessions, according to Rāmī. "She had the tirelessness of the peasant [*fallāḥ*] and exerted the effort of a *fallāḥ* if the case required it." "She personally supervised the entire preparation of any recording," working until its completion without consideration of mealtimes or rest.[18] She was meticulous and tried to perfect all aspects of her performers. No concert tape was aired over the radio without her approval, which required her hearing the tape more than once. She even involved herself in the selection of excerpts for listener request programs and background music for her interviews.[19]

The dates on which new songs were premiered were usually fixed in advance. During the 1960s and 1970s, new songs received press attention ahead of their premieres. The name of the poet and composer, details of the orchestration, information about the process of composition and the rehearsals were published in newspapers. The text itself occasionally appeared on the day of the performance or the day after.

Beginning in the mid-1950s Umm Kulthūm and her *firqa* made studio recordings prior to the first performance of most songs. The records were thus available for immediate sale after the premiere, and, as an added benefit, she could be certain that her accompanists knew the song well before a live performance. The process of recording was often lengthy, especially for the songs by ʿAbd al-Wahhāb who was as meticulous as she was. The introduction to "Intra ʿUmri," which lasted four minutes, took almost five hours to record. "Amal Ḥayaati" took sixteen hours and "Hādhihi Laylatī," fifteen.[20]

Editing the tapes was undertaken with similar exactitude. Where, in the early 1930s, Umm Kulthūm approved or disapproved recordings herself, during the 1950s she acquired help. Her principal assistant was her nephew, Muḥammad al-Disūqī.[21] His duties expanded until, at the end of her life, he functioned as her primary representative and aide. The engineer Sayyid al-Maṣrī then assumed responsibility for editing recordings.

Even recordings labeled "live" were edited and sometimes were composites of several performances. In one instance, ʿAbd al-Wahhāb requested that the syllables *Inta ʿum-* from one tape be patched to the syllable *-ri* from another, which was done. Excessive clapping and audience response were excised as were mistakes: "Sometimes she would go one way and the *firqa* would go another. Did we want to keep *that*?!" al-Maṣrī explained.[22] As a result, the only actual reproductions of concerts exist on the tapes in the radio archives and in the collections of aficionados who recorded performances from broadcasts.

"Choice, exactitude, work and revision" characterized her approach to her productions. Musicians described her effort as extraordinary and exemplary. Balīgh Ḥamdī articulated their common attitude that "her care for her art as a whole is fifty times greater than any other singer. If every new singer understood that and gave to her art one fourth of what Umm Kulthūm gives hers, we would have at least ten really worthwhile singers."[23] Only a few of her contemporaries, Nādira, Laure Daccache, and Suʿād Muḥammad among them, were both interested in and capable of working with poetry and music as Umm Kulthūm did. The work and dedication of poets and composers was considered absolutely essential to her results. Few singers commanded the commitment of these artists that she did. This view of Umm Kulthūm and her musicians' work persists, even among her detractors.

But, ultimately, creativity in Arabic music is collective and depends on listeners. "The concept of 'listening,'" Racy writes, "which in the modern West implies a cerebral aesthetic process distinct from the physical sense of 'hearing,' may be contrasted with the *ṭarab* related concept of *samāʿ*, which in common Arabic usage means both 'listening' and 'hearing' and, like the related Sufi concept of *samāʿ*, 'auditioning,' presented music as a truly holistic experience."[24] The popularity of Umm Kulthūm's "first Thursday" concerts, the character of her idiom, and the styles in which she sang depended on the engagement of listeners. What did they hear? What did she encourage them to hear? And what were the consequences of the interaction of artist and audience in the long run?

The Concerts

When the curtain rose, the theater audience saw Umm Kulthūm, modestly but elegantly dressed, seated next to the *qanungi* in the first row of the ensemble. Her dresses for the stage often took the form of an elaborate, bejeweled woman's *jallābiyya*. In the late 1920s, she developed a conservative elegance in her style of dress not unlike that of the wealthy women in whose houses she performed. She purchased rich cloth for dresses. She acquired furs and jewelry. She no longer wore a head covering. Most entertainers of the 1930s and 1940s adopted the glamorous style popularized by American film stars, and, to a certain extent, Umm Kulthūm also followed current fashions. However, her dresses almost always had sleeves and relatively high necklines, in accordance with Egyptian principles of modesty. Listeners applauded her for maintaining a dignified bearing on stage. "She wore contemporary dresses, but she never abandoned the spirit of the country, its traditions, its customs . . . and its modesty."[25]

Her hairdo during her last thirty years was almost always styled in some sort of bun or more elaborate chignon. This was one more link to her own past and to her audience of working-class Egyptians. According to her husband, she was most comfortable with a personal appearance that matched what she had been brought up to believe was appropriate. "She was very conservative," he said. "She was a real *bint il-riif*. . . . Her dress, the shape of her hair indicated her *bint il-riif* character."[26] She was an elegant and stylish daughter of the country.

Gradually her *balāṭ*—that noisy coterie of supporters in the 1920s—gave way to the more dignified *sammāʿiyyūn,* literally "listeners," devoted audience members who attended all of Umm Kulthūm's concerts and knew her repertory well. They sat in the front rows during her performances, some for more than thirty years. She received them as visitors in her dressing room during intermissions. She noticed, people said, if anyone was missing, as illustrated by the following representative story, told by a musician:

> An old *ʿumda* lived in Alexandria and attended all of Umm Kulthūm's concerts. He bought two seats, one for himself and one for his coat and hat. When he didn't appear at one concert, Umm Kulthūm sent the emergency service [*būlīs al-najda*] after him during an intermission. It transpired that the *ʿumda*'s father had died and he was in mourning. He came to the concert anyway with the police. He is still alive in Alexandria.[27]

During the later years of her life, Egyptian listeners sometimes waited as delayed charter flights or private planes from abroad landed and foreign concertgoers made their way to the theater.[28] Perhaps as many as fifteen hundred people participated in these performances, calling out compliments as her singing went on and requesting repetitions of lines and stanzas. This audience was important to her; she catered to them, sang to their moods, played with words or lines they liked, and reveled in their approbation. As a young girl, she said she could not sing without a live audience. Aḥmad Rāmī accompanied her to recording sessions and mimed encouraging responses from behind a glass partition.

Generally solicitous of her audience, in her later years Umm Kulthūm nevertheless disparaged what she called the "clowns" who interrupted with whistling and acclamations and attempted, in her opinion, to call attention to themselves rather than to the music.[29] She cultivated the knowledgeable reactions of the *sammāʿiyyūn* at appropriate points in the song. They played an important role, as she appreciated the response of informed and supportive listeners. Virtually everyone who came into contact with her, however casually, noticed her attentiveness to her audience, frequently remarking that "She cared much about people's opinions," "She was concerned about the audience's tastes," or "She really respected her audience." The degree of her concern, viewed by musicians in particular, set her apart from many other singers.

The opening sounds of performances were instrumental sounds. Newly composed instrumental introductions became the norm in Umm Kulthūm's repertory in the late 1920s and undoubtedly owed much to the influence of Muḥammad ʿAbd al-Wahhāb and Muḥammad al-Qaṣabjī's musical thinking. These introductions replaced short, familiar pieces in the *maqām* of the song to follow (*dawālīb,* s., *dūlāb*). Beginning, in Umm Kulthūm's repertory, with the syncopated instrumental introductions composed by Aḥmad Ṣabrī al-Najrīdī and continuing through the newly composed introductions to her monologues and the later *ughniyyāt,* instrumentalists played longer and more distinctive portions of the songs. ʿAbd al-Wahhāb's compositions contained a higher percentage of instrumental music than any others in her repertory. For instance, the introduction to al-Sunbāṭī's love song "Laa ya Ḥabiibi" (1965) occupied about three-and-a-half minutes and that for al-Mawjī's "Lil Ṣabr Ḥuduud" (1964) slightly less than four minutes; the introductions to "Amal Ḥayaati" and "Intra ʿUmri" by ʿAbd al-Wahhāb lasted about six-and-a-half and seven minutes respectively. Instrumental interludes were proportionately longer in ʿAbd al-Wahhāb's songs as well.[30] Many innovations took place in these instrumental sections, when Umm Kulthūm was not singing, and they often featured Western musical styles and dancelike passages.

New instruments and electronics greatly increased the number of sounds available to musicians to the delight of almost everybody. Since nuances of color are critical constituents of style, electronics and new instruments greatly expanded an important medium of musical expression. Moreover, as Stephen Slawek argues in the case of Ravi Shankar, while his compositions for sitar and orchestra may be seen as imitations of Western models, they may also be seen as appropriations of a powerful symbol of Western culture for Indian music, securing a new venue for Shankar and presenting the two cultures on equal footing.[31]

Egyptian composers absorbed Western instruments constantly, and listeners generally did not hear the sounds as "foreign." "Foreignness" depended on other characteristics. Connoisseurs missed the delicate sound and interplay of the smaller *takht,* and said so. But generally the new instruments and techniques in and of themselves were not seen as detrimental to the character of contemporary Arab music.

One reason was that the size and instruments of an ensemble, while attractive and attention-getting, were less important determinants of style than the role played by the ensemble in performance. Umm Kulthūm insisted that the singer be the focal point of the performance and the leader of the ensemble. This perpetuation of old Arab practice helped lodge her style in the domain of the authentic almost regardless of instrumentation.

When the instrumental introduction was almost over, Umm Kulthūm rose, holding in her hands the silk scarf that was her hallmark, and began what would be three to six hours of singing. Listeners at home heard enthusiastic clapping when she stood up. She customarily used the first song, called a *waṣla,* to take stock of the mood of her audience and to "warm them up" if necessary with a familiar and popular song. New songs were featured as the second *waṣla.* She frequently left the selection of other songs literally until the last minute—until she had seen the audience. This allowed her to gain a sense of them, to tailor the closing *waṣla* to their reaction, and to accommodate her own fatigue without disrupting a previously announced program. She rarely sang a song that was more than ten years old.

At the start of her first line, the number of instruments decreased to a handful, the remainder engaging only in interludes and a few cadences. Accompaniment to Umm Kulthūm's vocal lines remained light, sparing, and often heterophonic. This style of accompaniment was more difficult to attain the larger the ensemble became, and the solution she reached was to limit the number of instrumentalists who accompanied the vocal line to about six or fewer, and, when more accompanists were playing, to limit those who were allowed to add improvisations. Only her inner circle of accompanists, the men who had worked longest with her and were seated nearest her on stage, improvised along with her.

Umm Kulthūm led her accompanists; she determined when and how many reiterations of a phrase would occur, and she initiated improvisations, followed by her accompanists who added their own contributions between her phrases. Only on rare occasions did she sing along with a rigidly metrical accompaniment played by the entire ensemble. The dominant position accorded the solo singer while she was singing maintained a historic relationship and permitted freedom for her improvisations and varied repetitions. These lay at the heart of her musical idiom and identified her songs as indigenous in the ears of her listeners.

Until 1966, the concerts consisted of three songs (or *waṣalāt*) with intermissions of thirty to sixty minutes between them. The concerts began at 9:30 P.M. and invariably lasted well past midnight. A likely model of a lengthy performance might be:

10:30–11:40 First *Waṣla*
Intermission: 50 Minutes
12:30–2:40 Second *Waṣla*
Intermission: 50 Minutes
3:30–4:15 Third *Waṣla*[32]

The timing and length of her performances reflected old and important ideas associated with good singing and *ṭarab:* the pleasure of listening to a wonderful singer all night; the excellence of the singer who could enchant her audience until dawn; the marvelous strength of the voice that could sing until daybreak. The dispersement of time in her performances as a whole was a significant factor in her association with Arab tradition. She insisted on this schedule even when she sang in Paris in 1967, to the amazement of French officials and the non-Arab audience. The length of her concerts, which extended to seven hours ending at 3 A.M., set a new local record. "Not even for Wagner" had the Olympia Theater remained open so late, and it was reported that special permission had to be obtained in advance from the city authorities.[33]

During the 1960s, younger listeners became impatient of the long concerts and the long songs. They said that modern life did not allow hours of listening to a single song and that the whole idea was out of step with contemporary reality. In a review of one of her concerts in 1966, Kamāl al-Najmī observed that their length had become excessive from another point of view: "Last night," he wrote, "Umm Kulthūm sang 'Aruuḥ li-miin' until 4 A.M.!" Ten years earlier, he correctly observed, she would have finished by 3 A.M. at the latest. What was responsible for this protracted length was the growing number of audience requests for repetitions of lines and entire sections. Al-Najmī suggested that this behavior had extended beyond its normal and desirable role, and that the requests had taken on a life of their own, not directly related to musical appreciation.[34] Essentially, audience members shouted for repetitions no matter what she did.

Umm Kulthūm took this opportunity to reduce her program to two songs, an understandable decision since she was then over sixty years old, but her style of rendition and the audience response remained the same. A 1968 performance of "al-Aṭlāl" occupied an hour and seven minutes, after which she rested for an hour and then sang "Hādhihi Laylatī," for over an hour. In 1972, "Inta 'Umri" lasted two hours and a performance of "Laylat Ḥubb" in 1973 was longer still.[35]

Outside the concert hall the much larger audience that sustained her over the years rarely if ever came to a concert. They sat in homes and coffeehouses, with friends and relatives, wherever a radio could receive the general program from Cairo. For, as Racy writes,

> *ṭarab* music itself can be emotionally experienced outside the immediate ecstatic and interactive ambience that originally led to its creation. Whether in the form of recordings of live performances . . . or radio broadcasts . . . *ṭarab* works become ecstatic codes capable of establishing a *ṭarab* ambience for the culturally trained and musically initiated listener.[36]

Her concerts reached beyond Cairo into towns, villages, and camps, beyond the boundaries of Egypt, throughout the Arab world via the radio, and her audience consisted principally of people who never attended a concert. These listeners, as much as the concertgoers, evaluated, compared, complained, raved, and glorified her. Not only her performances but talk about the performances became pervasive. This audience, their attention and their talk, created the space in which she became "the voice of Egypt."

"Her voice . . . !"

Umm Kulthūm's voice itself brought sighs of appreciation. Ordinary listeners used ordinary language for the sound of her voice. For them it was simply "powerful," "beautiful," or "amazing." The speech of experts directs attention to its more specific qualities. They speak of the power, clarity, and bell-like resonance of her voice. Their words offer ways of hearing the nuances she learned and cultivated.

The power of her voice—its volume, resonance, and resilience—that was noticed with amazement by listeners in the 1920s remained a salient characteristic of her sound throughout her life. But she also deployed many colors, among them *baḥḥa* (hoarseness), *ghunna* (nasality), falsetto, and an array of pretty and affective frontal resonances that constantly varied her sound and added impact to the sung text. Her listeners identify *ghunna* as an important marker of authentic singing. A writer for *Rūz al-Yūsuf* devoted a full page to praise of nasality, calling it "what pleases us in the voices of Sayyid Darwīsh, Muḥammad ʿAbd al-Wahhāb, and Umm Kulthūm." He likened Umm Kulthūm's voice to the "tones of a *mizmār*" (a double-reed instrument) and concluded that "the sweetest [quality] in her voice is that of *khanaafa*."[37] When Western culture accrued influence in Egypt, *ghunna* was one of the musical qualities that came to be considered undesirable among those interested in emulating the West. Partisans of European classical music apparently considered all kinds of nasality to be rustic, countrified, or unsophisticated. Racy identifies changes from nasal to nonfrontal resonance in the early twentieth century with Westernization:

accordingly, the nasal voice is the local voice and tone color an indicator of identity.[38]

Baḥḥa served at once as a beautiful feature of Umm Kulthūm's rendition and as a way to heighten the emotional impact of the text. It contributed to her most compelling performances, such as that of the religious *mawwāl* "Bi-Riḍaak,"[39] and was part of her rendition of almost every song in her repertory for as long as her voice was capable of producing it. Falsetto was linked with a trill, producing vibrant ornaments for the upper range of a line.[40]

Still, listeners rarely reacted to the first note she sang but, rather, to the first phrase. Her rendition of the words was what mattered.

"But Can You Understand the Words?"

"The song depends before all else on the words," Umm Kulthūm said. "If the words are beautiful, they will inspire the composer and the singer, and the composition will turn out beautifully and the rendition excellent. The more affective the text, so will be the song." "The words, in my opinion," she said, "are what is important [*al-fā'ida*] in music."[41]

Throughout her career Umm Kulthūm was known for her mastery of Arabic language and poetry. To her, it was fundamental: "The singer who does not articulate accurately cannot reach the heart of the listener and is not capable of perfect artistic rendition."[42] It was said that she "tasted each word."

Asked to explain *ṭarab,* the state of "enchantment" wherein the listener is completely engaged with a performance, Umm Kulthūm said that it was attained when the listener "felt" the meaning of the words.[43] Usually she sought to evoke meaning(s) in indirect ways, drawing the listener closer to the themes and emotions of the text, *taṣwīr al-ma'ná.*

Her skills in diction and *taṣwīr al-ma'ná* were invariably noted and appreciated by critics as well as by her larger audience. Bayram al-Tūnisī remarked that "Simple words acquire depth and beauty when she sings them." The scholar Ṭāhā Ḥusayn said that he "listen[s] to her a great deal. I enjoy her excellent delivery of the Arabic language, and I very much like the depth of her sensitivity to its meaning." Umm Kulthūm's artistry was "the art of the word, and the art of rendition, beyond her gift in singing."[44] It was frequently said that even one who did not speak Arabic would understand the meaning of a text from listening to her sing it, and this statement succinctly expressed perceptions, widely shared in Egypt, of Umm Kulthūm's particular skill.

Aḥmad Zākī Pāshā's vivid simile captures the essence of an important conceptualization with long roots in Arab culture, that of the closeness of poetry and music: "Poetry and music are two entities in the human soul having a single meaning, or two meanings for a single thing, as flowers and their scent."[45] Umm Kulthūm's linkage of text to melody pulled this conceptual wire into the twentieth century and electrified it in new uses.

Ibn Surayj (ca. 634–726), in his discussion of the expectations of a good singer, included good pronunciation and correct inflection of the Arabic case endings.[46] Surveying the history of Arabic song, Ibrahim Boolaky wrote that "Verses—countless in number—were admired not merely for their poetical content but also for their exquisite diction. The overall quality of the vocal expression of the time depended as much on the choice of words as on the skillful use of the human voice."[47] Musical genres often shared the names of the poetic genres to which their texts belonged, for instance the *mawwāl* and the *qaṣīḍa*. In the mid-nineteenth century Lane noted that "distinct enunciation . . . [was] characteristic of the Egyptian mode of singing."[48] Al-Khulaʿī devoted a long paragraph to pronunciation, urging professional singers of his day, whom he believed frequently were illiterate, to hire teachers to school them in language and grammar so as to avoid obvious errors in articulation and inflection.

A good comprehension of texts was also expected of singers and composers. The singer, according to al-Khulaʿī, must understand the syntax, grammar, and meaning of poetry, and choose songs appropriate in their texts to the tastes and understanding of the audience.[49] In practice, Racy found that "despite the elaborate melismas occurring frequently in the vocal line, the dynamic accentuation of the text [of *qaṣāʾid*], for example, the degree to which each text syllable was elongated or emphasized, was often reflected in the duration of the notes."[50] Clever plays on words (for instance, successive puns); allusions to historical, legendary, or religious figures or events; allusions to local happenings; and metaphors all contributed to the well-loved text. So too did rhyme, alliteration, and skillful use of sounds characteristic of the Arabic language, especially the emphatic consonants (*ḥ, ṣ, ḍ,* etc.).[51]

Ultimately the link of word to music was the essence of *ṭarab* in Umm Kulthūm's idiom. It explained why she was a paragon of Arabic singing, representing a turn away from the process of enchantment (*taṭrīb*) based on melodic invention alone,[52] a quality associated by Egyptian listeners with Turkish singing.

"She Was Good Because She Could Read the Qur'ān"

Egyptian listeners often link the various skills associated with proper delivery of the text—pronunciation, correct inflection, informed delivery, and *taṣwīr al-maʿná*—with the training required to recite the Qur'ān, thus investing these aesthetic requirements with age and weighty significance. As Boolaky wrote,

> Indeed when Prophet Muhammad began to recite the words of the Revelation, the professional poets of Arabia themselves realised that none of their poems could possibly match the verses of the *Qur'an*. Thus, besides the Revelation, it was basically the transmission of the *Qur'an* by Prophet Muhammad which prepared the ground for the successful establishment of traditional Muslim vocal art-forms in the world.[53]

Although it is not considered to be song (and conservative Muslims reject any connection between the two), recitation and song share fundamental principles. Egyptian observers have argued that Qur'anic recitation is the foundation of Arabic song, although its sound is unique. As Nelson describes it,

> Its characteristic sound is reproducible and therefore necessarily organized according to a set of underlying principles. The system of organization has certain special features that distinguish Qur'anic recitation from other cultural forms such as music. . . . The organizational system is not self-contained, but shares patterning principles such as cultural values and aesthetic orientation, with other modes and forms of Egyptian society.[54]

The elements shared by the recitation of the Qur'ān, the singing styles of the *mashāyikh,* and Umm Kulthūm's style of rendition include correct pronunciation, sensitive expression of textual meaning, attention to the unity of the textual phrase, and use of vocal tone colors.[55]

Recitation is governed by an elaborate system of rules known as *tajwīd.* According to a modern manual, "Tajwīd, in the technical sense, is articulating each letter from its point of articulation, giving it its full value."[56] Rules mandate the nasalization of certain syllables when they appear in the context of particular combinations of consonants. Rules for duration require the reader to regulate the length of syllables by counting two to six beats. Nasalization affects the duration of the syllables, and the entire system produces rhythms particular to the recitation of the Qur'ān, unlike the meters of poetry.

A secondary aim in the melodically elaborate *mujawwad* style of recitation is *taṣwīr al-maʿná.* For the singer and composer, the affective treatment of a text often involved the depiction, shaping or heightening of its meaning, sense, or idea. Nelson observes that *taṣwīr al-maʿná,* as applied in recitation of the Qur'ān, refers "more to mood or emotion than to meaning," and that "techniques for correlating melody with meaning [are] limited only by the imagination of the reciter."[57] Correct treatment of text, including *taṣwīr al-maʿná,* produced an effect perceived as the fusion of sound and meaning:

> Ultimately, scholars and listeners recognize that the ideal beauty and inimitability of the Qur'an lie not in the content and order of the message, on the one hand, and in the elegance of the language, on the other, but in the use of the very sound of the language to convey specific meaning. This amounts to an almost onomatopoeic use of language, so that not only the image of the metaphor but also the sound of the words which express that image are perceived to converge with the meaning.[58]

Clear articulation was essential to the correct recitation of the Qur'ān and also to many prayers. "The word," according to popular understanding, "is the foundation of religious song."[59] The link between treatment of text in singing and recitation of the Qur'ān formed a fundamental piece of the conceptual framework for discussions of musical competence: "If [recitation of] the Qur'ān is the foundation [of musical training], [then] the tongue is properly trained, and spreads in its possessor good execution, vibrant tone, melodiousness, and correct shortening of final consonants."[60]

During the twentieth century, the reciters and singers of religious song came to be viewed as the principal repository of Arabic song and singing. Their style and repertory were identified as historically Arab and *aṣīl.* Dāwūd Ḥusnī's son, himself a musician and teacher, explained the relationship as follows:

> The Qur'ān is the basis of all music. It allows for improvisation but also has a system of strict rules. People *min al-mashāyikh* know the

> rules but they also know the means of improvisation; as a result of their training they understand the meaning of texts, and also their pronunciation is better than those without the same background.[61]

With performers such as Salāma Ḥijāzī and Zakariyyā Aḥmad moving readily between the world of recitation and religious song and that of urban stage and theater, careful treatment of text became linked with Muslim classicism conceptually and practically.[62] Zakariyyā explained this quality in Umm Kulthūm's idiom:

> By virtue of her memorization and reading of the Qur'ān, she acquired experience that made her capable of giving to each word or each letter what was appropriate to correct pronunciation. From habit over the years, it became part of her nature, and her delivery of the letters was perfected to the point where her listener can clearly perceive every word she sings.[63]

When the rendition of a song features the type of clear pronunciation associated with the recitation of the Qur'ān, it strikes a familiar chord for the listeners, establishing a link of shared experience between the singer and themselves. Listeners may not be capable of articulating the rules of recitation but often they can hear when others apply them or break them. As Pierre Bourdieu writes about Western classical music,

> a lover of classical music may have neither consciousness nor knowledge of the laws obeyed by the sound-making art to which he is accustomed, but his auditive education is such that, having heard a dominant chord, he is induced urgently to await the tonic which seems to him the "natural" resolution of this chord, and he has difficulty in apprehending the internal coherence of music founded on other principles.[64]

This knowledge, he writes, is acquired "by slow familiarization, a long succession of 'little perceptions.'"

Shared knowledge produced the assessment of Umm Kulthūm as "naturally gifted," listeners and singer alike having been slowly familiarized with constitutive elements of an aesthetic. In this case, however, what was learned was not the cultural property of the privileged few, but was and is widely shared by all strata of society. Significantly, folk repertories, which would be equally familiar throughout the society, are not, in this case, what is claimed as the source of cultural authenticity. The learned poetry and linguistic skill of the best of the *mashāyikh* claimed greater authority.

El-Hamamsy captures the central place of the sound and idea in the shared culture of Arabic speakers:

> By perpetuating a community of language the Qur'ān kept alive a community of culture—a process which was reinforced by the use of the Qur'ān as a basic teaching text throughout the Arab world. . . . Reverence for the Arabic language transcends sectarian considerations so that one finds an Egyptian Copt such as Makram Ebeid acknowledging that his powerful oratory owed much to the study of the Qur'ān.[65]

In an eloquent discussion, Timothy Mitchell writes that "the force of the phrase gathers not simply from the various references of the separate words, but from the reverberation of senses set up between the parts of the phrase by their differing sounds." Mitchell argues, correctly in my view, that pleasure in the sounds and meanings of words, and even the power of words of comfort, instruction, or charm against the powers of evil textures the lives of ordinary people.[66] My own experience suggests that it is nearly impossible to overestimate the impact and relevance of the sound of recitation in Egyptian cultural practice.

Qualities shared with Qur'anic recitation formed the stable core of Umm Kulthūm's singing styles, to which other "new," "modern," or even foreign qualities were added as musical fashions changed. In relying on this fundamental style, Umm Kulthūm linked herself artistically to the *mashāyikh*. Through her performances, she and her audience maintained and strengthened the presence of the *mashāyikh* and the associated practices and concepts about culture within Egyptian society. This practice of performing and listening at once drew from and advanced a particular set of values and a view of culture and its potentials grounded in Muslim, Egyptian, and Arab practices.

"She Gave Us Back the Qaṣīda"

The concept of *turāth* or heritage in Egyptian music includes the systems of melodic and rhythmic modes and also compositional genres, ways of structuring music and specific pieces. Some pieces, notably the large repertory of difficult *muwashshaḥāt*, have served as teaching pieces. These often beautiful songs are rarely performed but have been used by singers to develop their vocal skills and increase their command of the *maqāmāt,* together with their knowledge of *turāth.*

However, in general, audiences demand new songs (or new interpretations of songs), not reproductions of older pieces. Innovation is expected, with the caution that the result be compatible with the essential aspects of the musical culture.[67]

As a young singer and even as a performer of "modern" or "advanced" songs such as those by al-Qaṣabjī, Umm Kulthūm was linked to the *turāth.* As her career progressed, this connection grew stronger, and after her death songs from her repertory came to be considered part of the Arabic *turāth.*

The compositions she sang were usually carefully conceived and drew upon classical models in important ways. She learned to command the *maqāmāt.* Almost all of her songs were based on *maqāmāt* and constructed along the familiar lines of the arch: beginning low in the range of a *maqām,* ascending in the initial *maqām,* modulating and descending to close in the original mode.[68] Most of her songs used familiar and well-loved modes: *rāst, bayātī, nahāwand,* and *huzām.*

She introduced new *qaṣā'id,* a quintessentially Arabic genre, virtually every year of her career. In the late 1920s and 1930s, a time when her colleague Muḥammad ʿAbd al-Wahhāb and others advocated the invention of new musical genres, she sang *adwār* hearkening back to the nineteenth-century repertories of ʿAbduh al-Ḥāmūlī and Muḥammad ʿUthmān.[69]

Her performances, even of the new songs of the 1960s and 1970s, manifest the impact of *turāth* in their relationship to the older *waṣla,* or suite of instrumental and vocal pieces. In her later repertory the instrumental introduction typically included two or three sections of two to four phrases (one to two minutes each), metrical and nonmetrical, with one or more instrumental solos often fashioned as improvisations (*taqāsīm*). Then the vocal part usually opened with several slow, nonmetrical phrases, followed by a metrical interlude (*lazma*) and a metrical vocal section or stanza. A lengthy *lazma,* often in an Arab or Western dance rhythm, was usually included at the midpoint of the composition, and vocal improvisation took place after that interlude. The structure of these performances, and their length, often over an hour, resembled the Arabic *waṣla,* and Umm Kulthūm, in fact, employed the term to denote each of the two or three songs that constituted her concerts.[70] As illustrated below, the *ughniyya* and *waṣla* involve similar concepts (metrical/nonmetrical, more improvised/more fixed) in similar variable sequences.

	Waṣla	*Ughniyya*
1.	Metrical instrumental piece	Instrumental introduction, metrical and nonmetrical
2.	*Muwashshaḥ* (metrical vocal piece)	First vocal stanza or section, often nonmetrical
3.	*Taqāsīm*	Instrumental *lazma* (metrical)
4.	*Layālī*	Second vocal stanza or section
5.	*Mawwāl*	
6.	*Qaṣīda* or *dawr*	Last section with improvisation

An important relationship between *waṣla* and *ughniyya* lies in the collective disposition of time in performance. Both genres are formed jointly by performers and audience who could stop a musician in any number of places, urging lengthy repetitions. Thus, in musical content, shape, and rhythmic structure there were clear parallels between the *waṣla* and Umm Kulthūm's newer songs, and this forged one more link between Umm Kulthūm and her Egyptian-Arab musical heritage.

"She Never Sang a Line the Same Way Twice"

Umm Kulthūm's principal contribution to Arabic song came in the artistry of her renditions. Although she sang precomposed songs that eventually became familiar to her audience and she repeated successful inventions, each of her renditions was believed to be unique. Her musical creativity enabled her to spontaneously produce multiple versions of a single line, "over fifty in a row" according to stories about her concerts.[71]

Arabic song historically involves not the replication of music but the reinterpretation of familiar models. While the "main contours" of a song in performance remain "fixed and identifiable" and "the order of its segments is not altered,"[72] the song is supposed to be varied from one performance to another: "Composers handed down to the performers a skeletal framework which consisted of the naṣ [text], laḥn [melody], and iḳāʿ [rhythmic mode]. To this skeletal framework, performers added ornaments, cadential formulae, and improvised entire sections."[73] The performer's responsibility for the sound of the performance was equal to or greater than that of the

15. Umm Kulthūm singing at Ewart Hall, the American University in Cairo, 1939 (photo courtesy of Dār al-Hilāl).

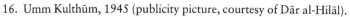

16. Umm Kulthūm, 1945 (publicity picture, courtesy of Dār al-Hilāl).

17. Umm Kulthūm performing in Abū Dhabī (photo, Mahmoud Arif).

18. In an elaborately decorated *jallabiyya* with her trademark handkerchief (photo, Mahmoud Arif).

19. Umm Kulthūm (photo, Farouk Ibrahim).

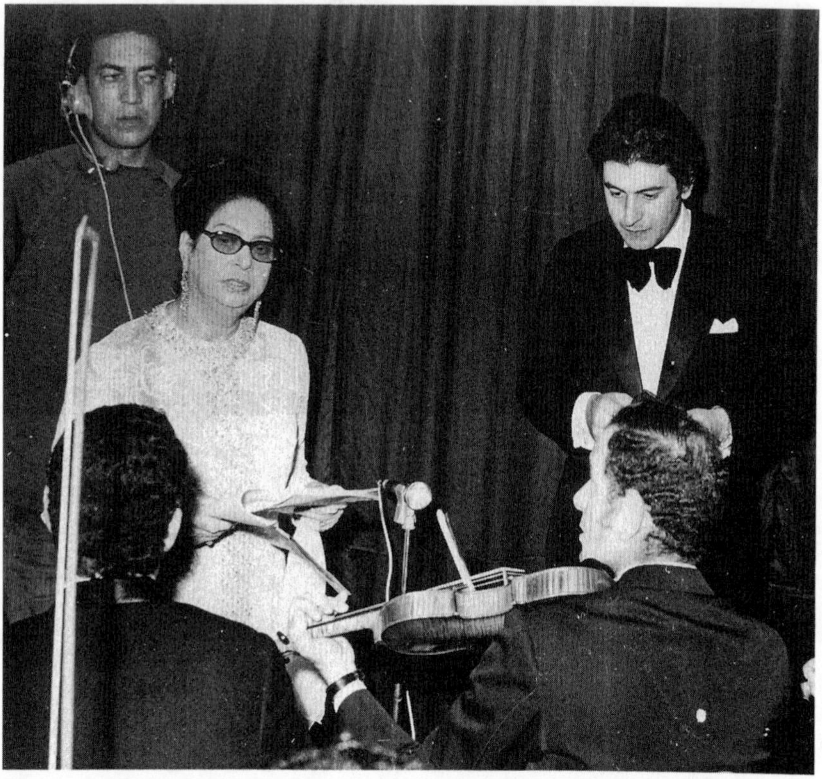

20. Umm Kulthūm, talking to members of her ensemble (photo, Mahmoud Arif).

21. Riyāḍ al-Sunbāṭī (photo, Mahmoud Arif).

22. Umm Kulthūm in Libya (photo, Mahmoud Arif).

23. Umm Kulthūm's funeral (photo, courtesy of *al-Ahrām*).

24–25. "The Voice and Face of Egypt": Acknowledging applause with a common Egyptian gesture—and (facing page) feeding a water buffalo (photos, Farouk Ibrahim).

composer. Responding to audience reaction, the singer controlled the length of the composition and the relative importance of its component lines or sections.

Unless the song began with a particularly popular phrase, Umm Kulthūm sang several lines (often an entire stanza or section) before requests for repetitions were made. People applauded and cried "Allāh!" or "Ya kariima, ya sitt!" at the ends of lines or sections. Vociferous and prolonged applause followed favorite lines (such as "Give me my freedom, set free my hands" from "al-Aṭlāl") and also occurred at the beginnings of sections of improvisation. The audience might bring the performance to a complete halt at these points, and a good rendition included at least three or four such stops. Occasionally audience members stood up to applaud or to call out compliments. Some whistled, a noise previously considered out of place and crude. When Umm Kulthūm appeared abroad, audience reaction tended to be more exaggerated than at home; men stood on their chairs and occasionally attempted to approach the stage. Even in Cairo, audience behavior almost became institutionalized: by the 1960s, concertgoers acted as though every performance was her best, and their acclamations and calls for repetitions extended performances by a good deal.

To formulate her multiple iterations of lines, she relied primarily on the techniques she used for her delivery in general: her point of departure was the text, which she divided, sometimes truncated, to present partial or different meanings. Melodic excursions first occurred on the individual words; eventually the entire line became fragmented and subjected to variations, often very small ones: slight rhythmic displacement, the introduction of unexpected silences, the addition of ornaments, and the extension of cadences.

She knew the *zakhārif*. These historic vocal ornaments included attacks of notes from slightly above or below pitch, slides from one pitch to the next, repetitions of a small melodic motive at a new pitch level, and shifts of rhythmic accent. A singer might add new melodic material to a previously sustained note, introduce unexpected silences, add one or more grace notes before a pitch, or add trills, mordentlike figures, and tremolo.[74]

Extensive melodic invention proceeding from the established *maqām* usually occurred in one of three places: early in her career she began songs with improvised *layālī;* throughout her career, other improvisations took place at a point about three-quarters through the song, and at cadences.

Sometimes the focus moved from the words themselves to melodic excursion, and the text thus became a pretext for invention.

The textual meaning was drawn out and the musical sound varied through alteration of vocal tone colors. Umm Kulthūm integrated *ghunna, baḥḥa,* and falsetto into a vocal line. Her voice seemed to slip from one color to another. Coloristic change at once engaged *taṣwīr al-ma'ná* and vocal virtuosity. These colors contributed aesthetic beauty to the line, added variety to the rendition, heightened the meaning of the text, and localized the rendition by infusing it with qualities recognized as part of historically Arab vocal style.

Song texts did not require particular treatment. The ideal of *taṣwīr al-ma'ná* simply mandated that the meaning of the text be the focal point of the rendition and that the singer draw out and enhance the poem somehow or other. The link between the vocal device and the word or phrase was not necessarily direct. In "Udhkurīnī," for instance, Umm Kulthūm nasalized the word "nāshiran" (spreading) in this phrase: "Udhkurīnī kullamā 'l-fajru badá nāshiran fī-'l-ufqi a'lām al-ḍiyā' (Think of me whenever the dawn breaks spreading in the horizon banners of light). Nasality did not highlight the literal meaning of the word or phrase, but strengthened her expression of the emotion of the entire section of the song, the misery of the abandoned lover.

Probably because of the importance of nasality in the recitation of the Qur'ān, *ghunna* suggested religious themes. Umm Kulthūm used it to begin "Salū Qalbī," a *qaṣīda* in honor of the Prophet's birthday, even though the initial phrase has no direct religious association and would not be nasalized according to the rules of *tajwīd*.

In most cases, the text seemed to be the single driving force for the rendition, the raison d'être for the song, and the foundation upon which all decisions regarding improvisation or variation were based. A concert performance of "Nahj al-Burda" showed the careful delivery of each line that characterized her style. Her variations typically occurred on textually significant lines, for instance one that described God's command to Muḥammad to carry his message to the people. Umm Kulthūm's rendition was focused upon the word "Allāh." She spent over ten minutes on lines that described the unique role of the Prophet Muḥammad: "You [Muḥammad] reached a heaven that cannot be flown into on wings nor approached on feet; it is said that every prophet has his place; oh Muḥammad, this is the throne, accept it." These lines constituted the climax of the song text as constructed by Umm Kulthūm and Rāmī. Thus the choice of this place for musical elaborations flowed from textual considerations. Her varied repetitions, centered on the words "heaven" and "Muḥammad," involved nasalization, falsetto, varied divisions of the phrase and of rhythmic placement of syllables, but nothing disturbed the syntax of the line or the clarity with which the words were delivered. The musical rendition served the text and constantly drew attention to its meaning.

Most of the texts she sang were less weighty than "Nahj al-Burda," but the words still anchored her rendition, and her variations neither altered nor obscured the sense of the line. Often she dwelt upon pastoral images of the Egyptian countryside, familiar and beloved to all Egyptians. In the love song "Faakir lamma Kunt Ganbi" she repeated the phrase "I wish I were like a wave on the Nile," varying her rendition of "wave on the Nile" by changing vocal timbre, extending the consonants *m* and *n*, and the length of the phrase itself (see example 8). Here, her melodic alterations consist of changes in the approach to a pitch, the attack, or the addition of a few new pitches or melodic figures in place of a previously sustained note, illustrated in her variations on the word "Nīl" (Nile). She was particularly fond of melodic sequences. Her inventions tended to be stepwise explorations of a genus of the mode of the piece (here, *kurd*) or that of a related mode with the same or similar principal pitches: conservative, historically Arab modal treatments. Her melodic figures were often linked to rhythmic shifts: melodic additions were frequently cast rhythmically as triplets.

The construction of her variations manifested the fundamental priorities of her style: the text took precedence over virtuosic musical invention. Virtuosity was necessary to her idiom but melodic invention was virtually never at its heart. Umm Kulthūm's varied repetitions were varied treatments of the texts, intended to bring the listener closer to the mood of the line with each successive iteration. The tools she brought to bear were tone color, rhythm, and articulation rather than melodic excursions that might obscure the words.

A critical point in the rendition was the cadence or *qafla* (pl., *qafalāt*). Umm Kulthūm's inventions at cadence points were her most extensive. She added *qafalāt* that at once heightened the impact of the phrase and displayed her melodic invention. These moving cadences, affective endings for lines or sections, sealed the meaning of the text and resolved the musical

Example 8. Excerpt from "Faakir lamma Kunt Ganbi"

tension of the phrase. "If you can't do *qafalāt,*" Nelson quotes a critic as saying, "you can't do Arabic music,"[75] and indeed failure to conclude the phrase effectively ruined a performance. The *qafla* was a point at which singers could demonstrate command of the *turāth* by quoting short passages from other compositions or famous singers and by utilizing all the resources of the *maqām* to construct an effective cadence.

Muḥammad ʿAbd al-Wahhāb, among many others, remarked on Umm

Kulthūm's "warm cadences that kindled passions and enchanted [the] audience." In his view Umm Kulthūm distinguished herself by her "manner of rendition, her genuine Egyptian *qafla*, and her articulation of the text." "She became famous for her *qafalāt:* the *qafla* never eluded her and never slipped from her grasp."[76]

Her *qafalāt* sometimes consisted of short phrases familiar as closures in a particular *maqām;*[77] other times they were made from new material, especially in the interior phrases of a song. The *qafla* occasionally generated new musical tension before bringing its phrase to rest. In most respects, it was analogous to the Western cadence inasmuch as some were less definitive than others and resembled half-cadences. A single performance included only three or four major *qafalāt,* usually ending the main sections. Cadences for phrases within these sections had less impact. The placement of significant *qafalāt* depended upon the dramatic structure of the text and its musical setting, on the one hand, and the rendition of the text by the singer, particularly the number and content of varied repetitions of phrases, on the other. The singer might introduce major *qafalāt* not conceived by the composer in the course of her rendition.

Umm Kulthūm's cadences took a number of musical shapes, their effectiveness lying in the link between the musical content of the cadence and that of the musical and textual phrase it closed. However, she rarely ended a highly melismatic phrase with a melismatic cadence, nor a syllabic phrase with a short cadence. The *qafla* usually either resolved musical tension already created in the phrase or took the phrase in a new and unexpected melodic direction when the preceding phrase was relatively plain.[78] "Raqq il-Ḥabiib" includes a variety of *qafalāt* (see example 9). The first excerpt ends the first half of the performance. She extended the last syllable of an otherwise metrical line, prolonging the *qafla* and drawing the listener along with her invention in *nahāwand.* In the second instance, she concluded a long series of varied repetitions centered on the final syllable of the line "Sihirt astann*aah*" (I stayed up waiting for *him*) and closed the entire section with a single, crisp delivery ending with syllabic treatment of the line "w-ashuuf khayaalu qaaʿid ganbi" (seeing his phantom sitting beside me).

The confluence of these techniques in a series of renditions is illustrated in the colloquial song "Ana Fi-ntiẓaarak" (see example 10). Her renditions of "ʿAayiz aʿraf" show a slightly varied articulation of the descent from C# to A, variation in tone color, and the addition of a few pitches, all in

Musical Example 9b

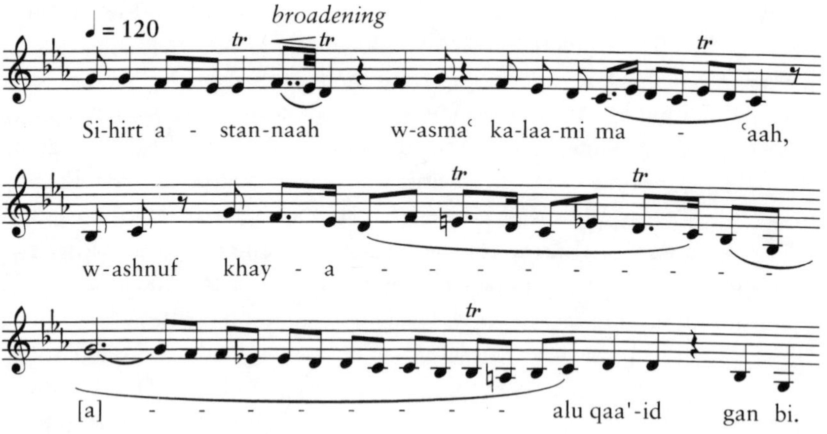

Example 9. Two excerpts from "Raqq il-Ḥabiib"

the context of limited melodic change typical of her style. Using repeated triplet figures, flourishes of neighboring notes, and the sounds of the words themselves, Umm Kulthūm drew attention to two significant words, "angry" (*ghaḍbaan*) and "someone else" (*insaan*).[79] Slight rhythmic displacement occurred in virtually every reiteration. She characteristically extended the *qafla*, prolonging the A and then adding pitches to the longer note in stepwise motion over the genus *ḥijāz*. The phrase was broken apart in her later improvisation on the section (see example 10b, below on p. 156).

The style of accompaniment provided by her ensemble supported Umm Kulthūm's multiple renditions. The principal accompanist in example 10 was the *ʿūd* player who shadowed the vocal line, plucking the significant pitches and maintaining the meter. The violins played sustained principal pitches. This style of accompaniment, notated for the first line of the example, dominates the song. The style changed slightly with the line "Khalletni . . . ," with violin and *qānūn* players adding embellishments during vocal rests. The *riqq* was audible for the first time following the second rendition of "Khalletni." In the latter part of the example, the principle accompanists alternated shadowing Umm Kulthūm's improvisations; here the percussion is barely audible and the meter supplied by the *ʿūd* player. The skill of accompaniment lay in correctly following the singer, anticipating her improvisations, and adding embellishments without interfering.

As a result of Umm Kulthūm's varied repetitions, the length and shape of a song changed from the original composition and among performances of the same song. For instance, extensive variations of two lines from "Udhkurīnī" occupied twelve minutes of a fifty-two-minute performance or 23.1 percent of the total performance time.[80] Umm Kulthūm's manipulations substantially altered the composition and shifted the emphasis from one place to another within the musicopoetic structure.

A good illustration of the results of this process is a comparison of two performances of "Ghannii li Shwayya Shwayya," one from the film *Sallāma* and the other a concert rendition marketed on commercial cassette (table 1). The first performance occupied less than five minutes while the second lasted almost half an hour. The musical process of the concert version corresponded to those of most of Umm Kulthūm's performances. The opening lines were sung in a relatively straightforward manner. In succeeding stanzas, certain lines were repeated more than others. She broke the phrases apart and moved farthest away from her compositional model

a.

Example 10a. Two excerpts from "Ana Fi-ntiẓaarak"

Example 10a. (continued)

roughly three-quarters of the way through the song. The closing lines were sung directly, in a manner similar to that of the beginning.

Umm Kulthūm's performance of a song ultimately dominated its constituent parts. The effect of her varied repetitions and her shaping and reshaping of songs in performance was to create with and for the audience the mood of the poem she sang and to involve the audience completely in this mood.[81]

b.

*break in tape probably made by editor

Example 10b.

Table 1. "Ghannii li Shwayya Shwayya": Versions from Concert and Film

Concert Version	*Film Version*
Instrumental intro. A (=line 1), A 1, 1, *lazma* A, A, 1, 1, *lazma* A, A	*Ṭabla & nāy* intro. A 1, 1, *lazma* A
2, 2, 3, 4, 5, *lazma* A, A, 2, 2, 3, 4, 5, *lazma* A, A	2, 2, 3, 4, 5, chorus 1, 1
6a, a, b, 6, 6, 6, 6a (with chorus), 6a, 6a, 6a, 6a, 6a, ab, *lazma* B (=6), B, 6a, *lazma* B, B, 6a, 6a, 6, 6, 7a, 7a, 7a, 6, 7a, instr. vamp, 6a, 6, 7a, 7a, 7a, 7a 7, 6a, 6a, 6a, 6, 7, 8, 9 (=5), *lazma* A, A, *lazma* C (=10)	6, 6, 7, 8, 9 (=5), chorus 1, male solo 1, chorus 1
10, 10, 10, 10a, b, b, 11, 12 (=5), *lazma* A, A, 10a, 10a, 10, 10, 10, 11, 12 (=5), *lazma* A, A	10, 10, 11, 12 (=5), chorus 1, chorus 1
13, 13*, 13**, instr, vamp, 13, instr. vamp, 13, 13, 13, 13a, b, 13a, b, 13a, 13a, 13, 13a, 13a, 13, 13, 14, 15 (=5), *lazma* A, A, A, 13, ***, 13, 13, 13, 13, 14, 15 (=5), *lazma* A, A	13, 13, 14, 15 (=5), chorus 1, chorus 1
16a, 16, 16, 16, 16, 16, 16a**, instr. vamp 16a, instr. vamp, 16a, instr. vamp, 16a, 16a, instr. vamp, 16a, 16a, instr. vamp, 16a, instr. vamp, 16a, 16a, 16, 16, 16, 16, 17, 18 (=6), 18, 19 (=7), 20 (=8), 21 (=5)	16, 16, 17, 18 (=6), 18, 19 (=7), 20 (=8), 21 (=5), chorus 1 interrupted by dialogue
TIME: 23 minutes	TIME: 5 minutes

* Phrase ends with a long *qafla*.
** Ensuing renditions of line are highly improvisatory.
*** The concert version is peppered with compliments and applause from the audience; at these points, however, the applause brings the performance to a halt.

Accessible sources do not permit a tracing of the aesthetic components of her renditions through Arab history. But clearly they resonate in historical documents. George Sawa's interpretation of the following story from al-Iṣbahānī's *Kitāb al-Aghānī* defines the presence of creative rendition and its value in Arabic singing historically:

> A good transmitter was uncreative, and often considered not so excellent a performer, a bad transmitter was creative, and often considered an excellent performer.
>
> "I [al-Iṣbahānī] was informed by Muḥammad ibn Mazyad who said: Ḥammād the son of Isḥāq informed us saying: I asked my father:

> In your opinion who is better, Mukhāriq or ʿAllūyah? He said: My son, ʿAllūyah is more knowledgeable as to what comes out of his head and more knowledgeable in what he sings and performs [on the lute]. If I were to choose between them both as to who will teach my slave singing girls, or if I were asked for advice, I would choose ʿAllūyah: for he used to perform vocal music [well] and compose with artful mastery. Mukhāriq, with his [masterly] control over his voice and his [consequent] overabundance of ornaments, is not a good transmitter because he does not perform even one song as he learned it and does not sing it twice the same way because of his many additions to it. However, should they meet with a Caliph or a [wealthy] commoner, Mukhāriq would win the favor of the assembly and get the reward because of his nice[r] voice and abundant ornamentation." (11:334)
>
> Mukhāriq's musical twin was Muḥammad ibn Ḥamzah, an excellent singer whose constantly changing interpretation made him likewise an impossible and useless teacher (15:359).[82]

Umm Kulthūm's renditions moved older practices through the twentieth century. Their histories are better known by the educated elite. Nevertheless other listeners sensed historical depth in her style as well and claimed her music as importantly their own, *aṣīl,* authentically Arab. "If you want to know what Arab music is," a young man told me, "listen to Umm Kulthūm."

While the people in the concert hall participated directly in the performance, the impact was felt no less strongly by listeners in their homes, for whom a concert by Umm Kulthūm became a distinct genre of musical experience. She succeeded in overwhelming her listeners with the emotional impact of her texts. For critics, it was this aspect of her renditions that produced the numbing effect they disliked. For the many aficionados, it was the essence of her artistry. For virtually everyone, her renditions were evidence of musical mastery in a coherent and well-developed Arabic idiom. The Sufi leader, the Arabian horse, the player of the *mizmār,* and the reciter of the Qurʾān came together in the sound of Umm Kulthūm's repertory and in her performance practice.

Seven

Umm Kulthūm and a New Generation

The days have passed . . .[1]

Following the glorious performances and growing list of accomplishments of the 1940s, Umm Kulthūm suffered a succession of physical and other personal distresses. She contemplated retirement.

Health problems plagued Umm Kulthūm every few years for much of her life beginning in the 1930s. She became ill with liver and gallbladder ailments in the late summer of 1937.[2] Related difficulties afflicted her throughout her life.

In 1946, personal dilemmas thrust themselves on her in such a way as to disrupt her professional activities for the first time in her life. During the summer, she suffered an upper respiratory inflammation that led to the diagnosis of a thyroid problem later that year. The physical symptoms of this ailment, the ramifications of treatment, and her fear for her voice combined to cause serious depression. She worked sporadically and spoke of retiring. One of few people privy to her personal feelings later said that at no other time before or since had she seen Umm Kulthūm in such a state of despair.[3] Her recovery was a prolonged process. She was treated at Bethesda Naval Hospital, ostensibly at the suggestion of the American ambassador to Egypt.

She also sought treatment for a chronic inflammation of the eyes, said to be aggravated by the bright lights of the stage and film. The thyroid problem persisted and required repeated visits to hospitals in Egypt and abroad.[4]

In 1947, her mother died. The two women had lived in the same house for all of Umm Kulthūm's life, and she took her mother's death as a severe blow. Later, during one of her trips to the United States for medical treatment, her brother Khālid died.[5] At roughly the same time she suffered the termination of a romantic involvement and a subsequent failed marriage.

Questions about her personal life, especially that of why she did not marry, followed Umm Kulthūm from the time she began her career in Cairo. In the 1920s she was linked with a number of men, including the poet Aḥmad Rāmī. Her apparent strong will, sharp tongue, and the absence of any lasting close personal involvements prompted the assessment that "she has no heart." Another suggestion was that, "like Greta Garbo," she had been disappointed in love early in life and could not love another.[6]

By dint of fame and her efforts to improve her manners and general education, Umm Kulthūm rose in Egyptian society to the point of socializing with members of the elite.[7] In about 1946, Sharīf Ṣabrī Pāshā, one of King Fārūq's uncles, proposed to marry her. The union was immediately barred by the royal family, causing much grief to Umm Kulthūm. That such a marriage could have been contemplated seriously at all was a source of amazement to many observers. However, having succeeded in attaining the position she had, Umm Kulthūm seems to have believed that this would be possible and was gravely disappointed when it was not.[8]

Feeling the disappointment of the broken engagement and the burden of bad health, she suddenly agreed to marry Maḥmūd Sharīf, a fellow musician and vice president of the Musicians' Union. The marriage was dissolved within days, regarded by both parties as a mistake, amid a tremendous outcry of protest from Umm Kulthūm's fans who attacked the character, personal status, and abilities of Sharīf, "as if the man had not a single good quality."[9]

Finally she married one of her doctors and a longtime audience member, Dr. Ḥasan al-Ḥifnāwī, in 1954. Like so many others, al-Ḥifnāwī had been brought to Umm Kulthūm's concerts and introduced to her by Aḥmad Rāmī. Born in Asyut in 1915, Dr. al-Ḥifnāwī was raised in a conservative atmosphere similar to Umm Kulthūm's. Both were familiar with rural Egypt and the values and behaviors common to it. Both were ambitious. Both were successful. Al-Ḥifnāwī finished medical school in 1940 and became one of the most noted skin specialists in the Arab world. However, in addition to the learning and elegance that both of them acquired, they retained a sense of connection with rural or small-town Egypt. For her part, Umm Kulthūm displayed this like a banner, constantly reinforcing her identity with most Egyptians. Dr. al-Ḥifnāwī was less a public figure; however, he was described by his son, with a certain pride, as "a *baladi* [countrified] sort of man" in his personal life.[10] Her husband remained in the shadows when she appeared in public. According to family members and close friends, however he maintained the status of head of the household. She appreciated his accomplishments and strengths of character for, as many of her acquaintances agreed, "Umm Kulthūm hated weak men." This union met with the acceptance of her audience, apparently because, during the time of her illness, people came to see Umm Kulthūm as a human being with a personal life. And a doctor brought to the marriage a social status that was well suited to Umm Kulthūm.

She tried to resume her regular schedule of concerts as soon as possible after her treatment in the United States in 1949. However her health problems and attendant exhaustion persisted. These afflictions as well as external forces such as the curfew imposed in Cairo after antigovernment riots in January, 1952, which precluded concerts and other commercial entertainment, combined to make the season of 1951–52 "the worst in her history."[11]

July of that year saw the Egyptian Revolution that finally returned the country to the hands of Egyptians and ultimately brought to its leadership President Jamāl ʿAbd al-Nāṣir, one of the most charismatic rulers of the twentieth century and a personality with whom Umm Kulthūm became bonded in the public mind. Born to a working-class family, ʿAbd al-Nāṣir spoke with a voice familiar to the large majority of his compatriots. Despite the problems during the later years of his rule, he has remained a beloved figure to many Egyptians to the present day.

After the difficulties of the 1930s and 1940s and the decline of King Fārūq's reputation (owing to his questionable dealings with munitions during the Palestine War and his scandalous personal behavior), most Egyptians welcomed the new regime with hopefulness and relief. Charles Issawi described the atmosphere in late 1952:

> Perhaps more important than all these specific measures [promised by the new government] are the new feelings of self-respect, hopefulness, and unity which have emerged in Egypt. A few *çi-devant* pashas and wealthy men look back with nostalgia on the *douceur de vivre* of the *ancien régime,* but the overwhelming majority of the country, including the middle class, has rallied to the new government.[12]

Umm Kulthūm was no exception. Hearing of the revolution at her summer retreat in Ra'as al-Barr, she immediately returned to Cairo and commissioned Rāmī and al-Sunbāṭī to write an appropriate national song. The result, "Miṣr allatī fī Khāṭirī wa-fī Damī" (Egypt, which is in my mind and my blood), premiered shortly thereafter.

The bloodless revolution caused relatively little interruption in the everyday lives of most Egyptians. The changes that ensued took place over a period of time and affected people gradually. Thus most of the entertainers of the day continued to work through the revolution and years afterward. Umm Kulthūm's connections to the previous regime were not close enough to jeopardize her career, and the revolutionary government demonstrated eagerness to continue public entertainment, especially radio broadcasting, in an uninterrupted manner.[13] Her songs continued to be broadcast and she, along with most of her colleagues and competitors, made gestures of support and cooperation toward the new government and carried on with their lives.

Because of nagging health problems, Umm Kulthūm announced in late 1954 that she would limit her schedule and record only a few *qaṣā'id* of powerful and religious theme. Her 1955–56 season was reduced from the customary eight concerts to five.[14] She released very few new songs during this period, averaging only one per year. She was at the age when most singers retired and she was clearly slowing her pace.

Journalists immediately began to talk about possible "successors" and the name most frequently mentioned was Suʿād Muḥammad, a young Lebanese singer who had shown remarkable skill in performing Umm Kulthūm's repertory in the Lebanon. Borrowing her songs for public performances occurred more frequently outside Egypt than within the country. As the fame of the borrowers grew, their use of her music became annoying to Umm Kulthūm. She contended that the singer who originally recorded a song ought to receive royalties for others' performances.[15] It was not only the melody and words, she argued, but the manner of singing that was being copied to profit the copier and not the original artist. In 1952, she demanded a fee from a radio station in Damascus for broadcasting her tapes. In 1955, she issued an official warning to owners of music halls in Syria and Lebanon. She does not seem to have found any legal way to prevent this sort of imitation, but she used her considerable influence to discourage it.[16]

Her view of royalties was reflected in the argumentation of the case brought against her by Zakariyyā Aḥmad which was then in court. The accusation was that she had failed to honor her contractual obligation to obtain written permission from Zakariyyā for each of his songs she wished to have broadcast on the radio. (Royalties were determined on the basis of these permissions.) Umm Kulthūm's rebuttal was that she owed Zakariyyā nothing beyond the fee she paid for the initial composition. Ownership of the artistic product, she argued, was hers. She was the one who selected the text, presented the idea to the composer, "worked day and night" to develop the song and to create its final rendition. The composer, in her view, was an artisan from whom she obtained a part for a product and who should be paid a simple fee for that.

Zakariyyā, on the other hand, wanted 4 percent of the proceeds of records sales rather than the flat fee of 200 £E per song that the Cairophon Record Company offered. His demand proceeded from an old grievance; the prevailing view among recording industry executives was that Umm Kulthūm (or the recording company with which she contracted) "always" paid Zakariyyā less than either al-Qaṣabjī or al-Sunbāṭī and that he finally became angry about it. Public opinion was on Zakariyyā's side. *Rūz al-Yūsuf* depicted him as "an artist defending his art and his future," compared to Umm Kulthūm, "who loves herself more than her art and refuses to extend a helping hand."[17] The case was finally settled out of court in 1958.

Nor was Zakariyyā alone in disputing his pay. For years she did not pay al-Qaṣabjī for "Raqq il-Ḥabiib," one of his most famous and successful songs. From time to time her accompanists expressed consternation at their pay as well, for instance in 1952, when Aḥmad al-Ḥifnāwī, Muḥammad ʿAbduh Ṣāliḥ, and Ibrāhīm ʿAfīfī, "faithful and devoted players," demanded shares of Umm Kulthūm's fees for broadcast recordings. Once a tape or record was made, or a concert given, pay for the accompanying instrumentalists was complete. They took no percentage of record sales nor royalties of any kind. Thus the instrumentalists probably made less money from their work on Umm Kulthūm's songs than anyone else involved in the performance. Although she sounded sympathetic, she was apparently not especially forthcoming with money to meet these demands.[18]

Such argumentation of disputes and negotiations of compromises were not unusual in Egyptian society. Each party had a right to argue his or her claim. The cases reveal the workings of power among individuals. Of the composers who worked with Umm Kulthūm, Zakariyyā and Riyāḍ al-Sunbāṭī were stronger personalities by far than Muḥammad al-Qaṣabjī. Zakariyyā and al-Sunbāṭī argued with her, sued her in court, left her company. For her part, Umm Kulthūm capitulated more often to al-Sunbāṭī than anyone else, probably because the idiom she sought depended on his skills more than anyone else's. She was prepared to dispense with al-Qaṣabjī's and Zakariyyā's compositions, but not with those of al-Sunbāṭī.

The National Songs and "Rābiʿa al-ʿAdawiyya"

Encouraged by the authorities in the new Ministry of Information and National Guidance that set policy for Egyptian Radio, virtually every singer made efforts to record songs in celebration of Egypt and its new regime. These pieces were rooted in the commemorative poetry and songs for the monarchy and earlier. During the 1950s, their production formed a sweeping trend which lessened in the 1960s but persists to the present day. Between 1952 and 1960, Umm Kulthūm sang more national songs than at any other time in her life; they constituted almost 50 percent of her repertory, and roughly one-third of her new repertory after 1960.[19]

Many, especially the earlier ones, were martial in style, featuring large orchestral accompaniment with brass instruments and timpani, chordal harmony, quadruple meters, and often a men's chorus. A few became especially beloved, notably "Miṣr Tataḥaddath ʿan Nafsihā" (Egypt speaks of herself, 1952) and "Wallaahi Zamaan Ya Silaaḥi" (It's been a long time, oh weapon of mine, 1956). (The latter was adopted as the Egyptian national anthem.)[20] This style was accepted by the Egyptian public as an outgrowth of military music in general, which had been cast in a European mold since the early nineteenth century. Most singers included similar songs in their repertories, but the songs rarely retained popularity over a period of years.[21]

In the hands of Bayram al-Tūnisī, Muḥammad al-Mawjī, and Riyāḍ al-Sunbāṭī, the patriotic song took on the color of other popular songs. European instrumentation and harmony were replaced with the instruments and styles of traditional Egyptian musics. A characteristic feature of the *mawwāl* appeared in Bayram's text "Ṣoot il-Salaam."[22] "Baʿd il-Ṣabr ma Ṭaal" included familiar Egyptian dance rhythms and "Ya Salaam ʿala ʿIdna" incorporated a *nāy* melody into its otherwise European orchestral setting.

As Umm Kulthūm's reputation in the Arab world grew, she was invited to provide national songs for other countries. She recorded songs for Kuwaiti National Day twice during the 1960s and an anthem for Iraq.[23]

During the mid-1950s Umm Kulthūm recorded the radio program, later a film, entitled "Rābiʿa al-ʿAdawiyya."[24] The story was that of the life of a saint, Rābiʿa, known to Muslims from biographies and folk hagiographies. The legends about her "give us a clear ideal of a woman renouncing the world and its attractions and giving up her life to the service of God,"[25] thus conforming to Umm Kulthūm's stated objectives of the time. The songs from this production, along with five love songs, two *qaṣāʾid,* and six patriotic songs constituted all of Umm Kulthūm's new work between 1948 and 1956.

At the same time, she began to fashion herself as a public spokesperson for causes. For the first time she advocated particular social and political issues.

She had granted few interviews in the 1930s and 1940s. When she did, she discussed only topics having to do with her professional life. She was not, she said, a social star, but a singer and a citizen of Egypt and from those positions only would she speak.[26] Beginning in the late 1930s, Umm Kulthūm began to make a few public statements about herself and then about political issues. Her first autobiographical statement appeared as a series of articles in *Ākhir Sāʿa* in 1937 and 1938.[27] Through these statements and with interviews she began to construct a consistent public persona and to articulate the way in which she wanted to be characterized and remembered.

By the 1960s, she was willing to address the nation with her opinions. Asked for an interview on a nonmusical topic, she responded, "Certainly. I have much that I want to say to the Egyptian people just now."[28] In her political voice, she usually gave expression to widely shared sentiments. She used her visible position to articulate what, she said, any decent Egyptian thought. She offered support for the Egyptian soldiers who fought in Sinai in 1948, prompting Egyptian Radio to broadcast the songs they requested at the appropriate times. After the defeat at al-Fālūja, she invited the entire battalion of soldiers who fought there to a reception at her home, thrusting herself into conflict with the head of the war ministry in doing so. He argued that, in light of the defeat and the ensuing scandal concerning munitions which had by that time been linked to the palace, any celebration was out of order. Her reply was unequivocal:

> I have made my invitation. If you would like to come, you are welcome. If not, it is your choice. As for the others, I have invited them in order to express my appreciation as a citizen of Egypt for their struggle and sacrifice in the Sinai. My sentiments have not changed and my invitation stands.[29]

The Free Officers of the Egyptian army were among the defenders of al-Fālūja, and this reception may have been her first meeting with Jamāl ʿAbd al-Nāṣir.

Friendship developed between Umm Kulthūm and ʿAbd al-Nāṣir during the 1950s, and the connection between the two figures remains strong in the collective memory to the present day. "She was a powerful weapon for him," people said, suggesting that he made political use of her performances. But this use of music was nothing new: during World War II, British, German, and Italian broadcasting stations all tried to get recordings, even endorsements, from popular singers to draw listeners and suggest support for their messages. It is reasonable to believe that audiences were inured to the practice. At any rate, it is unlikely that Umm Kulthūm (or any other commercial artist) would have objected to the inclusion of her performances on Egyptian international broadcasts.

Umm Kulthūm and ʿAbd al-Nāṣir had much in common: both were from the lower classes and had utilized opportunities for upward mobility new in their lifetimes. Both were powerful personalities who became skilled at reaching the Egyptian population. Both drew upon similar images for their public identities: *fallaḥiin* and *abnaaʾ il-riif*. "Listen to ʿAbd al-Nāṣir's speech nationalizing the Suez Canal," a friend recommended. "You will feel you are afraid of nothing!" ʿAbd al-Nāṣir used many references to the people of Egypt and later to the unity of Arab peoples. He coupled the language of oratory with that of ordinary speech. He played on Egyptian heartstrings by championing sovereignty and Egyptian control of resources to create a renovated version of "Egypt for Egyptians." ʿAbd al-Nāṣir's public speeches were compelling performances.

"Although she did not at first intend this," Niʿmat Aḥmad Fuʾād said, "President ʿAbd al-Nāṣir gained much from his association with her. He always liked her and he took the opportunity to befriend her." He decorated her with state awards, featured her on international radio broadcasts and invited her as a close family friend would be invited to break the fast at his home on the first night of Ramadan. Umm Kulthūm supported the policies of the revolutionary government and cultivated friendships with a number of the new national leaders. ʿAbd al-Ḥakīm ʿĀmir, Jamāl Ṣalīb, and Muḥammad Ḥasanayn Haykal were "frequent dinner guests" at her home.[30] She became a participant in the formulation and administration of cultural policy, serving on several committees for music formed by government ministries.[31] These positions provided forums in which she advanced her views on music teaching, broadcasting, performance, and government funding for musical institutions. She reminded Egyptians of their national heritage through her expressed opinions as well as her musical style.

"A New Stage"

When Umm Kulthūm recovered her health, she did in fact return to the stage, beginning a phase in her career that was immediately perceived as a "new stage."[32] Although her practice of learning and performing stayed more or less the same and her distinctive idiom remained, the style of her new songs shifted. She began to sing long love songs solicited from the younger generation of writers and composers.

Lyricists more than poets, the new writers produced texts in colloquial Arabic, simple in language, direct and fluid of expression compared to the terse phrases of Bayram al-Tūnisī and Badīʿ Khayrī. The new composers utilized large ensembles to accompany vocal lines that were melodically simpler than those of Riyāḍ al-Sunbāṭī, and more dependent on the small leaps embedded in Western popular tunes than Zakariyyā's.

While most of her previous songs had been lengthy in performance, the new ones were simply longer compositions. The extended song texts were further augmented by longer instrumental introductions and interludes in compositions by the young composers who had taken inspiration from al-Qaṣabjī and ʿAbd al-Wahhāb. A dramatic high point in the production of new love songs was her collaboration with ʿAbd al-Wahhāb in 1964.

Among the poets who began writing for Umm Kulthūm were Ṣalāḥ Jāhīn, popular among young leftists, Ṭāhir Abū Fāshā, who wrote the texts for "Rābiʿa al-ʿAdawiyya" and a few other songs, and ʿAbd al-Fattāḥ Muṣṭafá and ʿAbd al-Wahhāb Muḥammad, who wrote patriotic songs and love lyrics. Their texts were characterized by direct conversational vocabulary combined with colorful turns of phrase exemplified by ʿAbd al-Wahhāb Muḥammad's lyric, "Lil-Ṣabr Ḥuduud":

Matṣabbarniish bi-wuʿuud wi-kalaam maʿsuul wi-ʿuhuud,
Ana ya ma ṣuburt zamaan ʿala naar wi-ʿadhaab wi-hawaan,
W-ahe ghalṭa wi-mush ḥatʿuud.

(Don't console me with promises and honeyed words and vows,
How long I have borne fire and torment and shame,
That's a mistake, and it won't happen again.)

The conversational vocabulary and syntax condensed rich meaning into a few words. Poetic use of expressions "kalaam maʿsuul" (honeyed words) and "ahe ghalṭa" (that's a mistake) make the lyrics of Muḥammad among the most interesting of the work of the young poets that she sang.

Umm Kulthūm also sought texts from popular lyricists of the day such as Mursī Jamīl ʿAzīz, Aḥmad Shafīq Kāmil, and Maʾmūn al-Shināwī.[33] The topic of these texts was invariably a familiar expression of romantic love, in simple and direct language:

> *Kull leela wi-kull yoom ashar li-bokra fi-ʾntiẓaarak ya ḥabiibi*
>
> (Each night and day I sit awake until the morrow, waiting for you, my love)

or

> *Il-Ḥubb kullu . . . ḥabbeetu fiik . . . il-ḥubb kullu wa-zamaani kullu ana ʿishtu liik, zamaani kullu.*
>
> (All love . . . I loved in you . . . all love, and all my life I lived for you, all my life.)

Gone from this style are Rāmī's personifications of birds and Bayram's clever epithets. These lyrics pour out emotion directly and sometimes redundantly.

Common themes in her new songs continued to be separation, love lost, and the lover waiting, typical of her entire repertory. Separation was usually caused by the departure of the man from the woman. Pain, anger, and frustration were common emotions as the protagonist of a song typically awaited some action on the part of her beloved. Such lyrics generalized easily from amorous situations to other social and even political situations that engendered frustration, pain, and waiting. Thus the line "Aʿṭinī ḥurriyyatī, aṭliq yadayya" ("Give me my freedom, set free my hands," from the song "al-Aṭlāl") was linked by listeners variously to the struggles of the Palestinians and Arabs against the West and of Egyptian citizens against ʿAbd al-Nāṣir's oppressions. Later, "Wi-Daarit il-Ayyaam" (The days have passed), originally a lyric of romantic love, was moved by listeners into the memory of ʿAbd al-Nāṣir's death. Probably the most popular texts were those that admitted multiple and various interpretations.

For Umm Kulthūm, texts had to be susceptible to varied repetition in performance. This requirement led her toward lyricists working specifically in the song market and away from the work of other young and talented poets, such as Fu'ād Ḥaddād, ʿAbd al-Raḥmān al-Abnūdī, and Ṣalāḥ Jāhīn, whose work did not lend itself to segmentation and repetition of single words, phrases, or lines. Like Bayram, Ḥaddād and al-Abnūdī successfully captured the flavor of daily life in their poems. Other singers, including Sayyid Makkāwī and ʿAbd al-Ḥalīm Ḥāfiẓ, sang their texts to the great enjoyment of audiences. But Umm Kulthūm retreated from the path struck by Bayram, Badīʿ Khayrī, and others to the well-worn commercial avenue. The new poetry by Ḥaddād and the others, terse in formulation and realistic in sentiment was, for Umm Kulthūm, the road not taken.[34]

The arrangements made by Umm Kulthūm with her young lyricists were businesslike, generally without the personal loyalty that characterized her relationship with Rāmī. New situations arose. In about 1960, Umm Kulthūm heard a song entitled "Allāh ʿa-'l-Ḥubb," composed by Muḥammad al-Qaṣabjī and recorded by Suʿād Muḥammad. "Where," she pointedly asked al-Qaṣabjī, "did you get that text?!" It transpired that ʿAbd al-Fattāḥ Muṣṭafá, the author of the lyric, had sent it first to Umm Kulthūm, who was still considering its possibilities when she heard it over the radio, sung by a competitor. The poet had left it in her hands for a period he considered to be long enough. Tired of awaiting her decision, he notified Egyptian Radio that the text was available and was able to sell it to Suʿād Muḥammad.[35] Umm Kulthūm was unaccustomed to this treatment.

As she turned to younger poets, Aḥmad Rāmī's role as her lyricist declined. He remained a good friend and consultant, and he wrote lyrics for other singers until the 1970s, when he suffered from the tribulations of old age.

Whereas Umm Kulthūm's production of new love songs began in earnest in 1956–57, she was frankly looking for new composers as early as 1952. Her search resulted from both practical and artistic factors. Her relationship with Zakariyyā Aḥmad had been disrupted by the lawsuit, and she was consistently disappointed with al-Qaṣabjī's work. She had worked with no composer other than Zakariyyā, al-Qaṣabjī, and al-Sunbāṭī since 1931, and the last of her earlier composers had died in 1937, leaving her dependent on al-Sunbāṭī alone. This situation was unsatisfactory to both of them. She needed more variety in her new repertory. The usually taciturn al-Sunbāṭī complained that working with Umm Kulthūm was extremely time consuming and precluded other projects, and that it required constant adjustments to her opinions. She was clearly in need of someone new.

The process of finding new composers was gradual. She studied the styles of the young men before approaching them. Apparently the first to be considered was the popular song writer, Amīn Ṣidqī, but the results were unsatisfactory. She then approached composers Muḥammad al-Mawjī, Kamāl al-Ṭawīl, and Balīgh Ḥamdī, all three of whom had written successful songs for the popular movie star ʿAbd al-Ḥalīm Ḥāfiẓ and the young singer Najāt al-Ṣughayyara.[36] Al-Ṭawīl wrote "Wallaahi Zamaan ya Silaaḥi" and set two texts for "Rābiʿa al-ʿAdawiyya." Their work together ended soon thereafter. Al-Mawjī began with national songs and two songs for "Rābiʿa al-ʿAdawiyya." The success of his love song "Lil-Ṣabr Ḥuduud" led to another, "Isʾal Ruuḥak." Umm Kulthūm described this song as "thoroughly Arab" in character, and her remark typified critical response to al-Mawjī's style both as a composer and as a sensitive singer.[37]

In 1957, Umm Kulthūm contacted Balīgh Ḥamdī.[38] She was on the verge of concluding a recording contract with the Misrophon company, owned by Ḥamdī's friend, singer-actor Muḥammad Fawzī. Fawzī provided the introductions and later negotiated the terms of their collaboration. Sayyid al-Maṣrī, eventually Umm Kulthūm's principal recording engineer, then worked for Misrophon. Balīgh's "Inta Feen wi-ʾl-Ḥubb Feen?" (Where are you and where is love?) became the first of his love songs for Umm Kulthūm, the first of her songs to be edited by al-Maṣrī and the first to be recorded for Misrophon.[39]

Beginning with the premiere of "Inta Feen" in 1960, Balīgh wrote a new song for Umm Kulthūm almost every year until 1974. He composed melodies typically characterized as "light" (*khafīf*), much different from what she had been accustomed to sing by Zakariyyā and al-Sunbāṭī. Like ʿAbd al-Wahhāb and al-Qaṣabjī, he experimented with choral accompaniments, large orchestras, and new instruments. However, sensitive musicians claimed that one could hear in his melodies the influence of Zakariyyā as well.[40] Virtually everyone, including Umm Kulthūm, viewed Balīgh's songs for her as essentially pleasant tunes. His style was criticized by those who regarded it as trivial compared to the sophistication of al-Sunbāṭī's melodic lines and the cultural depth of Zakariyyā's. However, Balīgh's songs fared well commercially and found permanent places in her repertory, not only in Egypt but throughout the Arab world.

Very late in her career, Umm Kulthūm worked with Sayyid Makkāwī, whose style followed in the path of Zakariyyā. "Ya Msahharni" (1972) was the single completed result of that work, but another of his songs was in preparation when she died. There was occasional talk of her performing a song by the composer and movie star Farīd al-Aṭrash, but no collaboration resulted.[41]

The young composers with whom she worked in the 1950s were as eager as their predecessors to have Umm Kulthūm sing their songs. For these young men she offered particular advantages: Balīgh Ḥamdī learned a great deal about composition not only from her but also from the experienced older musicians in her ensemble. Her recordings provided virtually certain and continued financial success. Composition of a successful song for Umm Kulthūm was a credential, a certificate of attainment as a composer, that positively affected future opportunities and fees.[42] Whereas work with Umm Kulthūm had certainly been advantageous for al-Qaṣabjī, al-Sunbāṭī, and, to a lesser extent, Zakariyyā, they had all "come up together." The new generation of composers considered the invitation to work with Umm Kulthūm as the turning point of a career.

Collaboration with ʿAbd al-Wahhāb

By far the most dramatic step Umm Kulthūm took in developing new repertory was her collaboration with Muḥammad ʿAbd al-Wahhāb. Through their careers, the two were frequently linked in the public eye. They were of the same generation and had enjoyed similar protracted and spectacular success in Cairo and in the Arab world, she as a singer and he, increasingly, as a composer. Their public lives were peppered with suggestions that they collaborate on such projects as a film about ʿAbduh al-Ḥāmūlī and Almaẓ, a production of the ever popular Arabic love story "Majnūn Laylá," or as composer and singer for a new song.

ʿAbd al-Wahhāb began his career in musical theater about 1917 and became a highly regarded singer and composer. His principal mentor was Aḥmad Shawqī, who wrote numerous elegant lyrics for him to sing. Umm Kulthūm became acquainted with ʿAbd al-Wahhāb during the 1920s. Both remembered their first meeting at one of the salons of Cairo, the home of Maḥmūd Khayrat al-Muḥāmī, where they entertained the other guests with a rendition of Sayyid Darwīsh's "ʿAla Qadd il-Leel."[43] For years, Umm Kulthūm and ʿAbd al-Wahhāb moved in overlapping musicoliterary circles. The poet Kāmil al-Shināwī described a soirée attended by the actress Camellia, the lawyer Fikrī Abāẓa, the playwright Tawfīq al-Ḥakīm, ʿAbd al-Wahhāb, Umm Kulthūm, and others. Umm Kulthūm listened to a *qaṣīda* that al-Shināwī had written and declared that, if ʿAbd al-Wahhāb would compose it, she was ready to sing it. He did and she did, apparently on the spot. On another such occasion, ʿAbd al-Wahhāb and Umm Kulthūm entertained the audience, ʿAbd al-Wahhāb singing Umm Kulthūm's "Ana Fintiẓaarak," and she singing his "Jabal al-Tawbād," and both collaborating in a rendition of ʿAbd al-Wahhāb's "Majnūn Laylá."[44]

ʿAbd al-Wahhāb starred in a number of successful films during the 1930s and 1940s for which he also wrote the music, and thereafter he was viewed as a prestigious and innovative composer. A self-proclaimed modernist, he evinced extensive interest in new instruments and commanded a wide variety of styles, Arab and Western.

The two artists' different artistic objectives discouraged collaboration. These were clear in the 1920s, when ʿAbd al-Wahhāb associated himself with experimentation and Umm Kulthūm associated herself with "Egyptianness." ʿAbd al-Wahhāb integrated disparate musical styles to produce sometimes startling pieces. His innovations were often rhythmic, borrowing from popular dance, both Western and Arab.[45] Umm Kulthūm pointedly criticized this approach in 1942: "If this 'modernization' is composing dance music or foreign music, and setting the words of a song to its rhythms, I regard it as chaos, not modernity." She opined that, while one might study European music to learn its means of powerful expression and to integrate these with Arab musical procedures, Western musical styles should never be adopted "as they were."[46]

Her words helped Umm Kulthūm to define an artistic and social position for herself vis-à-vis ʿAbd al-Wahhāb that lay at once close to the *fallāḥa*—suspicious of the foreign and proud of her own heritage—and to politicians and intellectuals who were turning away from Western models. There is no reason to believe that her words did not reflect her actual opinion; however expression of these sentiments was expeditious at the time and no doubt also helped Umm Kulthūm, a fierce competitor, to hold her ground against ʿAbd al-Wahhāb in the business of commercial music.

Temperamental difficulties existed between the two as well. Each preferred center stage. Each attempted to impress a personal stamp of artistic character on any work. Umm Kulthūm retained the suspicion of ʿAbd al-Wahhāb generated by Munīra al-Mahdiyya's fiasco in "Cleopatra."[47]

From time to time the two were in direct competition. Both ran for president of the Musicians' Union during the 1940s and early 1950s. Conflicts occurred, which one or the other of them remembered years later. For instance, during the 1940s, ʿAbd al-Wahhāb bought the lyric "Sahraan li-Waḥdi" from Aḥmad Rāmī. Umm Kulthūm, knowing this and aware of the beauty of the lyric, used her strong connection with Rāmī to obtain the text herself and gave it to al-Sunbāṭī to set. Her performance preempted ʿAbd al-Wahhāb's.[48]

Despite all of this, a few of the proposed joint ventures seemed to receive due and serious consideration from both parties, faltering somewhere in the processes of negotiation or artistic development. The prospect of working together never seems to have been viewed as impossible or unequivocally undesirable by either artist.

Ultimately, their collaboration was facilitated by mutual friends and business associates. Most close observers believe that the catalyst was President ʿAbd al-Nāṣir and his emissaries from the national government. From the beginning of his administration, ʿAbd al-Nāṣir displayed interest in the entertainment business. He maintained the older immigration policy that facilitated the residence of singers and actors from other Arab countries in Egypt. His use of radio and his belief in its importance are well known. In addition to promulgating his ideas, he advocated the use of radio as a means of uplifting the spirits of the people through national songs and other entertainment. People said he intervened to ensure that radio continue to solicit new popular songs, so that cheap entertainment would be available to everybody, ostensibly to help mitigate the bad effects of the economic problems facing the Egyptian people.

The president was an admirer and personal acquaintance of Umm Kulthūm and ʿAbd al-Wahhāb. In 1960, both artists were decorated with the Order of Merit by the Egyptian government. ʿAbd al-Wahhāb took this opportunity to make a complimentary speech about Umm Kulthūm. Some time later, possibly at the behest of ʿAbd al-Nāṣir, Field Marshal ʿAbd al-Ḥakīm ʿĀmir, a frequent visitor to Umm Kulthūm's home, began efforts to persuade both artists to agree to a collaboration.[49] Agreement was formally reached when Umm Kulthūm and ʿAbd al-Wahhāb were together again, performing for a concert in honor of Egyptian National Day. The president was in attendance and invited both artists to join the field marshal and himself at their supper table.[50]

However, both were still wary of each other. Umm Kulthūm feared that the vocal line of any song ʿAbd al-Wahhāb wrote would be overwhelmed by the instrumental parts and that she would be made to appear weak. ʿAbd al-Wahhāb, well aware of Umm Kulthūm's usual involvement in the process of composition and her command in the rendition of a song, feared that the song he wrote would, one way or another, be *mutakaltham,* or dominated by Umm Kulthūm to such an extent that his composition would become nothing but an insignificant vehicle for her vocal style.[51] Initially, the principal violinist from Umm Kulthūm's ensemble, Aḥmad al-Ḥifnāwī (who also worked for ʿAbd al-Wahhāb), and Umm Kulthūm's husband (who was friendly with ʿAbd al-Wahhāb) served as intermediaries. The compromise eventually reached was that ʿAbd al-Wahhāb would have carte blanche in composing the song, and that Umm Kulthūm would withhold comment until she saw the result and try to work with it as it stood.[52] The first product of their work was "Intra ʿUmri" (You are my life) which premiered in February of 1964 and quickly became one of her most popular and famous songs. Nine more followed. Others by ʿAbd al-Wahhāb for Umm Kulthūm were in progress at the time of her death.

The artists' apprehensions were not without foundation. Not two days after the premiere of "Inta ʿUmri," Umm Kulthūm served ʿAbd al-Wahhāb with a legal warning to cease and desist. She had learned that he had made a recording of the song himself, the first recording of his own singing in years. He was negotiating the sale of this highly valuable tape to Egyptian Radio. Umm Kulthūm's warning stated that if he released the tape in any fashion she would decline to sing the song herself ever again, would take the recording off the market, and would legally prevent Egyptian Radio from broadcasting it. ʿAbd al-Wahhāb's tape was never aired.[53]

The preparation and first performance of "Inta ʿUmri," and, for that matter, most of the other songs written for Umm Kulthūm by ʿAbd al-Wahhāb, were accompanied by unprecedented press coverage. Every possible opportunity for an article, an interview, or a commentary was taken. Not only trade publications and fan magazines but regular daily newspapers, even the prestigious *al-Ahrām,* featured full-page articles on the work of the two stars.[54]

ʿAbd al-Wahhāb's songs for Umm Kulthūm contributed greatly to the flavor of modernity that dominated her repertory during the last fifteen years of her life. The instrumental sections featured dance rhythms, both Arab and Western. As a younger man he had been prone to borrow melodies outright, but when writing for Umm Kulthūm he tended to borrow styles, composing his own tunes within their frameworks. "Amal Ḥayaati" featured a jazz instrumental solo in its introduction and a bit of American folk dance style in one of its instrumental interludes (see example 11). These sections demonstrated ʿAbd al-Wahhāb's great facility in absorbing the essential features of a wide variety of musical styles.

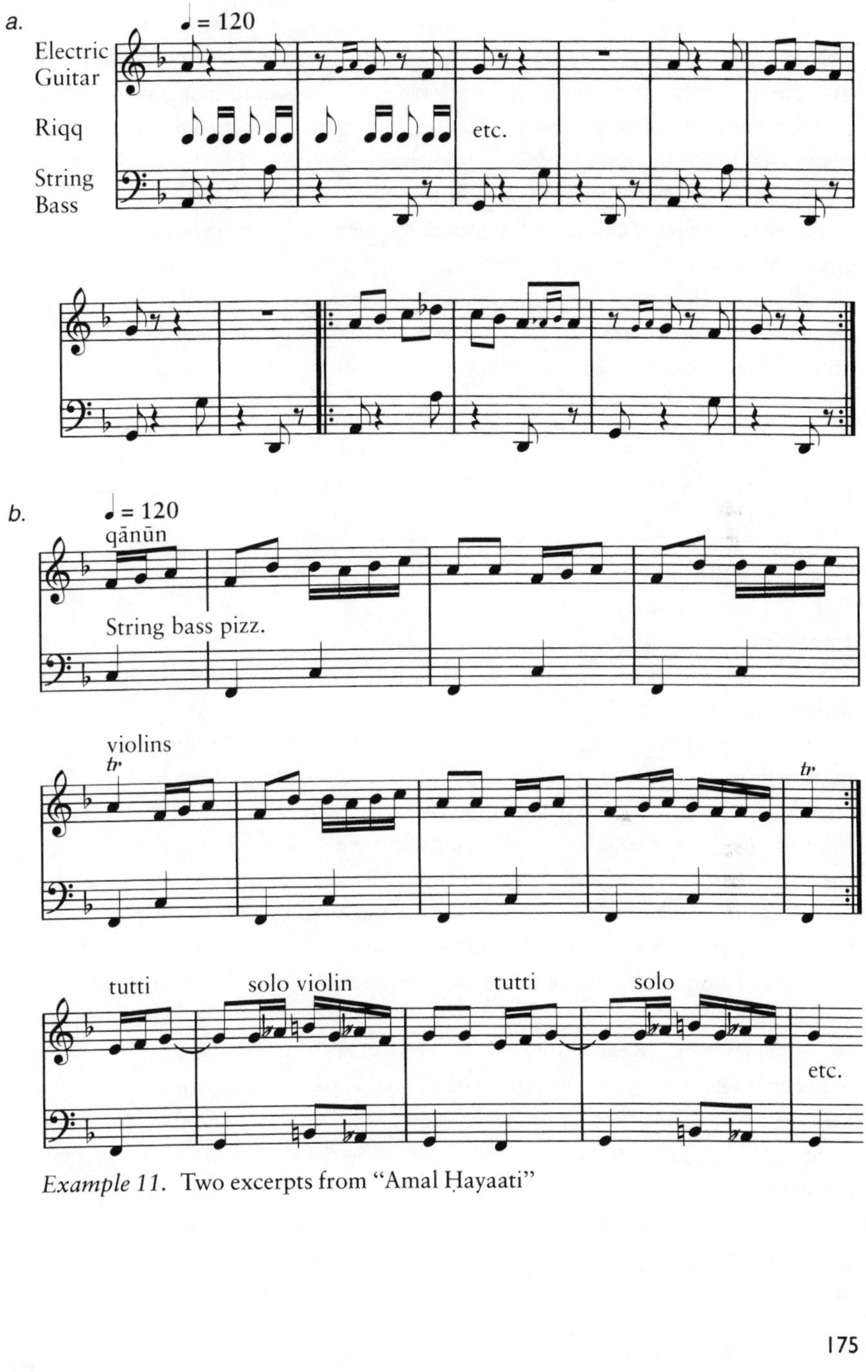

Example 11. Two excerpts from "Amal Ḥayaati"

Juxtaposition of styles distinguished his compositions from others. While "Amal Ḥayaati" was the most striking example in Umm Kulthūm's repertory, similar stylistic composites appear in "A-ghadan alqāk" and the instrumental introduction to "Wi-daarit il-Ayyaam." A popular view of his style was that "he cooks" (huwwa biyuṭbukh), taking "a little of this, a little of that." This remark was not complimentary. Critic Kamāl al-Najmī wrote that, while each line of ʿAbd al-Wahhāb's songs might be a stylistic gem, the songs as whole entities lacked unity.[55] They generally met with mixed reviews. "Inta ʿUmri," while a great commercial success, did not excite admiration among other composers. Reacting to the popular adulation for the song, Muḥammad al-Mawjī remarked,

> This is a dance more than a song. . . . The song is not a "miracle" [as it was popularly described]. I or any of a number of young composers could have written something like this. . . . I was expecting a song I could learn something from; but ʿAbd al-Wahhāb has been seduced by his [prior] success . . . so he used things he used with other singers before.[56]

Expressing the same sentiment, Balīgh Ḥamdī commented that "ʿAbd al-Wahhāb did not do anything! . . . and Umm Kulthūm is Umm Kulthūm. He did not add anything."[57]

However, within a month the song had "hit imaginary numbers in distribution in Egypt and the Arab world." It was *miliiḥ*, enjoyable, in contrast to her more serious repertory. ʿAbd al-Wahhāb and the lyricist Aḥmad Shafīq Kāmil divided profits of 250,000 £E ($575,000) at the end of the year from rights abroad. By June 30, 1965, receipts of sales of "Inta ʿUmri" in the Arab world outside Egypt amounted to £80,000 (sterling, or $224,000), and its popularity remained widespread thereafter.[58]

"Inta ʾl-Ḥubb" (You are love) and "Fakkaruuni" (They reminded me) raised more hackles among critics. One reviewer commented that the text of "Inta ʾl-Ḥubb" was so silly and devoid of serious expression that there was very little ʿAbd al-Wahhāb or Umm Kulthūm could have been expected to do with it. The general appraisal of "Fakkaruuni" was that it was not a song for the "Voice of *Qaṣāʾid*" but sounded like a song any ordinary singer might sing.[59]

Other songs, such as "Hādhihi Laylatī" (This is my night), "A-ghadan Alqāk" (Will I see you tomorrow?), and "Wi-Daarit il-Ayyaam" (The days have passed) were well received. But numerous critics believed that ʿAbd al-

Wahhāb's compositions and Umm Kulthūm's style of rendition were wildly incompatible, and that the songs could not stand comparison in the long run to those by Zakariyyā or al-Sunbāṭī. Nevertheless, from 1964 until 1973, ʿAbd al-Wahhāb's songs for Umm Kulthūm permeated entertainment and broadcasting. Since then, the repertory has acquired a place of its own as the principal exemplar of Umm Kulthūm's latest love songs.

The critiques of intellectuals and musicians distinguish the styles by which the two artists were known and the values, principally of modernity and authenticity, attached to them. However, popular appreciation of ʿAbd al-Wahhāb's songs for Umm Kulthūm indicates the degree to which both styles had penetrated cultural expression: whereas listeners could identify the differences between ʿAbd al-Wahhāb's and Zakariyyā's or al-Sunbāṭī's compositions, ʿAbd al-Wahhāb's songs were not or were no longer "foreign." Jazz, in the mid-1960s, was foreign; "Amal Ḥayaati," with its jazz-like introduction, was not.

The Resilience of al-Sunbāṭī's Songs

In the throes of Umm Kulthūm's stylistic change, Riyāḍ al-Sunbāṭī continued to produce love songs and *qaṣāʾid* on religious or patriotic themes that gained widespread and sustained popularity throughout Egypt and the Arab world.[60] As Umm Kulthūm began work with Balīgh Ḥamdī and al-Mawjī, and throughout the excitement of her collaboration with ʿAbd al-Wahhāb, al-Sunbāṭī produced lasting favorites including "Aquul lak Eeh," (What should I tell you, 1965), "Hagartak" (I left you, 1959), and "al-Aṭlāl" (Traces, 1966). After that, he wrote mostly religious and patriotic songs.

Al-Sunbāṭī willingly experimented with new instruments. He introduced a piano in "Arāka ʿAsīya ʾl-Damʿ," the only one of Umm Kulthūm's songs to feature the instrument. In the late 1960s he used electric guitars and organs. He did not, however, depart from the arch-shaped compositional framework, the Arab modes in recognizable formulations, and the subordination of the instrumental accompaniment, however large the ensemble, to the vocal line.

He was often described as a genius. Without attracting a great deal of attention to himself he compelled respect. His skills and strength of character forced Umm Kulthūm to accommodate him more often than she did others. Unlike al-Qaṣabjī, for instance, al-Sunbāṭī was rarely the brunt of her jokes and teasing. In her opinion, he was peerless in working with difficult Arabic poetry, brilliantly capturing the meanings of words and phrases in his melodic settings.[61] Critics believed he understood her voice well and wrote songs meticulously tailored to her abilities. Every singer, according to musicians and critics, needed such a composer in order to succeed.

His "Aṭlāl" became one of her best-loved songs. It was included in her concert in Paris in November of 1967, and she performed it in almost every concert series she undertook in the Arab world. Over the years it became a signature composition, frequently excerpted to evoke the memory of Umm Kulthūm.

The text was derived from two *qaṣā'id* by Ibrāhīm Nājī, "al-Aṭlāl" (Traces) and "al-Widāʿ" (The farewell). Most of the lines of the song came from the first, a neoclassical *qaṣīda* drawing on the images of wandering in the desert, coming upon old ruins, searching for something lost—a lover, a family, a home—common to the genre. The poem expressed the intensely personal feelings of torment and bereavement for which Nājī was known.[62] His language was contemporary, relatively direct in syntax, and accessible to listeners. He changed rhyme schemes with each section of the *qaṣīda,* an alteration of the old, single-rhyme scheme.

The lyric provided a striking instance of Umm Kulthūm's hand in editing the poetry she sang. To construct the song text, she created three-line sections from Nājī's quatrains, omitting the third of each group of four lines. She took her accustomed liberty in selecting stanzas from the much longer *qaṣīda,* rearranged the order in which they appeared, and replaced a few words. In the middle of the poem, she interpolated lines from Nājī's "Widāʿ." Of the thirty-two lines in the song text, lines 1–18 and 26–32 came from various places in "al-Aṭlāl." Lines 19–25 corresponded to lines 13–14 and 16–20 of "al-Widā."

Small emendations in texts were generally accepted and considered necessary and appropriate to the preparation of a text for singing. However, Umm Kulthūm's manipulation of Nājī's poems met with unfavorable criticism. The poet Ṣāliḥ Jūda wrote:

> This *qaṣīda* is not a mere song lyric, in which one can change the order of lines or drop lines with impunity; rather it is a narrative recording specific circumstances in historical order. . . . It is not possible to simply choose lines . . . and leave out others pursuant to some consideration about singing.[63]

If it were possible to complete the idea of a section in three lines rather than four, Jūda argued, the poet himself would have done so. In her defense, various authors pointed out that Shawqī himself had encouraged the selection and rearrangement of lines from his poems for the purpose of singing them. Several years later, Umm Kulthūm expressed her view that "the important thing is communicating the meaning that the poet intends, regardless of the number or order of lines of the *qaṣīda*."[64]

Al-Sunbāṭī's introduction consisted of contrasting sections; these did not simply establish the *maqām* of the piece (which is *rāḥat al-arwāḥ*) but included excursions away from it. Al-Sunbāṭī chromatically altered the augmented second, essential to the mode, twice to generate suggestions of various other modes (see example 12). The piece was composed for some twenty violins, three violoncellos and string bass, in addition to the *nāy, qānūn,* and *riqq*. The first recording also utilized timpani, cymbals, and triangle. The opening vocal line, however, was free of intrusion from the large ensemble and constituted a classical exposition of the mode. The declamatory style of the opening gave way to metrical rhythm as the poetic theme shifted to a fond memory of times past. Following the metrical section, the mode, which drifted through *bayātī* and *ṣabā* and changed to *nahāwand,* transposed upward, for the climactic line "Give me my freedom, set loose my chains." The new mode was based on a five-note species resembling the beginning of the Western minor scale, and, at this point, al-Sunbāṭī wrote a triadic bass line; however, the line functioned within the ensemble in the same way that an *ʿūd* or *qānūn* might, plucking out fundamental pitches of a mode at the lower octave. In the same section, the *nāy* part, improvised by the player, hearkened back to the accompanimental practices of earlier and smaller Arabic ensembles.

In Umm Kulthūm's performances, the song had two climactic points, one at the line "Give me my freedom, set loose my chains," located about one-third of the way through, and the second, about two-thirds through, after modulations through forms of *rāst, bayātī,* and *kurd,* at the line "Has love ever seen ones so intoxicated [with love] as we?" Here, al-Sunbāṭī wrote a popular Egyptian rhythm in the accompaniment.

Umm Kulthūm often indulged in direct text-painting using this line. Her varied repetition of the word *sukārá*ʾ (intoxicated ones) featured melodic excursions with unexpected accentuations thought to be suggestive of the irregular motion of one under the influence of alcohol. Her literary and

Example 12. Maqām Rāhat al-arwāḥ and excerpts from the introduction to "al-Aṭlāl"

musical skills were such that she could play on the words without deviating from the proper meter. When she sang "al-Aṭlāl" in Paris in 1967, an inebriated admirer approached the stage. Umm Kulthūm, who had reached the line in the poem, "Has love ever seen such intoxicated ones as we?" continued her performance by improvising "Have we ever seen such drunkards among us?"[65]

The *qaṣīda* concluded by completing the melodic arch with a descent to the final pitch of *rāḥat al-arwāḥ.* In the course of the descent, however, al-Sunbāṭī again altered the pitches of the critical augmented second to suggest *kurd* and *nahāwand,* transposed. The vocal ending, one octave higher than the opening (not an uncommon closing) was followed by an ornamental scale played on the string bass, built on the final pitch but not in the fundamental mode.

Several of the climactic lines took on political meaning: "Give me my freedom, set free my hands! I have given freely, I held back nothing. Ah, how your chains have made my wrist bleed. . . ." In 1966, these lines were perceived by some as addressed to the repressive measures of ʿAbd al-Nāṣir's government. After the Egyptian defeat of 1967, they took on a wider meaning, suggestive of the bondage in which many Egyptians felt the entire Arab world to be held. The lines were repeated "everywhere," as listeners assigned them new meanings. Over time, Umm Kulthūm and her listeners moved the poetic meaning between romantic and political themes.

"Al-Aṭlāl" was widely considered to be a musically sophisticated, popular, new *qaṣīda.* Its success illustrated the vitality of a historically Arabic compositional model as well as the flexibility of that model in accommodating the continuous absorption of new features. These, whether developed from closely or distantly related repertories, did not seriously disturb the underlying character of the genre.

The Ughniyya

Over the years Umm Kulthūm, together with her composers, established the *ughniyya* as a model of new Egyptian song. They produced a style of love song, sometimes called the "long song." Such songs typically began with an instrumental introduction three to six minutes in length. The introduction included several sections, at least one of which was metrical, usually based upon a popular Western or Egyptian dance rhythm, and at least one nonmetrical, improvisatory section similar to the traditional *taqāsīm* for a solo instrument. The solo instrument might be the electric guitar.

The voice usually entered with several nonmetrical lines (sometimes an entire stanza) with light accompaniment. The second stanza or group of lines was typically metrical and concluded the first half of the song. One or two instrumental interludes (*lāzimāt*) appeared in the first half. A longer instrumental section marked the median point of the song and was usually based on a dance rhythm. Most of the vocal invention occurred in the second half of the song, and the instruments played a lesser role. This section was the climax of the song and the ending itself was usually rendered with little fanfare.

Rhythmic innovation was a significant marker of the genre. Al-Sunbāṭī, especially, showed great skill in shifting from one temporal framework to another in his pieces.[66] The introduction of triple meter (sometimes called *fals,* borrowed from "waltz") had long been viewed as an interesting innovation and persisted in the new long songs.

Dance rhythms, Western and Egyptian, played a large role in the songs of al-Sunbāṭī, ʿAbd al-Wahhāb, and the younger composers. By contrast, Zakariyyā's *ughniyyāt* for Umm Kulthūm rarely exhibited striking contrasts or included these rhythms. Shifts in his songs were subtle, and the overall effect was of rhythmic homogeneity.[67] The essential rhythmic unity and absence of Western dance patterns cast Zakariyyā's *ughniyyāt* close to al-Sunbāṭī's *qaṣā'id* in style and to classical Arabic song generally.

The typical format for the love songs was sometimes applied to *qaṣāʾid* as well, especially by ʿAbd al-Wahhāb. "Hādhihi Laylatī" and "A-ghadan Alqāk" assumed the pattern of the modern *ughniyya* and its characteristic rhythmic innovation.

In some cases the large instrumental ensemble playing a metrical rhythm actually set the pace of the piece for Umm Kulthūm to follow, removing her, momentarily, from her accustomed position as the leader of the group. This rhythmic relationship represented a fundamental and important departure from her characteristic style and a turn away from historically Arab practice. Combined with the multitude of dance rhythms, it accounts for the often-voiced criticism of the new songs as being "nothing but dance."[68]

Umm Kulthūm's first *takht,* constituted in 1926, consisted of four or five men. The group expanded dramatically with the production of the film *Widād* to include a violoncello and string bass as well as more violins. In 1961, the size of the *firqa* stood at about eighteen: eleven violins, two violoncellos, a string bass, a percussionist, and the players of *ʿūd, qānūn,* and *nāy.* With the compositions of Muḥammad ʿAbd al-Wahhāb, the *firqa* expanded again as men were hired to play electric organ, piano, saxophone, accordion, electric and acoustic guitar, and various percussion instruments. Composers added the *nāy* and the *duff,* commonly associated with religious music, to reinforce religious themes in texts. The *nāy* alone often accompanied pastoral texts such as "Shams il-Aṣiil" and "Qaṣīdat al-Nīl," both of which evoked the river Nile. The *firqa* for "Inta ʾl-Ḥubb" (1965) featured twenty-seven players, for "Amal Ḥayaati" (1965), forty-five. In 1969, the permanent *firqa* numbered twenty-eight members.[69]

Many of Umm Kulthūm's new songs were vocally simpler and relied more heavily on instrumental flourishes than had her earlier ones. "I'll tell you," a violinist confided, "she had aged a little. What did she do?—The 'rhymthic' style of the young people." The earlier songs by al-Sunbāṭī "needed the strong voice of a young person." In the 1960s, "he simplified songs for her."[70] Instrumental music in dance rhythms provided part of the means for this simplification of the vocal line. As she aged, her compositions were pitched lower than her earlier songs, as she lost some of the upper range of her voice. The number and variety of *māqamāt* in which she sang declined, with a great many songs cast in *rāst, bayātī,* and *kurd,* and such modes as *shūrī* and *nakrīz* were excluded. Her voice aged well, and she never seemed to lose interest in performing or in engaging in the struggles for authority and power endemic in the business of commercial music. But she made adjustments. She acquired a sporadic heaviness of color that became noticeable in the 1950s.[71] A huskiness resonating in the chest replaced the high-pitched falsetto and *baḥḥa* of her earlier years. It approached a hoarse moan and was appreciated as highly expressive.[72] This strong cry also suited the shift of her persona from the sympathetic ingenue of the 1930s and 1940s to the strong-willed older woman of the 1950s and later. Her physical strength and vocal control allowed her to continue giving long performances late in her life. After the 1950s, pride of place accrued to her musical experience and imagination; the fast-paced high pitches and sweeping ascending lines that proliferated in the songs of her youth disappeared.

The Widening Market

Under President ʿAbd al-Nāṣir the number of radio stations, the power of transmission, and hours of broadcast dramatically increased as "Egypt . . . probably committed more resources to the establishment and programming of its radio and television systems than any other developing country."[73] Radio retained its popularity until the advent of the cassette tape player.

Broadcasting remained Umm Kulthūm's primary means for reaching her audience until the end of her life. She clearly understood the importance of radio in Egypt, all the more so after the development of the inexpensive transistor radio, when she said,

> We are in the transistor age. Thus broadcasting has become the weightiest of the arts. No one can stop it, no one can stand in its way. Everyone is able to listen to radio anywhere. Because of that I am a believer in the need for unlimited concern about broadcasting.[74]

In 1960, Umm Kulthūm participated in the opening of the Egyptian television station, and thereafter many of her concerts were videotaped and became part of television programming. She did not allow all of her concerts to be filmed, as she felt the commotion and particularly the bright lighting would annoy her audience. Especially for the first or second concerts of a new season, she did not want television cameras present. When they were there, she insisted on selecting the cameramen herself and objected to some of the photographic procedures. In her view, the television audience should see the concert from the same perspective as the theater audience. Close-up shots were forbidden: "If he comes any closer," she complained of a cameraman, "he'll photograph my thoughts!"[75] As usual, she had her way, and available videotapes of her concerts in general uniformly reproduce views from the middle of the theater.

Her recording company, Misrophon Records, was taken over by Ṣawt al-Qāhira, the Egyptian state recording company, in 1964. Her contract was acquired by Ṣawt al-Qāhira and remained substantially unchanged for the rest of her life. The company retained sole rights for distribution in perpetuity. Umm Kulthūm guaranteed at least three new songs per year. The company guaranteed the best possible recording equipment and that each song be recorded at least twice and the best result chosen. The company granted Umm Kulthūm the rights of final approval, the choice of her own accompanists (to be paid by the company), and a guarantee of 2,000 £E per recording and 27.5 percent of the proceeds of sales (except for national songs for which she received only the percentage of sales). Should another artist negotiate a more lucrative contract, Umm Kulthūm would automatically receive the higher figure as well. The high percentage and the amount of musical and editorial control over the result distinguished this from a standard artist's contract.[76]

While she always strove for the best contract possible with recording companies and radio, there is no evidence that she attempted to extract the last conceivable piaster from her concert audience. Potentially, she could have commanded much more than the 700 £E (about $1,600) she claimed as a fee for her services. However, ticket prices for the concerts remained virtually unchanged from the 1950s onward, ranging from 50 piasters to 5 £E (about $1.15 to $11.50). The cost of most tickets was between 2 and 3 £E ($4.60 to $6.90). Seats in the first rows (which were in fact unavailable to the general public as they were purchased every year by the same people) were 5 £E. Asked about raising ticket prices to bring them in line with the prices charged for other first-rank entertainment in Cairo, Umm Kulthūm replied, "No. We are not going to 'trade' in tickets." Unchanging ticket prices helped to guarantee a supportive and enthusiastic group of listeners in the theater which was extremely important to her.[77]

The Concerts for Egypt

Her continued popularity and the fees she was able to claim led Umm Kulthūm to the conception of the biggest benefit fund-raising effort of her life, her concerts for Egypt after the defeat in the 1967 war. The war had cataclysmic effects in Egypt and sent tremors—political, economic, and cultural—throughout the Arab world. The defeat came at a time when "the expectations raised by Nasserism had not been met: the general standard of living had not shown any appreciable rise, Egypt was involved in a disastrous war in the Yemen, corruption was perceived to be widespread, and political dissent was severely curtailed."[78] With the defeat in the 1967 war, every aspect of life was suddenly subject to reevaluation, especially by intellectuals. They decried what they believed had led to the disaster, namely collective delusions of grandeur, pride, lack of concern with the real problems of the Arab world, and lack of critical approaches to their solution. Umm Kulthūm, to many of them, symbolized this corpus of problems with her long performances and pride in local culture that they viewed as avoidance of real economic, social, and political distress. They tired of newspaper articles devoted to her wardrobe, wealth, and associations with ruling elites.[79] Her lengthy renditions bored the impatient young and annoyed critical intellectuals who, while willingly acknowledging her musical abilities, objected to the self-satisfaction her performances seemed to induce in listeners, distracting them from active involvement in issues of the day.

Sometimes deliberately Umm Kulthūm cramped other singers and other styles. Listeners sometimes complained about Egyptian-centered aspects of her style and persona and their centralizing effect on commercial and expressive culture. Throughout her career she maintained her supporters among the landowning class. This group effectively controlled radio. As an eminent intellectual pointed out, "While some of the personalities in this class changed after the [1952] revolution, the attitudes of members of this class and their position in Egyptian society did not." As an artist, Umm Kulthūm was "good enough that it isn't difficult to like her." The conflict was not with her music so much as the lack of choice. And it was hard to ignore the interests that intellectuals felt she represented.

Umm Kulthūm's concert series may have been a response to the accusation that she was "one of the reasons for the June defeat because her voice numbs the people instead of arousing them."[80] She began in Egypt, giving concerts, aided by governors and other local officials, in four Delta provinces. These were huge events, held in athletic stadiums or in large tents in an available open space. One of the first of these, in the city of Damanhūr, was held in a makeshift theater set up on about nine acres of public land.

Thirty-five hundred tickets were sold for between 3 £E and 100 £E each ($6.90 and $230) and a total of 38,000 £E ($87,400) was raised. Her 1972 concert in Alexandria was attended by thirty thousand people and netted 64,000 £E ($147,200) and forty kilograms of gold jewelry worth an additional 36,000 £E ($82,800).[81]

Her international concerts began in Paris at the Olympia Theater in November of 1967. This was the first and only time Umm Kulthūm performed outside the Arab world.[82] It was originally scheduled before the Egyptian defeat. In September of 1967 she announced that her income from the Paris concerts would be donated to the national treasury, and thus began her international crusade for Egypt. By 1970 she had performed in Tunisia, Libya, Morocco, Lebanon, the Sudan, and Kuwait, and she had collected £186,000 (sterling, or $520,000) outside of Egypt, 523,000 £E ($1,202,900) from her provincial tours, and 24,000 £E ($55,200) in jewelry donated by women. She continued her efforts in Iraq, Bahrain, Abu Dhabi, and Pakistan until, at the time of her death, she had contributed over 1,100,000 £E ($2,530,000), much of it in gold and hard currency, to the government.[83]

As part of this endeavor, she conceived the idea of creating a special song for each country in which she was invited to sing. She solicited texts from well-known local poets and gave them to one of her composers, usually Riyāḍ al-Sunbāṭī, to set. The new songs were premiered at concerts in the country represented. While the texts were not necessarily patriotic in nature, the overall effect of her performance was to evoke national pride. She produced songs on poems by al-Hādī Ādam from the Sudan, Jūrj Jirdāq of Lebanon, Muḥammad Iqbāl of Pakistan, and the popular Syrian poet, Nizār Qabbānī.[84]

Aided by a diplomatic passport granted her by the Egyptian government in 1968, her trips took on the characteristics of state visits. She was escorted to the Cairo airport and received at her destination by officials of high rank. She made well-publicized visits to local events and places of historical or cultural interest. These concerts contributed greatly to Umm Kulthūm's stature as a cultural leader as well as substantially augmenting the national treasury. More than a musician, she became "the voice and face of Egypt."[85] They did nothing to ameliorate the criticism of intellectuals, however, who continued to regard her as a conservative force with too-strong connections to the ruling elite.

"The Fallaḥiin are My Self"

Concomitant with her growing role as a public figure, Umm Kulthūm's performances in Egypt extended into speech about herself, her songs, and Arab music. As an older woman and a cultural authority, she talked about her commitment to Arab and Egyptian models and aesthetics:

> We must respect our artistic selves. . . . Take, for instance, the Indians. They show great respect for themselves in art and in life. Wherever they are, they insist on wearing their own clothes and in their art they are intent on asserting their own independent personality, and, due to this, their music is considered one of the best and most successful forms of music in the entire world. This is the way to success for us in music.[86]

Like many of her contemporaries, she distinguished between imitation of foreign style and adoption of selected qualities. She praised Egyptian literary figures Ṭāhā Ḥusayn, Maḥmūd ʿAbbās al-ʿAqqād, Muḥammad Ḥusayn Haykal, and Ibrāhīm al-Māzinī as effective writers because of their thorough study of both Arabic and European literature; each had arrived at a successful combination of good qualities from both sources:

> Music must express our oriental spirit. It is impossible to present the listeners with foreign taste. They won't accept it. If it is possible in other arts such as painting, for example, to depend on European taste and styles, that is because the audience for plastic arts is limited, drawn from the narrow circles of the intellectuals. But music and song draw the audience from all the people of various classes and levels of education. . . . Those who study European music learn it as one would learn a foreign language. Of course it is useful. But it would be silly to expect that this European language become our language.[87]

Her various performances characterized Umm Kulthūm as an Egyptian and Arab Muslim. They distinguished her from competitors, notably Muḥammad ʿAbd al-Wahhāb, who wore smoking jackets, conducted large orchestra-like ensembles of men in tuxedos, and fashioned himself a composer in the Western sense of one who created "pieces" that would be reiterated exactly.

When Umm Kulthūm talked about herself, she emphasized these aspects of her background: she linked herself to the *mashāyikh* and to *fallaḥiin* (peasants) and *abnaa' il-riif* (sons and daughters of the countryside). Her public image, built from song and speech linked to these two concepts, developed slowly as she learned to control her communication with the press.

Both the religious *shaykh* and the *fallāḥ* are important images in Egyptian society. These models are strong characters, men and women alike. In a simple, direct way, by describing herself in this language, Umm Kulthūm correctly identified her cultural and social background as one shared with hundreds of thousands of Egyptians. In effect, she produced herself, visually, aurally, and conceptually, from these ideas.

From her first autobiographical statements she talked about her rural origins. During the 1930s, a journalist wrote:

> If you asked any of our star female singers about her life, she would smile and say that she did not know in exactly what year she was born, but that, when she was a child, she remembers the servant carried her on her shoulder and placed her on the balcony of her father's palace in order to watch the demonstrations on the day the English arrested the late Sa'd [Zaghlūl] Pāshā and exiled him to Malta . . .[88]

> No singer or actress in Egypt talks to you about her past without mentioning the majestic and prestigious house in which she was raised . . . except one. . . . One only boasts today saying frankly that she was born poor, from a good family yes, but poor and that she knew poverty and deprivation . . . then thanks God for the blessings she has today and praises God for all of it, and that is Umm Kulthūm.[89]

As she aged she drew closer to this image. Describing her identity, she gave voice to characteristics and associations many Egyptians would like to believe are true:

> They [*fallaḥiin*] are simple people . . . but they have hearts of gold. They were my first audience. Whatever success I have realized goes back to them. They are the real masters of this country because they are the source of goodness, generosity and love in it. . . . The country is the foundation and source of the city. If you live in the city, you live in exile but in the village you live with your relatives and friends.[90]

She evoked this identity constantly in the last fifteen years of her life. "My childhood," she wrote, "was not different from that of many sons of my country [abnaa' baladi]." "The *fallaḥiin* are my self," she said. "They are my youth. They are my life. They are the broad foundation from which I emanated."[91]

Umm Kulthūm linked herself to *abnaa' al-balad* and to *fallaḥiin* in many indirect ways. Claiming, in an interview, that her chief entertainments were reading and taking walks, she happened to mention that she liked to walk in the rain. The interviewer quickly responded that people who like to walk in the rain were usually very sensitive and attempted to draw her into a discussion using the language of creativity and sensitivity that was in vogue at the time. Umm Kulthūm stopped this by interjecting simply "il-maṭar kheer" (rain is good), a common expression used by farmers for Egypt's infrequent rains. Following this exchange, the interviewer continued to query her about nature, asking what sort of scenes she liked. Responding to her answer, he exclaimed "But that's a picture of a village!" "Well, we are *fallaḥiin,* or didn't you know that?" she replied. The hapless broadcaster persisted, asking what kinds of flowers she liked.

> UMM KULTHŪM: Local ones.
> INTERVIEWER: What fruits do you like?
> UMM KULTHŪM: Each in its own season.[92]

Depending on simple language and common expressions, she insistently responded, in this and many other situations, as an ordinary Egyptian might, eschewing the position and tastes of the wealthy and urbane woman, the experienced international traveler who summered in Europe, which indeed she also was. She presented herself as an ordinary, dignified Egyptian who had become educated and elegant. Her insistent identification with villagers and *fallaḥiin* became an essential component of her public identity.

She described those she admired in similar terms. About singer Muḥammad ʿAbd al-Muṭṭalib she said:

> He is a son of the country, a real man [*ibn il-balad* and *gada*ʿ]. He has tones and cadences that are real Egyptian "folk," typical of the strong Egyptian male, who, in his voice, makes you laugh or makes you happy because he is a strong man in a time when this quality is vanishing. *Awlaad il-balad* are becoming ashamed to be *awlaad il-balad.* . . . I have observed that television has depicted them to us as thieves and hashish-smokers instead of the brave and heroic figures [they really are].[93]

El Hamamsy drew a general image of *awlād al-balad* widely recognized in Egypt:

> They live in the older, less Europeanized quarters of Cairo; many of them still wear traditional robes or galabeyas; they speak Arabic with-

> out intrusion of foreign words, and use the customary salutations and proverbial expressions with which their language is richly endowed; they still observe many of the older customs and ceremonial behavior which in earlier times were practiced by most Egyptians; they have preserved the male-dominant Muslim family pattern with its emphasis on strict codes for women and for sexual behavior; they eat traditional foods and listen to traditional Arabic music; the baladi coffeehouse is still an important source of entertainment. . . . There may well be among them educated as well as wealthy individuals. The most important criterion is the extent to which a person follows the old ways and identifies himself with *awlād al-balad.*[94]

The category is broad, and as El-Hamamsy writes, "today's Copts who live in the traditional quarters and exhibit traditional outlooks are now called *awlād al-balad.*" El-Hamamsy identifies an important attitude toward this identity: "Whereas in an earlier day, more . . . aspired to be considered *awlād al-zawwāt* [from the upper classes], recently the pendulum has swung the other way. People now find it awkward to be designated as *awlād al-zawwāt,* and many are anxious to prove their peasant or *ibn al-balad* background."[95] Umm Kulthūm's public behavior formed part of this shift in attitude.

The language used to describe Umm Kulthūm as a *fallāḥa,* as *aṣīla, min al-mashāyikh* is laden with value. Examples of this usage abound in everyday life. Responding to the suggestion that a women's group would have to deal responsibly with a particular situation, one woman's response was "Ma ʾḥna kullina fallaḥiin"—"But, we are all *fallaḥiin*"—implying "of course, we will act responsibly." In another case, the president of a charitable organization criticized a village leader's apparent attempt to profit from the group's day-care center, saying "Law kaan aṣiil"—"If he were a real Egyptian [village leader]"—he would not be corrupt, he would be an honest and good man.

Umm Kulthūm emphasized her origins *min al-mashāyikh.* "I was given a religious upbringing," she said to an interviewer, and added her view that it was necessary to read the Qurʾān to "be strong." "My first teacher," she said "was the Qurʾān."[96] She recited quietly in stressful situations, in her car on the way to a performance or in a plane about to take off. Her repertory included numerous songs with religious themes, and she often identified these as her favorites. In her later years, she made pilgrimages to Mecca and initiated an official inquiry that determined she was a descendant of the Prophet Muḥammad through his grandson Ḥasan.[97]

Fallaḥiin and the *mashāyikh* are sturdy personae, close to the heart of the self-images of thousands of Egyptians in the twentieth century. Umm Kulthūm drew upon the positive qualities of these images. But it is worth noting that both are complex characters, not simple stereotypes. A certain ambivalence attaches to the common view of *mashāyikh* and *fallaḥiin* in turn. The qualities of stubbornness and ignorance are often associated with *fallaḥiin* by other Egyptians, exemplified in a characterization from a novel by Ṭāhā Ḥusayn: "He was a fellah with all the besetting sins of his kind, hunger for land, miserliness over money, and overweening anxiety to be the gainer in any and every transaction." Marsot writes, "the term 'fallah' is . . . used as a term of praise, to denote strength of character and solid worth, and as a term of blame, to denote crudeness and apathy—an ambivalence that is intrinsic to the fallah."[98]

In many contexts Umm Kulthūm appeared to be a demanding and opinionated woman with a biting sense of humor. Her character softened only slightly over the years, and, along with stories about her generosity, the people who worked with her consistently told stories that portrayed her as demanding, sometimes unreasonably so. She simply insisted that her preferences be ascertained in each and every instance. This behavior amounted to use of personal power in a manner familiar among Egyptian women and frequently associated with *fallaḥiin.* At bottom is the value of protecting one's interests and those of one's family, clients, or associates. Overlaying this is the process of enhancing one's personal status by demanding that others behave to suit oneself. Hers was a powerful public persona that affected popular perceptions and may have helped produce comparisons such as this one with another talented singer: "When Suʿād Muḥammad sang, people listened. When she was not there, no one thought of her. Umm Kulthūm was a constant presence."

Umm Kulthūm's public persona rested not upon simple and digestible ideals but upon complicated figures, active concepts with long roots in the society. She appeared as a *fallāḥa* "with all the besetting sins of her kind" and also with all of the solid worth, defined by Egyptians, never imported from abroad.

While she deliberately stressed certain aspects of herself and avoided discussion of others, what she said seems to have represented, in a simplified manner, her sincere opinions and views. Her public self was clearly a construction but it was neither artificial nor false; Umm Kulthūm simply learned to present herself in the way she wanted to be thought of and remembered.

The Repertory Not Sung

The health problems that plagued Umm Kulthūm throughout much of her adult life worsened as she aged. Her eyes remained hypersensitive to light and in her later years, she wore dark glasses almost all the time. Beginning in 1971, her health deteriorated dramatically. In March, she suffered a gallbladder attack which resulted in the postponement of two concerts. The following winter, she was struck with a serious kidney infection that forced the cancellation of two more.[99]

During the first concert of the following season, she felt faint. She sang the entire concert, but it was her last. Failing health caused her to cancel the remainder of the season and, although she constantly planned to perform again, she never did so. She spent her time from the winter of 1973 through the summer of 1974 traveling to Europe and the United States to kidney specialists and suffered continually from weak health.[100]

She did not stop working. ʿAzīz Abāẓa and Muḥammad ʿAbd al-Wahhāb prepared a *qaṣīda* for performance at the Lebanese Baʿlabakk festival to which Umm Kulthūm had been invited frequently in the past. Sayyid Makkāwī wrote a song for her entitled "Awqaati Btiḥlaww Maʿaak," and ʿAbd al-Fattāḥ Muṣṭafá wrote a text entitled "Law il-Hawa Yiḥki," none of which she lived to sing.[101]

For years she had wanted to record a recitation of the Qur'ān, for which she never received what she considered to be the necessary approval from the religious authorities. She had also planned to record a reading of "al-Qiṣṣa al-Nabawiyya," which she had not performed publicly since her childhood, in thirty half-hour segments. The poet ʿAbd al-Fattāḥ Muṣṭafá and Muḥammad ʿAbd al-Wahhāb were working on the version she would sing. Riyāḍ al-Sunbāṭī composed the *qaṣīda* "Intiẓār" for Umm Kulthūm, using a text by Ibrāhīm Nājī; it was eventually recorded by Suʿād Muḥammad.[102]

The song "Ḥakam ʿAleena 'l-Hawa" was scheduled for its premiere in the spring of 1973. As was her custom, she planned to record it before its first performance and did so with great difficulty on March 13, 1973. The recording occupied twelve hours. For the first time, she sang while sitting in a chair, quietly brought to her by an engineer who saw that she was too weak to remain standing. The concert at which the song was to have been premiered was canceled and the recording released, never having been performed for a live audience.[103]

In the summer of 1974, Muḥammad al-Disūqī approached Ṣāliḥ Jūda for a text suitable for the celebration of the October national holiday. This poem, which began "Qiidu Shumuu ʿil-ʿIid wi-Ghannu li-Miṣr," was completed and set to music by Riyāḍ al-Sunbāṭī, but never sung by Umm Kulthūm.[104]

On January 21, 1975, she suffered the kidney attack that led to her death. Her last illness was accompanied by a vigil of watchful Egyptians outside her home in Zamālik and, later, by a phalanx of reporters from all over the Arab world at the hospital. The Syrian national radio station installed an open telephone line to the hospital to provide its listeners with up-to-the-minute reports of her health. Egypt's principal newspaper, *al-Ahrām,* published daily bulletins on her health.[105]

She died of heart failure on February 3, 1975. Her funeral was to be held at the ʿUmar Makram mosque in central Cairo, the site of most funerals for well-known Muslims in the city. From there, the body was to be carried by pallbearers for a short distance to a vehicle that would take it to its final resting place.[106]

The crowds of Egyptians far exceeded the number anticipated, literally filling the streets of Cairo. People later observed that her funeral had been larger than ʿAbd al-Nāṣir's.[107] The funeral did not proceed as planned. The millions of Egyptian mourners took the body from the shoulders of its official bearers and bore it themselves by turns, carrying it for three hours through the streets of Cairo, eventually to the mosque of al-Sayyid Ḥusayn, believed to be one of Umm Kulthūm's favorites. There the shaykh of the mosque repeated the funerary prayers over the body and urged its bearers to take it directly to its burial place, reminding people that Umm Kulthūm was a religious woman who would have wanted to be buried quickly in accordance with Muslim practice. This was finally done.

Legacies of a Performer

In the 1990s, Umm Kulthūm has acquired a transcontinental audience much larger than any during her lifetime. Writers in many languages have propelled memories of her forward and created new narratives. Her life story appears internationally in didactic works for children. International chains of stores sell her recordings on compact discs. The World Wide Web features a home page for listeners interested in learning more about her or locating particular recordings. Her work has been moved into societies, places, and media that would have been unimaginable to her during her career.

But perhaps more significantly, she remains a forceful presence in Egyptian culture. The voices we have heard speaking during and after her lifetime help us to see why. They suggest some answers to the questions of who Umm Kulthūm was and why she became so important.

Umm Kulthūm was first and foremost a singer, and she was, in many ways, a typical musician. As a young star, the performances she undertook were similar to those available to other singers. She was one of a number of women who found in commercial entertainment a way to enlarge their audiences and to attain the fame and fortune they sought. Like most, she came from a working-class background and viewed musical performance as a means of upward mobility.

Like the most successful of the female entertainers, she was a shrewd business person. She was not merely a pawn of commercial businesses. Rather, throughout her career, she occupied shifting positions of power in relation to her patrons, whether individual or corporate, and to her competitors, colleagues, and clients.

In part, she constructed herself through transactions. The capacity to extract compensation constituted a form of power. Like a number of her colleagues, she obtained large fees for her performances, probably the most money paid to any singer in Egypt. She was demanding in contractual negotiations and financial arrangements. She insisted on receiving higher pay than others and was not afraid of being difficult or saying no. She seemed to ask for extraordinary amounts of money when she was unenthusiastic about a project, rather than simply decline it, and also used the high fees she obtained to assert her domination of commercial entertainment. Her money provided her with the power to choose and to modify opportunities as well as to choose her associates and coworkers.

Umm Kulthūm used commercial means to advance her position within the ranks of performers and the society at large. Acquisition of wealth was a means of upward mobility (although not usually effective by itself in Umm Kulthūm's day). Together, her musical abilities and business arrangements gave her the opportunity to control the quality of her work and the nature of her public persona. Thus she gained a great deal of authority in the cultural domain.

She defined virtuosic singing in the twentieth-century Arab world. She continued to sing well throughout her sixties, long past the age at which most singers retired; she outlasted much of her competition. Her renditions and discourse about them inform us of the art of Arab vocal virtuosity.

Umm Kulthūm gave life to historically Arabic song in a commercial environment. Her work presented Egyptians with song they believed proceeded from their own culture and was not copied from another. Egyptian discourse about Umm Kulthūm's singing directs our attention to qualities of voice, the use of sounds of letters and words, and the rendition of words and phrases. Innovations float around these conceptual wires, transforming genres, styles, and practices. They become new but retain links to the past. Saxophones, electronic keyboards, triadic arpeggios, and tuxedos created a modernity and asserted competence coeval with the culture of the hegemonic power. Correct treatment of language, use of the structural principals of *maqām,* performance proceeding from the concept of *turāth* represented by the *waṣla*—all these helped constitute *aṣāla,* authenticity.

Umm Kulthūm brought to the socially marginal role of musician the dignity and demeanor familiar to Egyptian women generally. Like many other Arab women, she understood the power she had and used it to advance her causes. She is often credited with having raised the level of respect for singers. As a stage personality, seven-year president of the Musicians' Union, member of several government committees, and cultural emissary to other Arab nations, she offered a model of public behavior for young women aspiring to careers in entertainment and other professions in the public eye. In this arena and in her advocacy for Egyptian and Arab cultural and political concerns, she earned a place as a historic figure as well as a singer.

She emphasized her connection to the "folk" without recourse to folk music, associating herself instead with the more obviously learned of traditional expressions, those emanating from the *mashāyikh*. She worked with materials—religious song and recitation, *qaṣāʾid, zajal*—already present in expressive culture and transformed these using new sounds overlaying a familiar vocal idiom. She rarely if ever invented stylistic practices or musical gestures, nor did she invent a tradition. Rather, she drew upon musical precedents having particular associations.

She identified herself with the best of the *mashāyikh* and of the ideal *fallāḥ* and asserted the consummate value of these identities. Over the years, people increasingly used the image of the *shaykh* and the *fallāḥ* as icons of authenticity. Umm Kulthūm came to be valued in these terms; it was a valuation she encouraged, thus contributing to and strengthening an ongoing discourse. The repetition of this idealized image of Egyptian society reproduced an ideology of the worth and longevity of Egyptian Arab culture that helped to form an alternative to that of the West.

The "other" being confronted was a complex and shifting entity. Egyptians, as Laila El-Hamamsy points out, have maintained a separate identity for themselves as *abnaaʾ al-balad,* children of the country, sometimes against their own leaders, many of whom were non-Egyptians over the past two centuries. *ʿUlamāʾ*, and by extension the wider realm of the *mashāyikh* were, on the other hand, "real leaders" who "had power over the masses, in whose life religion played a major part" and who "were the only means of intercession with the ruler available to the masses." They were also identified as *abnaaʾ al-balad,*[1] but, as we have seen, they were also subject to criticism. The "others" are those who are not "really" Egyptian (and these may include Egyptians), those who are not "really" Arab or Muslim, or specifically those who represent the West. The opposition is neither simple nor always uniform and clear.

Umm Kulthūm was not, as an Egyptian political scientist noted, a politicized person, but she functioned in a political environment. To the continued consternation of her critics, she persisted in asserting pride in Arab and Egyptian culture when many thought that past practices could well be submitted to constructive criticism. In the face of such criticism, Umm Kulthūm tacitly retreated to her position as a singer and never became the political voice that critical intellectuals desired. Her repertory, thus, had the effect, felt acutely by intellectuals and leftists, of creating the impression that everything was really all right, that the future could be left to fate, that no action was necessary. Hers was the persistent song of *ṭarab* culture and of Arabic poetry.

Umm Kulthūm sang a repertory that was generally inaccessible to Western listeners and often incompatible with those Western musical styles and practices that gained currency in the twentieth-century Middle East. The great acclaim directed at such a figure is particularly interesting in the context of Egypt: while it has often been considered the most Westernized of Arab lands, Western scholars, politicians, and other observers have frequently wondered at the reluctance of Egyptians to conform more readily to apparently desirable Western ways. Some have been astounded when Egyptians have aligned themselves with Islamic or Arab causes believed by Westerners to be incompatible with "progress." The breadth of support for Umm Kulthūm, reaching as it did into almost every social and economic class from peasant to ruler, testified to the vast appeal of constructions that could be viewed as indigenous, the deeply felt pride in Arab history and culture, and the support for Arab or Islamic alternatives to Westernization. The political position suggested by Umm Kulthūm's musical sound and public persona—a version of "Egypt for Egyptians" proceeding from indigenous values and precedents—proved unassailable. Thus Muḥammad ʿAbd al-Wahhāb was the "Musician of the Generation" but Umm Kulthūm was the "Voice of Egypt."

Yet, as Stephen Blum cautions, "We have good reason to be suspicious of those who claim that a culture 'speaks' through a single voice."[2] The "Voice of Egypt" appears to be a spectacularly successful individual, clearly an exceptional person in many aspects. Yet, just as clearly, her "voice" was and is a collective voice, constructed historically. The performances produced by a single individual, Umm Kulthūm, became widely shared within Arab societies and identified by vast numbers of people as important cultural property. They were a focal point for discussion and argumentation that informed later performances. The repertory of the "genius" gave voice to a system of values.

Despite claims to the contrary by herself and others, she was never a voice crying in the wilderness. She tried assiduously and consistently to construct a voice that millions would claim as their own. She was affected by the musical thought of al-Sunbāṭī, al-Qaṣabjī, and, long before she sang his songs, by ʿAbd al-Wahhāb. She was shaped by Egyptian intellectuals and by less elite listeners responding to their own lived experience. She may have "taught poetry to the masses," but the "masses" also taught her (and others) that they would learn it—that it mattered. The music she produced changed in response to these forces. Listeners now call her songs part of their heritage. Her work has become *turāth.*

She did not merely reflect social attitudes, she advanced them, promulgating a point of view, articulating a position, and feeding a strong and deep current of feeling. The major work of her life, her "Golden Age," contributed to two major cultural formations: neoclassicism and populism. As an artist she was affected by these formations which were in progress when she was just a child and ongoing at the outset of her career. She in turn affected them, strengthening them with her colloquial songs and modern *qaṣā'id.* Thus, drawing from musical styles associated with Arab and Islamic cultural heritage, Umm Kulthūm fed the river of expression with songs that were at once recognized as *aṣīl,* importantly Egyptian and Arab.

After the entry of a song into the repertory of the society, listeners used it for many purposes and moved its meaning through time and space. Umm Kulthūm's performances, like those of many popular entertainers, were adopted by political authorities to attract attention to the broadcasting of their messages. Texts originally conceived as love lyrics acquired political meanings in the late 1960s: the sense of love lost extended to loss of land, national status, and international dignity. After ʿAbd al-Nāṣir's death, the performances of Umm Kulthūm were used to evoke his memory, indirectly, under the unsympathetic Sadat regime. Shopkeepers tuned in to the Umm Kulthūm station for nightly entertainment, and two lengthy performances per day were commonly heard in the public domains of working-class people.

Umm Kulthūm's "Golden" repertory in its populist and neoclassical formations manifested a gradual acknowledgment of the failure of the West to offer sociopolitical models for Egypt. This music, these songs, figured in the large-scale process of "acknowledging" within the society. They were taken in by listeners, learned, recited, performed, and replayed over years. They contributed to the popular construction of Umm Kulthūm as one of them—a "real" Egyptian, an educated Arab, and a religious person.

In a more general way, to be a listener to Umm Kulthūm was to join many others in a validation of a communal social universe. To listen to Umm Kulthūm during her lifetime was to participate in a historically Arab behavior: listening, often in small groups, and responding to a good singer.

The structure of time during performances opens a window onto this phenomenon: Umm Kulthūm's concerts in Paris—consisting of "only" three songs but lasting over six hours—were not "just like the Opera." They were much different: that is what was reported in Egypt and what was appreciated there. A number of communities were imagined: the group of listeners, the local community (whether *ḥāra,* neighborhood, or village), the community of Egyptians, Arabic speakers, or sometimes a larger community, the Muslim *umma.* Performances, as Clifford Geertz wrote, "are positive agents in the creation and maintenance" of these sensibilities. Umm Kulthūm and her listeners collectively accomplished the repeated "enactment of cultural values."[3] The world represented by her performances, constructed from Arab and Egyptian values, is where many listeners have wanted to live.[4] Critics, on the other hand, usually intellectual activists, argued that this choice had become dysfunctional.[5] But, partly because ordinary Egyptians saw leftist critics as products of a failed West, Umm Kulthūm's world, her voice, the alternatives listeners heard, remained strong in Egyptian society.

In the 1990s, the uses of Umm Kulthūm's music and persona continue to change. The playing of her tapes on cassette recorders in the street is now often replaced by recitations of the Qur'ān and by young Egyptian stars singing "light" music. When young singers now endeavor to perform her songs they often sing only sections at a time. Her performances are less frequent over radio and television, although her cassettes are still widely sold and are still played in shops and taxis.

Her songs are becoming old. Almost her entire repertory, including songs composed as recently as 1965, has passed into the *turāth.* The *qaṣā'id* in particular are viewed as venerable pieces; few singers can sing them, but the songs offer models of composition and rendition to the ambitious student and devoted listener.

Musicians reuse the songs in a variety of ways. "Huwwa Ṣaḥiiḥ," for instance, formed the basis for an instrumental recording by Aḥmad al-Ḥifnāwī, a violinist from Umm Kulthūm's ensemble. The popular film composer ʿAmmār al-Sharīʿī recorded an electronic version produced on a sophisticated new system. A *mizmaar baladi* ensemble from Upper Egypt uses the melody as part of a recording of a quintessential folk performance.[6]

Her *turāth* is performed at the New Opera House by state-sponsored ensembles for Arabic music who offer skeletal versions of her songs. This type of performance of the *turāth* as a whole, traced conceptually and historically by Salwa El-Shawan, constructs "al-mūsīqá al-ʿarabiyyah" as public classical music for which "students learned to reproduce fixed pieces, and improvisation was discouraged or prohibited."[7] The performances are largely unsatisfying to cognoscenti, "but," as retired singer Laure Daccache reminded me, "at least we can hear the music."[8]

The audience for the national ensembles at the New Opera House remains much as El-Shawan described it: well-educated, upper middle-class people who like the music very well and see value in replication, in classical concerts following Western models. However, this audience becomes noticeably livelier, calling out praise and waving their printed programs wildly in the air, when the national ensemble for religious music appears. This group of men, with sparse accompaniment, sing the repertory of the *mashāyikh,* of ʿAli Maḥmūd, of Ismāʿīl Sukkar, and of Umm Kulthūm's father. Recited religious *qaṣāʾid* are sometimes part of their program. The solo vocalist's long lines are met with shouts of praise and encouragement, the male chorus chiming in for the refrains in the old style. This educated and well-off audience responds to the familiar old religious singing more than the replications of ʿAbd al-Wahhāb and Umm Kulthūm.

Some listeners, put off by the performances or by the opulence of the New Opera House—some indeed by the requirement that men wear jackets and ties—have left this venue in favor of informal music societies where solo singing in traditional styles can be heard. Young and old, upper middle class and working class jam a third-floor room at l'Atelier in Cairo to hear amateur singers, some very accomplished. The young Tahānī Muḥammad ʿAlī stands in front of the crowd wearing her *ḥijāb,* accompanied by her teacher, to sing exquisite versions of songs by Muḥammad ʿAbd al-Wahhāb and songs of Umm Kulthūm. One of Sayyid Darwīsh's sons, a former opera singer, leads group singing of his father's songs and gives his own affecting performances of "Ana Maṣri" and "Salma ya Salaama" with listeners joining in the chorus and calling out compliments.

Yet Umm Kulthūm remains today a model against which other performers are measured. Like Jamāl ʿAbd al-Nāṣir, she now belongs to a bittersweet time gone by. People often manifest nostalgia for her as some do for ʿAbd al-Nāṣir. Fond and respectful memories of both are recollected by working-class Egyptians for whom both represented the value, strength, and potential of local society and culture. Confronted for years with difficult economic problems, these listeners strain to live in the hopeful environment of the 1950s.

In order to see the importance of this music—and of the role of expressive culture in society—one must look at the *longue durée;* one must look historically as well as anthropologically. In the process of so viewing Umm Kulthūm's life, one sees that it is not simply speech that organizes reality, that creates a heritage or a tradition. It is also musicians working with sound, poets with words—artists working with materials in palpably similar ways. Artists' performances and audience response, in this case positive, carry the works through time, instituting practices and structural principles. Through her work, Umm Kulthūm opened a space for herself in the public domain of her society. Her performances offer an opportunity for the disputation and affirmation of more general values that extend beyond the aesthetics of music. Through this process the star performer, working within musical practice, acts to constitute cultural identity and social life.

Glossary

The following list provides a brief gloss of Arabic words used frequently in the text. The definitions should not be taken as complete explanations of terms and concepts which are, in some cases, rather complicated; nor does it account for the multiple meanings some words have when the alternative meanings do not pertain to music or performance.

Adāʾ***:*** Rendition, or the singer's musical presentation of a song.

Baḥḥa: A quality of hoarseness or a break in the voice considered to be beautiful and expressive.

Dawr (pl. ***adwār***): Virtuosic genre of song developed in nineteenth-century Egypt; the *dawr* typically includes two sections, the second of which features choral responses to solo renditions of lines and a virtuosic improvisation on the syllable "ah," called the *hank*.

Dūlāb (pl. ***dawālīb***): Short, familiar instrumental pieces used to introduce songs in the same *maqām*.

Faddān: A measure of land equal to 1.038 acres.

Fallāḥ, f. ***fallāḥa*** (pl. ***fallāḥūn***; colloq., ***fallaḥiin***): Egyptian peasants.

Firqa: Ensemble of approximately eight or more instruments.

Ghunna: "Sweet nasality," a desirable tone color in song.

Ḥadīth: (As an adjective) New, novel, recent, late, modern.

Īqāʿ (pl. ***īqāʿāt***): Rhythmic mode.

Khanaafa: Colloquial Egyptian term for "sweet nasality" or *ghunna*.

Laḥn: Composition or melody of a song.

Layālī: Vocal improvisation on the text "*ya leel, ya ʿeen.*"

Lazma (pl. ***lazmāt***): Instrumental interlude in a song.

Mazhabgi: Accompanimental singer.

Maqām (pl. ***maqāmāt***): Melodic mode on which a composition may be based.

Mawwāl (pl. ***mawāwīl***): Genre of song dating from the twelfth century that may take a variety of shapes; recent Egyptian examples frequently have four to seven lines of text on which a solo singer improvises; puns, creative rhymes, and other plays on words characterize this manifestation of the genre.

Monologue: Through-composed song developed in musical theater and characterized by the emotive, often virtuosic expression by a solo singer.

Mughanni, f. ***mughanniyya:*** Singer.

Muṭrib, f. ***muṭriba:*** Term applied to an accomplished singer, literally "one who enchants."

Mūlid: Celebration of a saint's day.

Muwashshaḥ (pl. ***muwashshaḥāt***): Sophisticated, metrical song believed to originate in Andalusian Spain.

Naṣṣ: Text of a song.

Qafla (pl. ***qafalāt***): Cadence.

Qaṣīda (pl. ***qaṣā'id***): Classical poetic genre characterized by a single rhyme scheme and meter throughout; a lengthy poem constructed of hemistiches and often treating themes and images having to do with wandering in the desert and coming upon something that had been lost; usually through-composed in musical settings.

Al-Qiṣṣa al-Nabawiyya: The story of the prophet Muḥammad's life, sung using a selection of texts, usually *qaṣā'id* and *muwashshaḥāt,* relevant to the topic.

Ṣāla (pl. ***ṣālāt***): Music hall.

Shaykh, f. ***shaykha*** (pl., ***mashāyikh):*** Learned religious persons.

Tajwīd: Rules governing the recitation of the Qur'ān.

Takht: Ensemble consisting of two to five players that formed the customary accompanying group for a singer at the turn of the century.

Talḥīn: Composition.

Ṭaqṭūqa (pl. ***ṭaqāṭīq***): Strophic, colloquial song noted for its simplicity.

Ṭarab: Enchantment, the complete engagement of listeners with a musical performance.

Taṣwīr al-ma'ná: Enhancing or depicting the meaning, sense, or mood of a text using music.

Turāth: Heritage, of music or other cultural forms.

Ughniyya (pl. ***ughniyyāt***): Literally, "song," this term is applied to songs usually having colloquial texts cast in a variety of musical shapes that frequently include a refrain or some other form of internal repetition.

'Umda: Village leader, roughly equivalent to a mayor.

Waṣla (pl. ***waṣalāt***): A suite of vocal and instrumental pieces which, at the turn of the century, constituted a genre of entertainment common at elite gatherings of men.

Zajal (pl. ***azjāl***): Colloquial poetry.

Notes

Chapter One

1. Personal communications from listeners; also Fu'ād, 461; see also Gordon Gaskill, "The Mighty Voice of Um Kalthum," *Life* vol. 52, no. 22 (June 1, 1962), 15–16, which is often quoted approvingly in Arabic.

2. "Ghannat lil-ḥubb—fa-jamaʿat 76,000 Junayh lil-Ḥarb" (She sang of love—and collected 76,000 £E for war), *Akhbār al-Yawm* (June 19, 1967).

3. Blum, "In Defense of Close Reading and Close Listening," 47.

4. My view on this point differs from some others expressed in earlier literature dealing with speech and music, notably C. Seeger's "Speech, Music and Speech about Music" (in his *Studies in Musicology, 1935–1975*); where Seeger sees speech as a separate phenomenon, I see it as an allied if not integral aspect of musical performance and listening.

5. Feld discusses a similar situation using these apt words in *Sound and Sentiment*, 46.

6. Those surveyed for this work include the magazines *al-Ṣabāḥ* (1921), *Kawkab al-Sharq* (1924), *al-Tamthīl* (1924), *al-Tiyātrū* (1924), *al-Sitār* (1927), *Rūz al-Yūsuf* (1925–), *Fann al-Sīnimā* (1933), *al-Masraḥ* (1925–27), *al-Mumaththil* (1926), *al-Kawākib* (1932–), and *al-Funūn* (1924), all of which deal primarily with performing arts; also *al-Ahrām* (1876–), *Ākhir Sāʿa* (1936–), and *al-Rādyū al-Miṣrī* (later *al-Idhāʿa*, then *al-Idhāʿa wa-'l-Tilīfizyūn*, 1935–).

7. If not completely accurate these are highly suggestive of the content of music programming. Substitutions were made when recordings could not be located or were found to be damaged.

8. Muḥammad Ḥammād in *Ākhir Sāʿa* no. 178–85 (November 1937–January 1938); *ʿAwaḍ;* the sections of the latter which are Umm Kulthūm's have been translated and published in Fernea and Bezirgan's *Middle Eastern Muslim Women Speak*. I refer here to substantial autobiographical statements, not isolated reminiscences or anecdotes told to interviewers who questioned artists on a variety of topics.

9. Cf. Lila Abu-Lughod's use of "discourse" "to mean a set of statements, verbal and nonverbal, bound by rules and characterized by regularities, that both constructs and is patterned by social and personal reality" (*Veiled Sentiments*, 186). Abu-Lughod distinguishes this from the linguistic meaning of formalized speech acts. She (and I) derive our usages from Foucault. Dreyfus and Rabinow call Foucault's usage his "interpretive analytics" (105, 104). Giddens mandates attention to the "range of discursive phenomena," including humor and irony, and to the signifi-

cance of the practical consciousness which informs action (*Constitution*, xxx). See also Ricoeur.

10. Blum, "Musics in Contact," 4, 5, v; similarly, Middleton writes, "It is certainly clear that words *about* music—not only analytic description but also critical response, journalistic commentary and even casual conversation—affect its meaning" (*Studying Popular Music*, 220–21). And Feld: "Locational, categorical, associative, reflective, and evaluative discourse, as varieties of interpretive moves, tend to be attempts to identify the boundaries that sound objects and events present in their structure and social organization. Interpretive moves in talk, then, are attempts to recreate, specify, momentarily fix, or give order to the things that take place so rapidly and intuitively when we experience musical sounds" ("Communication, Music, and Speech about Music," 15). See also Hugo Zemp, "'Are'are Classification," and "Aspects of 'Are'are Musical Theory," and Klaus Wachsmann, "The Changeability of Musical Experience."

11. Middleton, *Studying Popular Music*, 188.

12. Waterman, *Jùjú*, 9.

13. Middleton, *Studying Popular Music*, 92; "Music *use*," as Middleton suggests, "is no less part of 'social practice' than is production" (139). Compare Waterman, "Jùjú History," 66. For listening as performance, see Blum, "In Defense of Close Reading and Listening," 52 n. 15. Bourdieu analyzes the participation of the viewer in visual art in the production of culture in "Outline of a Sociological Theory of Art Perception."

14. Dreyfus and Rabinow, 72; also 61.

15. Clifford, *Predicament of Culture*, 22 n. 1; see also Ortner, 158.

16. Reyes Schramm, "Music and the Refugee Experience," 9.

17. Foucault, 100.

18. Ibrahim Abu-Lughod concluded 'the radio is the most effective medium for reaching villagers, even literate ones" (101); see also Issawi, 189 and Boyd, 11. Most researchers note that even the television sets that appeared in public places in about 1960 did not attain the popularity of radio (Fakhouri, 103; Boyd, 1; Wahba, 12–13).

19. Wahba, 53, who also observed that, in about 1969, it was "generally believed that there must be approximately one radio set (transistor or electrical) for every three inhabitants" (14); see also Chabrier, 39 and Fakhouri, 102–3; for a recent perspective on the role of the radio and other mass media among the Awlād 'Alī Bedouin of the Western Desert, see Lila Abu-Lughod, "Bedouins, Cassettes and Technologies of Public Culture."

20. Because of the various ways in which performances may be understood, as Middleton notes, "Listeners can also enjoy performances with which they are ideologically out of sympathy" (*Studying Popular Music*, 263; see also 214). This occurred in the course of Umm Kulthūm's performances.

21. Turino, "Structure, Context, and Strategy in Musical Ethnography," 400; see also 406–7.

22. Middleton, "Articulating," 40.

23. Giddens, *Profiles*, 197–98.

24. Williams, *Marxism and Literature,* 166, 157.

25. Following A. Seeger, "Everything is always partly defined by what it is not—by the other members of a set which usually are systematically related among themselves" (*Why Suyá Sing,* 25). Qureshi effectively describes Indic musics in terms of verbal and musical content in *Sufi Music of India,* 47.

26. See L. Abu-Lughod, *Veiled Sentiments,* 178.

27. Compare Sugarman, 198.

28. Personal communications from Kamāl Ḥusnī, April, 1983; al-Khulaʿī, *Kitāb,* 7; *al-Mūsīqá wa-'l-Masraḥ* no. 6 (July 1947), 210; compare Sawa, *Music Performance Practice.* "Modern," in this context, is one translation of the Arabic word "*ḥadīth,*" meaning new, novel, recent, late, or modern, which is often applied to the contemporary and innovative. Neither word should be taken to imply a single specific set of sociocultural properties, often implied in scholarly writing by the words "modern" and "postmodern."

29. El-Shawan, "al-Mūsīḳa," 44. While skilled singers are called *muṭrib* (f., *muṭriba*), others are merely *mughannī* (f., *mughanniya*), literally "singer," implying less artistry.

30. This is one of the main themes of Williams, *Marxism and Literature.*

31. Blum, "Towards a Social History," 217. Similarly, Middleton argues that positional values are the primary tools in the construction of subjectivity (*Studying Popular Music,* 251–52).

32. Waterman, "Jùjú History," 53.

33. The magnitude of this change is suggested by Williams' observation that "they [electronic transmission and related technologies] are always more than new technologies, in the limited sense. They are means of production, developed in direct if complex relations with profoundly changing and extending social and cultural relationships: changes elsewhere recognizable as deep political and economic transformations" (*Marxism and Literature,* 54).

34. Racy, "Music in Contemporary Cairo," 6, 16; El-Shawan, "al-Mūsīḳa," 23–87.

35. Nettl, 239–40; Kay Kaufman Shelemay raised the issue of the individual in her "Response to Rice," and Rice's *May It Fill Your Soul* proceeds from the musical experience of two individuals. Recent works by Veit Erlmann ("Conversation with Joseph Shabalala of Ladysmith Black Mambazo" and *African Stars*) and by Stephen Slawek ("Ravi Shankar as Mediator between a Traditional Music and Modernity") address issues surrounding well-known star performers.

36. Middleton, *Studying Popular Music,* 45; see also Manuel, 95.

37. Frith, "Essay review: Rock biography," 276–77.

38. Giddens, *Profiles,* 8; also his *Constitution of Society,* 171, and 2, 288.

39. Turino, "The History of a Peruvian Panpipe Style and the Politics of Interpretation," 130.

40. Williams, *Marxism and Literature,* 195.

41. Waterman, "Jùjú History," 66.

42. Williams, *Marxism and Literature,* 97; see also 58–62 and 70–71. Williams' works offer a cogent theory and applications of ideas of artists working with

materials. Compare Kathleen Stewart: "ways of talking . . . *produce* a social reality rather than merely 'express' an inner reality or 'describe' an outer reality" (45). Middleton applies similar ideas to popular music and identifies their roots in Gramsci's writing (*Studying Popular Music,* 8).

43. Williams, *Marxism and Literature,* 119.

44. Ibid., 132.

45. Ibid., 111, 173.

46. This bias is discussed by James Clifford in his introduction to *Writing Culture,* 11–12.

47. El-Hamamsy, 283.

48. Berque, 101.

49. Keddie, in Keddie and Baron, 14.

50. C. Nelson, 329; see also Blum, with reference to Barbara Hampton and Margaret Kartomi, in "Prologue," 19.

51. Clifford, *Predicament of Culture,* 5.

52. L. Abu-Lughod, *Veiled Sentiments,* 40–41. She also observes that "some of the most conspicuous changes prove superficial. Rather than heralding the demise of Bedouin culture and society, they merely demonstrate the Bedouins' openness to useful innovations and their capacity to absorb new elements into old structures," giving as an example the sacrifice of a sheep to celebrate the purchase of a new car (74). Robert Witmer aptly noted that "as has been disclosed time and again in the anthropological literature, non-Western societies adopt those aspects of Western technology and material culture they perceive as potentially advantageous to them almost immediately upon exposure" (250).

53. Mitchell, 54–55.

54. Ibid., and chap. 2, and 149.

55. Feld, "Communication, Music, and Speech about Music," 11–12.

56. See, for instance, Keddie and Baron, Beck and Keddie, Fernea and Bezirgan, Altorki and Mernissi.

57. Geertz suggests that artistic innovation often results from the "crossing of conceptual wires," by "disarranging semantic contexts in such a way that properties conventionally ascribed to certain things are unconventionally ascribed to others" ("Deep Play," *Interpretation of Cultures,* 447). One thus needs to see the particular identity of the various "wires." "A context," as Roseman writes, "is inextricably entwined with the concepts and actions of those participating in its creation. An imperfect consensus shared by the participants upholds the meaning granted to a given context" (133).

58. Blum, "Conclusion: Music in an Age of Cultural Confrontation," 257.

Chapter Two

1. "*Abnā' baladī,*" ʿAwaḍ, 72.

2. Muḥammad Ṣabrī al-Zalfī, "Mīlād al-Khālida Umm Kulthūm" (The birthdate of the eternal Umm Kulthūm) *al-Akhbār* (January 4, 1976); "Tārīkh Mīlād Umm Kulthūm al-Ḥaqīqī" (The real birthdate of Umm Kulthūm) *al-Ahrām* (February 1, 1975).

3. In Egyptian families, children usually adopt their fathers' name(s), shortening it to obtain an accurate and distinctive patronymic. Thus Umm Kulthūm's name was Umm Kulthūm Ibrāhīm al-Sayyid al-Baltājī and she generally used Umm Kulthūm Ibrāhīm. Women commonly retain their fathers' names after marriage.

4. Zakariyyā Aḥmad, "Kayfa Qābaltu Umm Kulthūm" (How I met Umm Kulthūm) *al-Kawākib* (April 1949), 20.

5. Shūsha, 7; ʿAwaḍ, 70; "ʿIndamā Ṭalabatnī Umm Kulthūm" (When Umm Kulthūm requested me) *al-Kawākib* no. 1592 (February 2, 1982), 17; "ʿUmdat al-Samīʿa Yaqūl" (The chief listener speaks) *al-Kawākib* no. 1592 (February 2, 1982), 13.

6. Egypt: Ministry of Finance, *Census*, 346.

7. Quoted in Fu'ād, 106–7; the *ʿumda* was the village leader, usually a relatively large landholder and a respected man with a strong personality.

8. ʿAwaḍ, 11, 14, 15; Shūsha, 7, 9; al-Maṣrī, 5.

9. The following discussion of Qur'anic recitation is dependent on K. Nelson, esp. chaps. 2 and 5 which provide detailed explanations of each of the concepts mentioned here.

10. Umm Kulthūm apparently wanted to attend because her brother did. She said her mother proved an effective advocate for financing her attendance, which was a significant difficulty for poor families (ʿAwaḍ, 11–12; Shūsha, 8, 9; "Maʿa Rafīqat Ṭufūlat Umm Kulthūm fī 'l-Qarya" (With a childhood friend of Umm Kulthūm in the village), *al-Jumhūriyya* (February 3, 1977); Ḥusayn, *Egyptian Childhood*, 26–27; Heyworth-Dunne, esp. 14–15; MacDonald, *Aspects*, 292, 293–94. Daughters of wealthier families were educated at home. Compare Ṭāhā Ḥusayn's description of a *shaykh* and his *kuttāb*, dating from about ten years earlier, in chaps. 5–10 of *Egyptian Childhood*.

11. ʿAwaḍ, 15, 28, 32; Muḥammad ʿAlī Ḥammād, "Min Dhikrayāt lā Mudhakkirāt," *Ākhir Sāʿa* no. 178 (November 28, 1937), 7–10; al-Naqqāsh, "Liqā'," 44.

12. Ibrāhīm Shafīq in al-Ḥifnī, 3:b.

13. Al-Ḥājja al-Suwaysiyya was the best-known female religious singer in the nineteenth century. She appeared wearing a long black wrap, head covering, and face veil, with her husband, son, and brother as accompanists. She moved from her home in Suez to Cairo where she performed regularly at the coffeehouse Monsieur Antoine near Azbakiyya Garden (Buṭrus, 92; al-Naqqāsh, "Aṣwāt Aṭrabat Ajdādanā," 153). Al-Khulaʿī listed al-Shaykha Faṭūma al-Bastiyya al-Ṭanṭawiyya as one of "the famous readers of the Qur'ān and the Story of the Prophet's Birth" (*al-Aghānī 'l-ʿAṣriyya*, 246; also 2d ed. [1923], 292). Sakīna Ḥasan was a noted religious singer in Cairo during the 1910s and 1920s. Later, al-Shaykha Munīra ʿAbduh and al-Shaykha Karīma al-ʿĀdiliyya became famous reciters of the Qur'ān whose recitations were frequently broadcast over Egyptian Radio throughout the 1930s (see, for example, programs listed in *al-Rādyū al-Miṣrī* (February 14, 1937), (October 2, 1937), (January 23, 1938), (March 20, 1938); also al-Shaykh Aḥmad Shaʿbān, "Aʿlām al-Munshidīn" (Stars of religious song), *Akhbār al-Yawm* (November 23, 1985)).

14. For example, the chorus might begin with two lines, followed by the soloist singing two different lines; alternatively, the chorus might sing the entire piece, interrupted somewhere in the middle by an improvised rendition of several of the lines by the soloist (*Kitāb Mu'tamar,* 166; M. Ḥāfiẓ, 199).

15. Al-Naqqāsh, "al-Mashāyikh wa-'l-Fann," 98.

16. Marsot, *Egypt's Liberal Experiment,* 20–21; similar descriptions appear in Ṭāhā Ḥusayn's autobiography, *An Egyptian Childhood,* 17, 39–44.

17. K. Nelson, 188.

18. This group included women as well as men. Women of means hired readers for special occasions and for comfort in sorrow. Many women are competent reciters.

19. Al-Ḥifnī, 1:75.

20. The involvement of singers and reciters in both religious and other performance is common in the Arab world. See Hassan; Touma, 52; Elsner, 460; Shiloah, 40, 46–47; Al Faruqi, "Status of Music," 64.

21. Al-Ḥifnī, 3:a–b; Racy, "Musical," 48; el-Kholy, 88.

22. The complex nature of Islamic religious expression has been examined by anthropologists Nancy Tapper and Richard Tapper in Turkey, who wrote, "The religious 'great tradition', guarded by the urban, literate elite, is seen as a sober, intellectual matter, everywhere the concern of men; the religious of the 'little tradition' are emotional if not ecstatic, common among illiterate rural communities, and particularly the concern of women. . . . These associations are misleading and often false. . . . Ordinary, day-to-day practised Islam . . . inevitably combines both 'orthodox' and 'popular' elements" (Tapper and Tapper, 70); Rahman discussed the common association of Sufism with popular Islam in chap. 9 of his *Islam.*

23. El-Hamamsy, 288.

24. Marsot, "Ulama of Cairo," 157.

25. *Al-Masraḥ* no. 35 (August 16, 1926), 26; Kāmil, "Alḥān Zamān" (January 18, 1986); M. Ḥāfiẓ, 243; 'Arafa, 54–56, 81–82; Rizq, 4:103.

26. 'Awaḍ, 11–12; Ḥusayn, *Egyptian Childhood,* chaps. 5–10; al-Khula'ī, *Kitāb,* 78, 85.

27. Dāwūd Ḥusnī, quoted in El-Shawan, "al-Mūsīḳa," 66; and Sāmī al-Shawwā, quoted in Fu'ād, 399.

28. One might identify the *mawwāl* as Egypt's "country" music, widely known in cities and towns as well, which tended to evoke nostalgia for the village and its ostensibly purer lifestyle.

29. Modern performance of the epic of the Bani Hilāl was the subject of recent studies by Susan Slyomovics, Bridgit Connelly, and Dwight Reynolds.

30. Racy's dissertation provides a detailed and thorough study of the industry and its impact up to 1932 to which my discussion is indebted (Racy, "Musical").

31. Between 1900 and 1910, Gramophone made 1,192 recordings in Egypt, 223 in Algeria, 221 in Tunisia, and 180 in Syria (Gronow, 255; Racy, "Musical," 79, 93).

32. *Rūz al-Yūsuf* observed in 1926 that "the phonograph has spread among all classes of people after its price went down and it became possible for any family

of moderate means to acquire one along with some records to fill the home with music" ("Asʿār al-Muṭribīn wa-ʾl-Muṭribāt" [The prices of singers], *Rūz al-Yūsuf* no. 48 [September 29, 1926], 14).

33. Sharing record players and later radios and television sets was common in the Middle East. For instance, Racy found that in Lebanon during the early decades of the century, "a sort of mobile disk jockey carried a phonograph into various quarters and towns playing records for a fee" ("Words," 420).

34. Shūsha, 12; ʿAwaḍ, 15, 16, 19; Fuʾād, 90.

35. Al-Shawwā, *Mudhakkirāt,* 37; most famous singers participated in these trips. The performers made their own arrangements, knowing there would be many festivities wherever the personage was. Ṣāliḥ ʿAbd al-Ḥayy told of traveling with Lord Kitchener's Delta tour in 1913, Khedive ʿAbbās's trip in the Delta in 1914, Ḥusayn Kāmil's tour of Upper Egypt, and King Fuʾād's visit to Ṣuhāj (*al-Rādyū al-Miṣrī* (January 23, 1938), 6–7; al-Yūsuf, 39).

36. This trip was particularly memorable because the wedding had been postponed. Since everyone in the village was privy to such information, it never occurred to the host that he would have to make an effort to tell the singers (ʿAwaḍ, 21, 25).

37. ʿAwaḍ, 16, 24.

38. *Al-Masraḥ* 27 (May 24, 1926), 15.

39. Umm Kulthūm, quoted in Fuʾād, 90.

40. Umm Kulthūm remembered the ticket price as 1 piastre for any seat. The family was paid 1 £E ($5) for their performance and expenses (ʿAwaḍ, 19; Fuʾād, 80; Shūsha, 12; Abū ʾl-Majd, 229).

41. The establishment was called Klūb Qināwī Ḥasanayn. Al-Shaykh Ibrāhīm's sensibilities seemed to have involved both his daughter's well-being and the propriety of singing religious songs to a drunken audience (Shūsha, 14).

42. Conversely, Umm Kulthūm reported an unusually quiet audience in Mīt Rūmī. The family had to perform their entire repertory six times in order to fill the evening. Afterwards, she said, al-Shaykh Ibrāhīm insisted that they learn new songs to forestall a similar embarrassment (ʿAwaḍ, 19, 20).

43. Cf. Azzam, 19.

44. Compare Al Faruqi's explanation of the denial of testimonial rights to professional musicians by all four Islamic schools of law: "The musician therefore becomes suspect not because he performs *mūsīqā* but because he takes on a profession that has negative social and moral associations in the culture. Such a choice reveals in him a lack of concern for his position in the community and a disregard for safeguarding his integrity and reputation" ("Music, Musicians and Muslim Law," 22). Condemnation of music on orthodox Islamic grounds was uncommon in Egypt. For a good discussion of the prevailing view of music held by the religious establishment, see K. Nelson, chap. 3.

45. Zakariyyā's father was referring to "Ya leel, ya ʿeen," the common text for vocal improvisation in which the words become meaningless (ʿAwaḍ, 47, 24, 79; ʿAbd al-Wahhāb, 30).

46. Behrens-Abouseif, 25; Nāhid Ḥāfiẓ summarized commonly felt sentiments, writing that Cairo during the colonial period "was a place of many vices, for ex-

ample gambling, licentiousness, usury, drunkenness, drugs and prostitution, all of which resulted from colonialism" (216).

47. Shūsha, 14; *al-Masraḥ* no. 27 (May 24, 1926), 15.

48. Until 1952, certain titles following proper names reflected social status. Among the most prestigious were Pāshā and Bey. Thus, for instance, ʿAdlī Pāshā Yakan was himself a Pāshā, and Yūsuf Wahbī Pāshā was the son of a Pāshā named Wahbī.

49. Al-Shināwī Pāshā's estate was located in Kafr Badamas; its administrator at the time was ʿAbd al-Muṭṭalib Afandī al-Muwaẓẓaf. Umm Kulthūm's pay for the event was reported to be 1.5 £E ($7.50) (*Umm Kulthūm: Qithārat al-ʿArab,* 99; Abū ʾl-Majd, 229). Laylat al-Miʿrāj is the commemoration of the prophet Muḥammad's midnight journey to heaven celebrated on the twenty-seventh of Rajab.

50. Both letter and contract appeared in a newspaper clipping entitled "Awwal ʿAqd li-Awwal Ḥafla li-Umm Kulthūm" (The first contract for Umm Kulthūm's first concert) found in the archives of Dār al-Hilāl and incorrectly attributed to *al-Jumhūriyya* (March 31, 1975). The article includes photographs of the sections translated above. The copies of the documents available to me were extremely difficult to read and the translations, while substantially correct, may not be exact.

51. ʿAwaḍ, 25; Muḥammad ʿAlī Ḥammād, "Min Dhikrayāt," *Ākhir Sāʿa* no. 183 (January 3, 1938), 29; Shūsha, 15.

52. ʿAwaḍ, 22; Shūsha, 12, 13.

53. Shūsha, 13–15; *Umm Kulthūm: Qiṣṣat,* 4; *Umm Kulthūm: Qithārat,* 99–100; Fuʾād, 100; ʿAwaḍ, 25.

54. First-class seats increased the comfort of the group but affected their appearance very little: the canny Shaykh Ibrāhīm managed to descend from the first-class door, no matter where the family sat, so that whoever met them at the station would be properly impressed with their status (ʿAwaḍ, 23–24, 77; Fuʾād, 89).

55. When rural Egyptians came to Cairo, they tended to settle among relatives or friends who were usually from the same village or region. Many of these groups retained rural customs and an identification with the area from which they came. They traveled home for holidays, family members came to visit them, and the urban groups absorbed new members as more people came from the countryside to find jobs in the city. The extent and nature of contact between villagers and city dwellers tended to render rural-urban social or cultural distinctions of little use in describing Egyptian society and culture: like the new Egyptian elite, working-class Egyptians maintained important relationships with both city and countryside. See Janet Abu-Lughod.

56. Their host was a local landowner, ʿAlī Abū ʾl-ʿAynayn, who invited the two men to perform in the open air on his estate. Many local villagers attended as well as household retainers and invited guests. Fuʾād places this meeting in 1920, Shūsha in 1919, Zakariyyā in 1919 and 1920 alternately, and Umm Kulthūm mentions no date at all (ʿAwaḍ, 28–29; Zakariyyā Aḥmad, "Kayfa Qābaltu Umm Kulthūm," 20; Abū ʾl-Majd, 233–34; Shūsha, 15; Fuʾād, 110).

57. Her letters were "simple expressions written in green ink . . . to remind me of her voice and my invitation" (quoted in Fuʾād, 111; see also facsimiles, [518–

19]; Zakariyyā Aḥmad, "Kayfa Qābaltu," 20). The extent of his help is difficult to assess, for the nature of their early relationship became obscured by lawsuits between the two during the 1940s and 1950s when many pertinent biographical statements were made by both. At that point it was in Zakariyyā's best interest to depict himself as essential to Umm Kulthūm's early success and in her best interest to ignore the matter completely.

58. The wedding was held at Kūm al-Shaykh Salāma near al-ʿAtaba al-Khaḍrāʾ. In his memoirs, Zakariyyā describes an event (which he called variously a wedding and a *mūlid* or saint's day) that he helped plan for Umm Kulthūm, probably this one (ʿAwaḍ, 30; Fuʾād, 111; Shūsha, 15; Abū ʾl-Majd, 234; Zakariyyā Aḥmad, "Kayfa Qābaltu," 20).

59. Again, the means of introduction seems to have been an estate manager responsible for family property near al-Manṣūra (personal communication from Medhat Assem, January 28, 1986); see also Davis, *Challenging Colonialism*, 40, 118, for locations of some of the family's lands.

60. Personal communications from Medhat Assem, January 28 and July 10, 1986; see also Assem, "Umm Kulthūm: al-Usṭūra al-Khālida" (Umm Kulthūm: the eternal legend), *al-Kawākib* no. 2082 (February 8, 1975), 22. All of these men were wealthy landowners and important nationalist political leaders. At the time of this gathering, ʿAdlī Yakan was minister of foreign affairs, ʿAbd al-Khāliq Tharwat was about to be (or had recently been) appointed prime minister. ʿAlī Māhir became minister of finance later in the 1920s. Luṭfī al-Sayyid was a newspaper editor and advocate for educational opportunity who served as rector of the Egyptian University from 1925 until his retirement many years later. For a good discussion of Egyptian political life during this period and the roles played by these and other Egyptian leaders, see Marsot, *Egypt's Liberal Experiment*. Because she had been brought to sing for the women, her father and brother were not immediately at hand, an unusual circumstance that almost certainly added to Umm Kulthūm's discomfort in the men's salon.

61. It was said that when al-Shaykh Ibrāhīm rented his first Cairo residence, he chose the place so as to be near the ʿAbd al-Rāziq house.

62. On May 1, 1921, she was the featured singer at one of the concerts honoring the return to Cairo of the nationalist leader Saʿd Zaghlūl. She appeared at various locations in Ḥayy al-Ḥusayn and in Ḥayy al-Nāṣiriyya near Sayyida Zaynab. Recollecting one of these events, a journalist reported that Umm Kulthūm was part of a program featuring other acts including a Nubian dancing troupe (*al-Masraḥ* no. 28 [May 31, 1926], 12; Abū ʾl-Majd, 234; Zakariyyā Aḥmad, "Kayfa Qābaltu," 20; Shūsha, 17; Fuʾād, 111, 129; "Umm Kulthūm: al-Ṣawt wa-ʾl-Ṣūra wa-ʾl-Usṭūra" *Rūz al-Yūsuf* [February 10, 1975], 18; *al-Kashkūl* no. 58 [June 25, 1922], 4, and no. 85 [December 31, 1922], 4).

63. Berque, 374, 622.

64. Especially bright boys from families with the means to do so might be sent to the Azhar University in Cairo.

65. For example, the 1907 census reported literacy rates of 6.6 percent for the Delta city of al-Sinbillawayn, 3.5 percent for the markaz or county of al-Sinbilla-

wayn, and 2 percent for the village of Ṭammāy al-Zahāyra, where Umm Kulthūm was born. Few women were educated at this time. In 1907, no literate women were identified in Ṭammāy, only .07 percent of the women in the county, and .42 percent of the city women of al-Sinbillawayn were counted as literate. Nationally, the proportion of literate women was no higher than 7 percent in 1919 (Egypt: Ministry of Finance, *Census,* p. 346; Cachia, *Taha Husayn,* 27); for general discussions of education in Egypt, see Berque and Heyworth-Dunne.

66. Ḥusayn, *Stream of Days,* 75; cf. Berque's description of learned men of the Azhar University and mosque: "Although the University had its dynasties, it was by law and in fact open exclusively to men of learning and piety. Thus, in a rigidly compartmented city, it was one of the few places in which freedom of movement on the social ladder was possible. The fame of a learned man transcended all inequalities of rank and origin" (79).

67. Following the French occupation of Egypt (1798–1801) and "a turbulent period when Ottomans, mamluks and British forces tried to put their candidates in power as governor," Muḥammad ʿAlī gained control of the government and ruled Egypt from 1805 until his death in 1848 (Marsot, *Short History of Modern Egypt,* 51–53).

68. Berque, 98, 445; Marsot, *Egypt's Liberal Experiment,* 52–59, and *Egypt in the Reign of Muhammad Ali,* 78.

69. Davis, *Challenging Colonialism,* 28.

70. Issawi, 42; also Davis, *Challenging Colonialism,* 29.

71. Berque, 510.

72. Zakī, 100.

73. Marsot, *Egypt's Liberal Experiment,* 16; Marsot also notes that merely owning land would not necessarily allow admission to the elite. Issawi observed that "the savings of the peasants tend to be used solely for the purchase of land," and also that "all those [of the professional class] who can do so hasten to mark their advent to affluence by the purchase of an estate" (Issawi, 138, 258).

74. Davis, *Challenging Colonialism,* 151.

75. Berque, 622.

76. Issawi, 258.

77. El-Hamamsy, 286.

78. Ibid., 286–89.

79. Davis, *Challenging Colonialism,* 8.

80. Berque, 374.

81. Zayid, 334. Zayid refers here to the spending of Khedive Ismāʿīl (who ruled from 1863–79) which effectively bankrupted the country and led to the establishment of the British Protectorate. One of Ismāʿīl's expenditures was the building of the Cairo Opera House.

82. Issawi, 42.

83. Lacouture and Lacouture, 67.

84. Berque, 239. Describing the operations of the Mixed Courts, Landes wrote that "the forms were generally observed in that the European was expected to prove his case; but the double standard was reflected in the different weights accorded

European and native testimony and interests: one man's word was worth more than another's, his limbs were more precious, his property more valuable. Only too often, the assertion of the Westerner was equivalent to proof, the presence of the Egyptian was evidence of responsibility" (323).

85. Goldschmidt, 181. Actress Rūz al-Yūsuf, for one, wrote that during World War I Egyptians recoiled from public entertainment, "leaving the cities to the drunken soldiers" (al-Yūsuf, *Dhikrayātī,* 28); see also Mitchell, 115–16.

86. Issawi, 47; Marsot, *Egypt's Liberal Experiment,* 45.

87. From the song "Ana Maṣri" in Darwīsh's play *Shahrazaad* (1921).

88. Khayrī, 101.

89. El-Hamamsy, 295.

Chapter Three

1. A conversation between poet ʿAbbās Maḥmūd al-ʿAqqād and playwright Muḥammad Taymūr, ca. 1920, recollected by al-ʿAqqād in "Rāya Mutawwaja bil-Ḥarīr," *al-Muṣawwar* no. 1306 (October 21, 1949), repr. in Shūsha, 88.

2. A swamp in the Azbakiyya quarter had been drained and landscaped in the style of the Bois de Boulogne at the behest of Khedive Ismāʿīl to form Azbakiyya Garden (Berque, 88–89). Ṣālat Santī was a relatively old and respectable entertainment establishment which featured well-known soloists and promising young singers as well. For instance, Salāma Ḥijāzī rented Ṣālat Santī for his first independent productions in 1905 (Kāmil, *al-Masraḥ,* 16).

3. Fawzī as quoted in Fu'ād, 120.

4. Solo singing between the acts of plays dated from about 1884; the famous singers of the nineteenth century, ʿAbduh al-Ḥāmūlī and Almaẓ, performed during entr'actes (Kāmil, *al-Masraḥ,* 9, 12). Muḥammad ʿAbd al-Wahhāb started his career in this way as did many others (ʿAbd al-Wahhāb, 27; "Faṭma Qadrī," *al-Tiyātrū* no. 4 [January 1925], 23).

5. Landau, 57.

6. Racy, "Musical," 70; Kāmil, *al-Masraḥ,* 9–19.

7. "This kind [of song] is characterized by a predilection for European tunes" (*Kitāb al-Mu'tamar,* 171).

8. Fu'ād, 134.

9. Al-Yūsuf, 91–92, 167.

10. Al-Ḥifnī listed the famous *ṣālāt* as El Dorado, Kawkab al-Sharq, Ṣālat Ilyās, Nuzhat al-Nufūs, the Luxembourg, the Alhambra, and Alf Layla (1:75). These establishments were sometimes called "clubs" (*klūb,* pl. *kulūb*) or "casinos" (*kāzīnū,* pl. *kāzīnūhāt*), although they were not usually private nor was gambling necessarily available.

11. Al-Yūsuf, 29.

12. A more detailed history of these women appears in Danielson, "Artists and Entrepreneurs."

13. *Rūz al-Yūsuf* no. 83 (June 9, 1927), 11; no. 48 (September 29, 1926), 15.

14. Cf. Racy's examples from the nineteenth century: the male singer, who typically "performed in ensembles containing a male singer, two or more vocal accom-

panists, and five or six instrumentalists who played the *qānūn* (a trapezoidal type of zither), the *ʿūd* (a lute), the *nāy* (a reed flute), the *kamanjah* (a spike fiddle) and sometimes the *riqq* (a small tambourine)," and Bamba Kashshar, a popular female singer whose ensemble consisted of "eight women: the head singer herself, two women who played the *darabukkah* (a pottery hand drum), three who played the *ṭār* (a large tambourine), one who played the *riqq*, and another who played the *ʿūd*" (Racy, "Musical," 24–25, 51–52, 155; M. Ḥāfiẓ, 195).

15. Al-Khulaʿī, *Kitāb*, 89–90. For further discussion of the Egyptian *waṣla*, see Racy, "The Waṣlah," and his review of "Waṣlah ghināʾiyyah."

16. In a review of one of the first of these, an anonymous author wrote, "Among the nuisances in the world about which we might complain is that we girls are prohibited from attending programs of music and song if we want to preserve our honor and our eyes from the sight of the hoards of people for whom morality has no meaning." Badīʿa's matinees provided an acceptable atmosphere, according to the writer (*al-Masraḥ* no. 50 [December 6, 1926], 13). Badīʿa's were probably not the first such performances; Beth Baron found references to theatrical matinees for women in newspapers dating from the 1900s (personal communication).

17. Maṣabnī; *al-Masraḥ* 48 (November 22, 1926), 16, wherein the author asserts that Badīʿa "proved again that women can do and obtain what they want"; *al-Ṣabāḥ* no. 105 (October 1, 1928), 11; *Rūz al-Yūsuf* no. 40 (August 4, 1926), 6–7; no. 74 (March 31, 1927), 18; no. 111 (December 1927), 17–18; no. 164 (March 18, 1930), 17; no. 176 (June 10, 1930), 17; no. 177 (June 17, 1930), 17; no. 178 (June 24, 1930), 16; no. 219 (April 25, 1932), 21; no. 233 (August 8, 1932), 26; al-Najmī, 127.

18. *Al-Masraḥ* no. 43 (October 18, 1926), 20; no. 87 (October 13, 1927), 11; *Rūz al-Yūsuf* no. 115 (February 21, 1928), 17. Among the exceptions were Layla Murād, whose father was a successful singer, and the Aṭrash children who came to Cairo with their mother to escape the fighting in their native Jabal Druze.

19. The word "improvisation" serves inadequately for the extemporized inventions that pepper Arabic musical genres. Racy explains: "The modern *ṭarab* jargon does not include a standard concept that means 'improvisation.' Similarly the modal theory expounding the various *maqāmāt* makes no distinction between 'improvisation' and 'precomposition' and provides only an implicit correlation between the unfolding of a mode and the application of a genre that is metrically free and suitably flexible. Furthermore, concepts such as *taqāsīm, layālī,* and *mawwāl,* despite their improvisatory nature, refer literally to such components as structure, text and literary content" ("Creativity and Ambience," 18).

20. A good example is his very popular "Fī ʾl-Layl." Among other features this song included a waltzlike section, and the *takht* was augmented by a violoncello and string bass. "Fī ʾl-Layl" was premiered in 1929 but represents the compositional style developed by ʿAbd al-Wahhāb and others throughout the decade.

21. Cachia, *Taha Husayn,* 25, 86–87, and 57.

22. Cachia, "Introduction" to Ḥusayn, *Egyptian Childhood,* [iii].

23. Aḥmad Ṣidqī, quoted in Ṣabrī, 2:229.

24. Al-Ḥifnī, 1:73–75.

25. Ibrāhīm al-Maṣrī, "al-ʿAql al-Miṣrī" (The Egyptian mentality), *al-Tamthīl* no. 15 (November 24, 1924), 10.

26. A good discussion of peasant involvement appears in Nathan Brown's *Peasant Politics in Modern Egypt.* The popular foundation of the uprising and its apparent aim, to return resources to local control, prompted Ellis Goldberg to argue that the revolution was a classical Marxian revolution (see "Leadership and Ideology in the 1919 Revolution").

27. Al-Najmī, 86, 87.

28. An example is "il-Gulla ʾl-Ginaawi," extolling the work of the potters of Qena in Upper Egypt and utilizing the local hard *g* in place of the Cairene glottal stop or classical *qāf.*

29. Khayrī, 16, 122.

30. The first line is from the song "il-Ḥilwa Dii" and the second from "Salma, ya Salaama," both of which are well known throughout the Arab world to the present day.

31. Cachia, *Taha Husayn,* 35.

32. The concept of authenticity in Egyptian Arabic is designated by the adjectives *aṣīl* and *aṣlī* as well as the noun *aṣāla.*

33. The agent rented the premises or arranged the fee with club managers, advertised the performance, and paid Umm Kulthūm after taking a percentage for himself. Like virtually every other entertainer in Cairo, she complained vociferously about the means these agents used to increase their shares of the profits. Unfortunately, her father was not particularly gifted in financial matters, and sometime after 1927 she assumed control of her contracts and finances herself.

34. "Dhikrayāt maʿa ʾl-Qaṣabjī," *al-Kawākib* (February 11, 1975), 33–35; based on a 1955 interview.

35. *Rūz al-Yūsuf* (June 26, 1926), quoted in *Umm Kulthūm: Qithārat,* 151; see also ʿAbd al-Wahhāb in *Widāʿan,* 24; Assem, "Umm Kulthūm: al-Usṭūra al-Khālida," *al-Kawākib* no. 1644 (February 1, 1983), 4; al-ʿAqqād in Shūsha, 88.

36. *Widāʿan,* 55.

37. Listeners remembered Umm Kulthūm singing "Subḥān Man arsalahu Raḥma li-Kull man Yasmaʿ aw Yubṣir" (Praise to Him who sent him out of mercy for all who hear and see), "Jalla man Ṭarraz al-Yasmīn" (Praise Him who decorated the jasmine), "Ḥasbī Allāhu Min Majīʿ al-Aʿādī" (God is sufficient for me against all my enemies), "Aqūl li-Dhāt Ḥusn Rawaʿatnī [?]" (I say to a beautiful one who has dazzled me), "Mawlāya Katabta Raḥmat al-Nās ʿalayk Faḍlan wa-Karaman" (My Master You ordained for Yourself kindness for the people, freely and generously). The last may have been Zakariyyā Aḥmad's setting of an older text (ʿAwaḍ, 20, 28, 32, 57; Buṭrus, 141; *al-Masraḥ* no. 27 [May 24, 1926], 15; Abū ʾl-Majd, 228–29; Fahmī, *Shaykh al-Mulaḥḥinīn,* 40; "al-Shaykh Zakariyyā Aḥmad," *al-Tiyātrū* no. 6 [March 1925], 25; Shūsha, 11; Fuʾād, 67).

38. *Kitāb Muʾtamar,* 165, 170; Fuʾad, 139; Racy, "Musical," 49, 53, 144. A few texts carried political messages such as "Edirne, oh sweet [place]," composed by Dāwūd Ḥusnī after the occupation of Edirne by the Bulgarians in 1912–13 (N. Ḥāfiẓ, 216).

39. "Ya qamara, ya qamara, ya qammuura, ya mḥanni deel il-ʿaṣfuura" (*al-Masraḥ* no. 23 [April 26, 1926], 16–17). Lyricist Yūnis al-Qāḍī inveighed against such texts (despite his own authorship of several successful bawdy songs) in *al-Masraḥ* no. 22 (April 12, 1926), 10.

40. "Irādat al-Shaʿb wa-Umm Kulthūm" (The will of the people and Umm Kulthūm), *al-Kashkūl al-Muṣawwar* no. 57 (June 18, 1922), 6–7. At another performance at an orphanage in a working-class district, she sang "new *adwār, ṭaqāṭīq* and monologs" with the orphans pounding out the rhythms and singing along ("Umm Kulthūm bayna ʾl-Talāmīdh" [Umm Kulthūm among the students], *al-Kashkūl al-Muṣawwar* no. 85 [December 31, 1922], 4).

41. *Al-Masraḥ* no. 13 (February 8, 1926), 14.

42. *Al-Masraḥ* no. 24 (May 3, 1926), 15; also, "There is no doubt that the beauty of Umm Kulthūm's voice and its strength and the effect it produces, all these factors cover and compensate for what is lacking in artistry (*al-Masraḥ* no. 29 [June 7, 1926], 20).

43. *Rūz al-Yūsuf* no. 33 (June 16, 1926), 15.

44. *Rūz al-Yūsuf* no. 160 (February 11, 1930), 16. "What the simple woman wants to say is that the 24 £E pay the rent only, apart from household expenses and the price of food and drink." Sensing impending disaster, Umm Kulthūm inadvertently compounded it by offering her guest money not to tell the story.

45. *Rūz al-Yūsuf* no. 179 (July 1, 1930), 16.

46. The song was "Qaal eeh Ḥilif" ("Dhikrayāt maʿa ʾl-Qaṣabjī," *al-Kawākib* [February 11, 1975], 33–35).

47. Another later monologue by Aḥmad Rāmī and Muḥammad al-Qaṣabjī, "Biʿidt ʿannak bi-khaṭri" (ca. 1928), drew similar criticism for the banality of its text, and Rāmī tried to deny having written it (*al-Ṣabāḥ* no. 105 [October 1, 1928], 12, and no. 106 [October 8, 1928], 4).

48. Umm Kulthūm, quoted in Fuʾād, 98.

49. ʿAwaḍ, 62–64.

50. Al-Naqqāsh gave the following humorous account of a rare foray by Muḥammad ʿAbd al-Wahhāb to a country wedding: He and his ensemble descended from the train in Banhā fashionably attired in silk smoking jackets, only to confront in dismay the necessity of traveling on donkeys to the place where the performance was held and to share a meal with the man who cared for the animals (al-Naqqāsh, "Shawqī wa-Ḥayāt ʿAbd al-Wahhāb," 93).

51. The marketing of the records was not as regular as this average may indicate owing to Umm Kulthūm's change from the Odeon to the Gramophone company in 1926 and to the logistics of recording, manufacturing, and shipping between Egypt and Europe.

52. *Al-Masraḥ* no. 33 (July 19, 1926), 20. The records were sold for 20 piasters each ($1.00), then the highest price on the market (*al-Masraḥ* no. 25 [May 10, 1926], 5–6). Making recordings was financially attractive to musicians, whose pay from this source was higher than from any other at the time, especially if they were paid a percentage of sales. The great Yūsuf al-Manyalāwī (d. 1911) had such a contract, the profits from which provided his estate with 1,200 £E ($6,000) an-

nually even sixteen years after his death (*Rūz al-Yūsuf* no. 99 [September 9, 1927], 14). Racy pointed out that a long-range effect of this financial opportunity was to institutionalize the star system and to widen "the gap between the successful recording artist and the not so famous musician" (Racy, "Arabian," 48).

53. It was said that Manṣūr ʿAwaḍ, Gramophone's Egyptian director, wanted to use Umm Kulthūm's repertory and public image to upgrade the respectability of his firm (*al-Masraḥ* no. 33 [July 19, 1926], 21). In fact, money seems clearly the compelling factor for both parties. Gramophone, which already marketed the recordings of such respected figures as Abū ʾl-ʿIlā Muḥammad and ʿAbd al-Ḥayy Ḥilmī, gained a singer who generated unprecedented sales, and Umm Kulthūm settled an excellent contract despite the fact that Gramophone had a deservedly bad reputation for sound quality.

54. Umm Kulthūm, quoted in Fuʾād, 166. Further discussion of recording contracts appears in Danielson, "Shaping Tradition" (255–58) and "Artists and Entrepreneurs" (300–303).

55. Her behavior in the early 1920s resonates with J. S. Eades's view that "an actor is not concerned with abstract problems of whether his choice of resources reflects 'ethnicity' or 'class consciousness'" (quoted in Waterman, *Jùjú,* 224).

56. Rāmī in *Widāʿan,* 60–61; ʿAwaḍ, 140; *al-Masraḥ* no. 31 (June 28, 1926), 11; Kāmil, *Muḥammad al-Qaṣabjī,* 31–32. Rāmī's first was "Khaayif yikuun Ḥubbak," set to music by al-Najrīdī and released by Odeon in 1924.

57. ʿAwaḍ, 34; Shūsha, 23; al-Naqqāsh, "Lughz Umm Kulthūm," 27, 44–45; Fuʾād, 174.

58. Shūsha, 24; Fuʾād, 174; *al-Masraḥ* no. 36 (August 30, 1926), 9; no. 26 (May 17, 1926), 15; and no. 29 (June 7, 1926), 20. Little information about Maḥmūd Raḥmī is readily available. He appears to have been a singer and percussion player engaged from time to time to coach singers; he was in charge of the singers for Jūrj Abyaḍ's theatrical troupe in the 1910s (Kāmil, *al-Masraḥ,* 21). On a very few occasions, Umm Kulthūm accompanied herself on the *ʿūd* ("Nādira, Amīrat al-Ṭarab," *al-Kawākib* no. 1768 [June 18, 1985], 46). Dāwūd Ḥusnī gave freely and frequently of his advice and assistance to young singers. Faṭma Sirrī and Asmahān are two others whom he coached (personal communication from Kamāl Ḥusnī, April 29, 1982; "Faṭma Sirrī," *Rūz al-Yūsuf* no. 106 [November 17, 1927], 20). Later, during the 1930s, Umm Kulthūm engaged Ibrāhīm Ḥajjāj to teach her to read musical notation, to play the piano, and to understand European music (Shūsha, 55; biographical information about Ḥajjāj appears in ʿAbd al-Ḥamīd Tawfīq Zakī, 227–32). She said that her father paid "huge sums" for her training, giving as an example Raḥmī's fee of 3 £E per month ($15) for daily instruction (ʿAwaḍ, 78–79; Fuʾād, 119; al-Maṣrī, 23; Shūsha, 67).

59. Abū Zayyān in *Umm Kulthūm: al-Nagham al-Khālid,* 11.

60. Al-Najmī, 87, 55–56.

61. ʿAwaḍ, 30, 32, 33. The song was "Jalla man Ṭarraz al-Yasmīn."

62. ʿAbd al-Wahhāb in *Widāʿan,* 26; personal communication, Kamāl Ḥusnī, May 2, 1982; al-Naqqāsh, "Lughz Umm Kulthūm," 27.

63. Personal communications from Medhat Assem (January 28, 1986) and

Dr. Buthayna Farīd (January 29, 1986), both of whom were acquainted with these women. Riḍá Bey was the head of the Arab Music Club. The Abāẓas are a large and prestigious Egyptian family.

64. *Rūz al-Yūsuf* no. 232 (July 25, 1932), 20.

65. Davis, *Challenging Colonialism,* 50; cf. the significance of the circle surrounding Luṭfī al-Sayyid described in Smith, 391.

66. Compare the events recorded by the slightly older Ṭāhā Ḥusayn regarding himself and his brother during their student days at the Azhar University (his comments are cast in the third person): "They had been rising in the world a little, thanks to their qualities of intelligence and scholarship, and also to the favour and approval which they had earned from the Imam [Muḥammad ʿAbduh]. They had formed friendships with one or two young men of well-to-do families, such as were to be found amongst the students of the Azhar at the time. They used to exchange visits with these rich young men" (*Stream of Days,* 75). Marsot wrote that "the profession of alim [religious scholar] was the most successful vehicle of social mobility for the lower classes, and especially for the fallahin" ("The Ulama of Cairo," 158).

67. Her early recordings feature accompaniment by a few instrumentalists, usually playing *qānūn,* violin, or *ʿūd.* These musicians were probably retained by the recording company, which insisted they be used regardless of a singer's practice in live performances. I am grateful to Jihad Racy for suggesting this explanation.

68. Al-Khulaʿī identified Umm Kulthūm as a prominent singer as early as 1921 along with Fatḥiyya Aḥmad, Munīra al-Mahdiyya, ʿAzīza al-Maṣriyya, Naʿīma al-Maṣriyya, Tawḥīda, and Tawaddud al-Shāmiyya (al-Khulaʿī, *al-Aghānī,* 245). *Rūz al-Yūsuf* featured Umm Kulthūm on its cover for the first time in March of 1926 and counted her among "the most famous female singers" alongside Fatḥiyya, Naʿīma al-Maṣriyya, Tawḥīda, and Munīra (no. 19 [March 10, 1926] and no. 18 [March 3, 1926], 7). In the spring of 1926, a plethora of newspaper polls appeared, asking readers to choose favorite singers, among Fatḥiyya, Umm Kulthūm, and Munīra. Fewer than 150 people responded; nevertheless much was made of the results. Fatḥiyya placed first in all categories and Umm Kulthūm third in all but one: she placed second in "affectiveness of voice." More importantly, the poll and the discourse following it helped to represent Umm Kulthūm as one of the three best singers in Cairo (*Rūz al-Yūsuf* no. 29 [May 19, 1926], 7; no. 31 [June 2, 1926], 14; no. 39 [July 28, 1926], 13).

69. *Al-Masraḥ* no. 30 (June 14 1926), 25. Ṣāliḥ ʿAbd al-Ḥayy was a highly regarded singer of the classical repertory of *adwār* and *mawāwīl.* He was known for his strong voice and for his affective rendition and musical skills.

70. *Rūz al-Yūsuf* no. 37 (July 14, 1926), 11.

71. *Al-Masraḥ* no. 26 (May 17, 1926), 15; also no. 31 (June 28, 1926), 11. The men's behavior, remaining by the side of their female relative as she appeared in public and acknowledging applause on her behalf, was an adaptation of mannerly behavior common in Umm Kulthūm's social stratum; the writer probably recognized this and chose to classify it as backward or "countrified."

72. See, e.g., *al-Masraḥ* no. 26 (May 17, 1926), 15, wherein the writer opined

that the song "Mawlāya Katabta Raḥmat al-Nās ʿAlayk" was inappropriate for an audience consisting largely of Christians and foreigners.

73. *Al-Masraḥ* no. 29 (June 7, 1926), 20.

74. Among the evidence supporting this suggestion is that Umm Kulthūm's first performance in her "new" style took place at a private party in Alexandria on August 5, 1926, less than three weeks after *Rūz al-Yūsuf*'s criticism was published on July 14. It is unlikely that this critique motivated a change that would have taken much more than three weeks to effect (*Rūz al-Yūsuf* no. 40 [August 4, 1926], 12, and no. 41 [August 11, 1926], 13).

75. *Rūz al-Yūsuf* no. 31 (June 2, 1926), 12.

76. He was reported to be concerned that working for a female entertainer was inconsistent with his dignity (*Rūz al-Yūsuf* no. 7 [December 7, 1925], 8; no. 178 [June 24, 1930], 16; ʿAbd al-Wahhāb in *Widāʿan*, 25).

77. *Al-Tiyātrū* no. 11 (August 1925), 21; Kāmil, *Tazawwuq*, 128; Mansī, 254–56; *al-Sitār* no. 5 (October 31, 1927), 24; *al-Masraḥ* no. 12 (February 1, 1926), 6; "What we want to see now is al-Shaykh Ibrāhīm in a smoking jacket," remarked *Rūz al-Yūsuf* in no. 43 (August 18, 1926), 13; al-Maṣrī, 11; Kāmil, *Muḥammad al-Qaṣabjī*, 33; *Rūz al-Yūsuf* no. 51 (October 20, 1926), 13.

78. *Rūz al-Yūsuf* no. 40 (August 4, 1926), 12, and no. 41 (August 11, 1926), 13; *al-Masraḥ* no. 41 (October 4, 1926), 5; Shūsha, 27.

79. *Rūz al-Yūsuf* no. 45 (September 8, 1926), 7.

80. Quoted in *Rūz al-Yūsuf* no. 52 (October 27, 1926), 9.

81. *Al-Funūn* no. 14 (December 20, 1926), 8.

82. *Rūz al-Yūsuf* wrote that Umm Kulthūm dispensed with them "with difficulty," and not altogether, for Khālid remained as a singer. "Either she does not want to or cannot get rid of the *mashāyikh* all at once" (*Rūz al-Yūsuf* no. 43 [August 18, 1926], 13; no. 45 [September 8, 1926], 7).

83. *Rūz al-Yūsuf* no. 90 (July 28, 1927), 12; no. 92 (August 11, 1927), 12; *al-Mūsīqá wa-ʾl-Masraḥ* no. 20 (October 1948), 795. Story after story about Umm Kulthūm's subsequent decisions mention the necessity of al-Shaykh Ibrāhīm's approval: for instance, "It remains to be seen whether Umm Kulthūm will agree and whether the *mashāyikh* . . . will accept" (*Rūz al-Yūsuf* no. 91 [August 4, 1927], 12).

84. *Rūz al-Yūsuf* no. 43 (August 25, 1926), 6.

85. *Rūz al-Yūsuf* no. 69 (February 24, 1927), 10; no. 72 (March 17, 1927), 18; no. 198 (November 30, 1931), 18.

86. Umm Kulthūm probably would have enjoyed this moment thoroughly had not Manṣūr ʿAwaḍ rushed into the fray and spoiled her advantage. With apparently the best of intentions he served Munīra with a legal warning to cease and desist (an *indhār*), claiming that Munīra's performances caused damage to his company. His action outraged the concertgoing public, most of whom liked Munīra. Journalists immediately asserted that Umm Kulthūm was afraid of the comparison, adding to her ire at the fact that ʿAwaḍ had as much as said publicly that Munīra could reduce Umm Kulthūm's record sales (*al-Ṣabāḥ* no. 103 [September 17, 1928], 4, 9; no. 107 [October 15, 1928], 25; *Rūz al-Yūsuf* no. 143 [September 11, 1928], 18; Fuʾād, 172).

87. *Al-Masraḥ* no. 34 (August 2, 1926), 26; no. 35 (August 16, 1926), 16. ʿAbd al-Majīd's preference for Munīra and his attacks on Umm Kulthūm were recognized as such. Munīra said she "supervised the magazine's editing and organization of articles and pictures." In *Rūz al-Yūsuf*'s opinion, "no newspaper or magazine served Munīra like *al-Masraḥ* under ʿAbd al-Majīd Ḥilmī" (no. 96 [September 8, 1927], 12; no. 58 [December 8, 1926], 14–15; *al-Ṣabāḥ* no. 83 [April 23, 1928], 11; ʿUthmān in *Widaʿān*, 47). A writer in *al-Funūn* remarked that the attack on Umm Kulthūm in *al-Masraḥ* was unwarranted and unnecessary (no. 20 [February 4, 1927], 9; no. 34 [May 22, 1927], 8).

88. *Rūz al-Yūsuf* no. 142 (1928) and *al-Nāqid* (October 17, 1927), both quoted in Fu'ād, 173, 400–401.

89. Dāwūd Ḥusnī had previously attempted to complete the opera but stopped work on it.

90. *Rūz al-Yūsuf* no. 68 (February 17, 1927), 13.

91. ʿAbd al-Wahhāb, 112–14.

92. Personal communication, Medhat Assem, January 28, 1986.

93. "Most people think these would be a serious threat to Munīra's records," commented *Rūz al-Yūsuf* (no. 91 [August 4, 1927], 12).

94. An excellent example is ʿAbbās Yūnis's "Klīyūbātrā: Bayna Munīra al-Mahdiyya wa-ʿAbd al-Wahhāb" (Cleopatra: Between Munīra al-Mahdiyya and ʿAbd al-Wahhāb), *Majallat al-Mūsīqá* no. 8 (August 1, 1936), 403–6.

95. Azzam, 7.

96. *Rūz al-Yūsuf* remarked that "Like Greta Garbo, Umm Kulthūm has an army of imitators who wrap themselves in a black robe and sing 'In Kunt Asaamiḥ.' . . . All they want is her position. . . . No one has yet succeeded" (no. 368 [March 11, 1935], 30).

97. When Saniyya Ḥasanayn failed to attract a substantial audience, Munīra dismissed her (*Rūz al-Yūsuf* no. 100 [October 6, 1927], 13; *al-Ṣabāḥ* no. 53 [October 3, 1927], 9–11; *al-Sitār* no. 4 [November 24, 1927], 10.

98. *Rūz al-Yūsuf* no. 162 (March 4, 1930), 16. *Rūz al-Yūsuf* reported seeing an exasperated agent, seeking a contract with Najāt, cast his eye on her entourage and ask, "All right, which one of you is her father?" thus insulting all of the "old men pretending to be young" who constituted her company. Najāt was one of the young stars recruited by ʿAbd al-Wahhāb for his films and, in general, she enjoyed a long career of films and concerts and the approbation of many critics.

99. *Al-Masraḥ* no. 43 (October 18, 1926), 20; *Rūz al-Yūsuf* no. 93 (August 18, 1927), 14; no. 92 (August 11, 1927), cover.

100. "The least we can say," sniffed *Rūz al-Yūsuf,* "is that this [Umm Kulthūm's action] is dishonorable" (no. 91 [August 4, 1927], 13).

101. *Rūz al-Yūsuf* no. 230 (July 11, 1932), 18, 31.

102. *Rūz al-Yūsuf* no. 110 (December 15, 1927), 15; also *al-Ṣabāḥ* no. 70 (January 30, 1928), 6.

103. Further details concerning the finances of Umm Kulthūm and other artists appear in Danielson, "Shaping Tradition," 230.

104. *Rūz al-Yūsuf* no. 122 (April 10, 1928), 16; no. 145 (January 22, 1929), 16; no. 132 (June 19, 1928), 19.

105. *Al-Mūsīqá* no. 6 (August 1, 1935), 38 and no. 12 (November 1, 1935), 36; *al-Idhā'a wa-'l-Tilīfizyūn* (March 11, 1972).

106. *Al-Masraḥ* no. 87 (October 13, 1927), 11; *Rūz al-Yūsuf* no. 223 (May 23, 1932), 30; *al-Mūsīqá* no. 8 (September 1935), 37–38.

Chapter Four

1. "Fi Ḥaflat 'Īd Mīlād Jalālat al-Malik bi-Qaṣr 'Abdīn," *Ākhir Sā'a* no. 137 (February 21, 1937), 21.

2. Racy, "Waṣlah," 398–99; see also *Kitāb Mu'tamar,* 164–65; *al-Masraḥ* no. 18 (March 15, 1926), 21; al-Ḥifnī, 1:73, 86–88; Racy, "Musical," 58; Touma, 53–54.

3. A through-composed song has no internal repetitions (unlike a strophic song). Unlike the *qaṣīda,* also frequently through-composed, the monologue texts did not adhere to norms of meter and rhyme characteristic of *qaṣā'id,* and the *qaṣā'id* tended to be syllabic, containing fewer melismas than the monologue, perhaps because the latter tended toward emotive expression where the *qaṣīda* was more closely tied to textual image. The individual lines of a *qaṣīda* generally conveyed complete thoughts and could be viewed as independent conceptual units, whereas in the monologue texts individual lines were more dependent on each other for meaning.

4. Other examples of this innovative style were "Khayaalak fil-Manaam" and "Ya 'Ishrit il-Maaḍi."

5. Over 500,000 copies were sold according to Shūsha (66); 250,000 and 1,500,000 are variously reported in Fu'ād (166, 128).

6. The term *zajal* would be applied to terse and highly colloquial verse and *shi'r* to poetry following classical literary models. In general, Rāmī's style lay closer to *shi'r* than *zajal.*

7. Compare Azzam's description of 'Abd al-Wahhāb: "'Abd al-Wahhāb managed to construct a larger ensemble but left aside harmony in favor of less intrusive Western elements. His melodies may occasionally outline chords, but they do so without functioning in a vertical sense. Chromaticism is used for dramatic expression and is undoubtedly a byproduct of Western influence" (324).

8. I. Saḥḥāb, 31.

9. Victor Saḥḥāb argues that Zakariyyā Aḥmad's and Muḥammad al-Qaṣabjī's innovations in *adwār, ṭaqāṭīq,* and monologues led to the development of the *ughniyya* (see esp. 93–140).

10. Similar bass lines appear in Dāwūd Ḥusnī's "Gannit Na'iimi" (1932) and al-Qaṣabjī's "Ḥaramt Aquul Bitḥibbini" (1938) among others. Zakariyyā's *dawr,* "Ya-lli Tishki min il-Hawa" included a section for bass and *nāy* and introduced triple meter in the second section while retaining most other features associated with a traditional *dawr.*

11. Badawi, 138. Good discussions of the romantic movement in the Arab

world appear in Badawi's book and also in Jayyusi's *Trends and Movements in Modern Arabic Poetry.*

12. Seventy songs, or about 70 percent of her repertory of the time. Sixteen different poets contributed thirty additional texts, and four of the texts were anonymous.

13. Jayyusi, *Trends,* 140–41; ʿAwaḍ, 33–34.

14. Smith, 409; Davis gives as an example of political engagement Ṭalʿat Ḥarb, the banker who underwrote substantial developments in Egyptian theater and film, whose house "became a salon during the late 1930s for prominent Egyptians, Palestinians, Iraqis and even members of the Saudi royal family who were concerned with the increasing power of the Zionists in Palestine" (*Challenging Colonialism,* 189).

15. This and other issues are discussed in detail in *Musique Arabe: Le Congrès du Caire de 1932.*

16. Statement made at a question and answer session at a lecture I gave in Alexandria, Egypt, May 24, 1992.

17. With Friday the Muslim religious holiday and Sunday the Christian, Thursday and Saturday nights were the prime occasions for evening entertainment.

18. *Al-Ṣabāḥ* no. 28 (April 11, 1927), 4.

19. Cf. *al-Nāqid* no. 1 (October 13, 1927), 12.

20. *Rūz al-Yūsuf* no. 141 (August 28, 1928), 16; no. 143 (September 11, 1928), 17. An agent, Ṣiddīq Aḥmad, arranged all of these concerts. Compare Fatḥiyya Aḥmad's schedule of two nights weekly at Ṣālat Badīʿa, *Rūz al-Yūsuf* no. 176 (June 10, 1930), 17; her agreement with Munīra to perform five nights weekly in "Cleopatra," *Rūz al-Yūsuf* no. 76 (April 21, 1927), 12; the demand in Ṣāliḥ ʿAbd al-Ḥayy's contract negotiations with Munīra to sing Mark Antony that he only work three nights per week (*Rūz al-Yūsuf* no. 91 [August 4, 1927], 12).

21. She sang at Cinema Ramsīs in 1931, from 1932–35 at Cinema Fuʾād, renamed Masraḥ Umm Kulthūm in 1933, in Ewart Hall of the American University from 1937–39 and, in the 1940s, at the National Club. She settled at Masraḥ Ḥadīqat al-Azbakiyya and Cinema Qaṣr al-Nīl in the 1950s, where she remained for the rest of her career, probably because of the large size of these two theaters (*Rūz al-Yūsuf* no. 195 [November 9, 1931], 22, and no. 200 [December 14, 1931], 14). Cinema Fuʾād seems to have been originally named Cinema Kleber, renamed Cinema Josy (or Josy Palace) in the 1920s, and then became Cinema Fuʾād, apparently ca. 1932 (*Rūz al-Yūsuf* no. 241 [September 25, 1932], 29; no. 246 [October 31, 1932], 25); see also concert programs dating from 1933, a number of which are available in the private collection of ʿAbd al-ʿAzīz al-ʿAnānī in Cairo, and in my own collection; *al-Rādyū al-Miṣrī* no. 133 (October 2, 1937), cover; no. 157 (March 2, 1938).

22. *Rūz al-Yūsuf* no. 241 (September 25, 1932), 29; her father's weakening health, indicated in 1928 and ending in his death in 1932, and Khālid's increasing responsibilities for the family's newly acquired property took them out of their former roles as her representatives. In the early 1930s, men with money to invest established music halls in the name of a popular female entertainer. Ṣālat Mārī

Manṣūr is one example. Badīʿa Maṣabnī and a few other women owned their own businesses.

23. Her audience, it was reported, included the entire Minyā police force, including those on duty (*Umm Kulthūm: Qithārat,* 118–19).

24. *Rūz al-Yūsuf* no. 115 (February 21, 1928), 16; also, for the first story, *al-Ṣabāḥ* no. 73 (February 21, 1928), 7.

25. The pilot had been trained for work in the new Miṣr Aviation Company, founded by Ṭalʿat Ḥarb and opened in 1932, in which many influential Egyptians took an interest (Davis, *Challenging Colonialism,* 134, 141); *Rūz al-Yūsuf* no. 208 (February 9, 1932), 25; no. 212 (March 7, 1932); *Majallat al-Mūsīqá* no. 4 (June 1, 1936), 202–4; *Ākhir Sāʿa* no. 148 (May 9, 1937), 41.

26. Ṭalʿat Ḥarb, representing Firqat Tarqiyat al-Tamthīl al-ʿArabī, the theater company his bank underwrote, approached Umm Kulthūm's father with these offers for the plays *Ṣabāḥ* and later *Ṭayf al-Khayāl* (Ḥammād, "Min Dhikrayāt," *Ākhir Sāʿa* no. 185 [January 16, 1938], 8–9; Fu'ād, 131–32). According to Badīʿ Khayrī, Umm Kulthūm wanted him to write the play and Najīb al-Rīḥānī to act and direct. Negotiations failed because another director was under contract to the troupe and al-Rīḥānī refused to act without also directing the play (Khayrī, 85–92). This must have occurred between 1922 and 1926 when the troupe disbanded (Kāmil, *al-Masraḥ,* 26).

27. Singer and *ʿūd* player Tawḥīda was reported to have at long last negotiated a contract that stipulated that she was not to be compelled to sit with customers nor to drink more than five glasses of cognac in one evening (Fu'ād, 158).

28. ʿAwaḍ, 57, 60–61. See also Danielson, "Artists and Entrepreneurs," 301–2.

29. During the late 1920s, Umm Kulthūm's entourage consisted of Manṣūr ʿAwaḍ, director of Gramophone Records, lawyer Būlus Armānyūs, Ḥifnī Bey al-Darīnī, formerly Prince ʿUmar Ibrāhīm's estate manager, ʿAlī al-Ḥamrāwī, a well-known merchant, al-Muʿallim Dabsha, a wealthy butcher, Ghālib al-Muhandis, a poet, Ḥasan Sharīf, a theatrical agent, and ʿAlī Bey al-Barūdī, Mannaʿ [?] Bey ʿAṭiyya, Muṣṭafá Naqrāsh, Muṣṭafá al-ʿAqīl, and ʿAbd al-Karīm whose professions are not indicated (*al-Masraḥ* no. 28 [May 31, 1926], 12; no. 31 [June 28, 1926], 11; no. 34 [August 2, 1926], 26; no. 51 [December 13, 1926], 4, 19; *Rūz al-Yūsuf* no. 25 [April 21, 1926], 13; no. 69 [February 24, 1927], 13; no. 61 [November 28, 1927], 14; no. 72 [March 17, 1927], 13; no. 113 [February 7, 1928], 17; no. 252 [December 12, 1932], 26; *al-Ṣabāḥ* no. 28 [April 11, 1927], 4; *Rūz al-Yūsuf* no. 2434 [?] [February 10, 1975], 18).

30. *Al-Masraḥ* no. 31 (June 28, 1926), 11.

31. *Rūz al-Yūsuf* no. 243 (October 9, 1932), 28. The memoirs of Badīʿa Maṣabnī include a lively description of Umm Kulthūm's *balāṭ* on pp. 228–29.

32. The suit was later dropped (*Rūz al-Yūsuf* no. 69 [February 24, 1927], 13).

33. *Rūz al-Yūsuf* no. 40 (August 4, 1926), 12; no. 95 (September 1, 1927), 13; no. 2434 [?] (February 10, 1975), 19–20. Rumor had it that Badīʿa Maṣabnī's *balāṭ* undertook to physically intimidate uncooperative critics (Fu'ād, 181).

34. *Rūz al-Yūsuf* no. 61 (December 31, 1926), 13.

35. Characterized as "the Pāshās and the Beys, notables and eminences who fill her house in Zamālik. They include someone high in the government, an important governor, a prince (or a prince-to-be), and a famous notable" (*al-Masraḥ* no. 31 [June 28, 1926], 11).

36. Khalīl Bey Thābit, then editor of *al-Muqaṭṭam,* Aḥmad Rāmī, and the members of her *takht,* among others, came to her house to visit and to transact business (ʿAbd al-Wahhāb in *Widāʿan,* 25; *Rūz al-Yūsuf* no. 129 [May 29, 1928], 18).

37. Fu'ād, 238.

38. *Rūz al-Yūsuf* no. 122 (April 10, 1928), 16.

39. *Rūz al-Yūsuf* no. 181 (July 15, 1930), 19.

40. "Ḥadīth Istaghraq ʿĀmayn," *al-Kawākib* (February 2, 1982), 18–19.

41. *Rūz al-Yūsuf* no. 194 (November 2, 1931), 18.

42. A discussion of this international trend, linked to the prevailing economic circumstances, appears in Gronow, 275.

43. Judging from record catalog advertisements and annotations in al-Maṣrī and Kāmil's index, the total number of Cairophon releases was no greater than twenty-five records over a period of approximately ten years. Many songs from the 1940s were not released as records at all at the time but were dubbed from radio tapes as much as ten or twenty years later (personal communication, Sayyid al-Maṣrī; compare El-Shawan, "al-Mūsīḳa," 102). For more information on recordings, see Racy, "Musical," and Danielson, "Shaping Tradition," 253–65.

44. Personal communication of Medhat Assem (January 28, 1986); El-Shawan, "al-Mūsīḳa," 105; Boyd, 3. Radio broadcasting in Egypt has been government controlled since 1934. I use the name Egyptian Radio to designate the growing number of radio stations broadcasting under the auspices of the state.

45. For more information on radio in Egypt, see Boyd, Wahba, and Danielson, "Shaping Tradition," 266–74.

46. During the early 1930s, ʿAlī Pāshā was Umm Kulthūm's physician; Dr. ʿAfīfī was the ambassador to London for a time and a personal acquaintance; and ʿAbd al-Ḥamīd Pāshā had been her admirer for years (personal communication, Medhat Assem, January 28, 1986).

47. Boyd, 4. Although licensing regulations allowed the compilation of statistics showing per capita radio ownership in the mid-1930s, most scholars agree that these are not good indicators of radio's growing impact.

48. El-Shawan, "al-Mūsīḳa," 114.

49. *Rūz al-Yūsuf* no. 257 (January 16, 1933), 29; no. 367 (March 3, 1935), 31.

50. Personal communication, Medhat Assem, January 28, 1986; also his article, "Umm Kulthūm: al-Usṭūra al-Khālida," *al-Kawākib* no. 1644 (February 1, 1983), 5. To answer her need for an audience, the faithful Rāmī often went with her to the studio and pantomimed encouraging responses (Shūsha, 31, 66).

51. Shūsha, 31; Fu'ād, 228–29.

52. The behavior of listening to the broadcasts with friends served as the basis for the plot of an Egyptian television serial in 1985. "Ḥulm Abū 'l-ʿIlā" featured as its main character a landowner from Upper Egypt who used to travel to Cairo on

the first Thursday of every month, not to attend Umm Kulthūm's concerts but to listen to them over the radio in the company of his Cairene relations.

53. *Rūz al-Yūsuf* no. 227 (June 29, 1932), 28.

54. Very likely these adversely affected attendance at plays and song concerts, but the available sources do not make this connection. According to Landau, silent films were first introduced in Egypt in 1904 (Landau, 157–60; Wahba, 57; Issawi, 189).

55. The search for ʿAbd al-Wahhāb's costar was extensive and well documented in the press. Umm Kulthūm was one candidate, but neither star would "cross to the other's side of the canal" to reach agreement (*Rūz al-Yūsuf* no. 239 [September 11, 1932], 28; no. 238 [September 4, 1932], 28; Shūsha, "Umm Kulthūm wa-Bidāyat al-ʿAṣr al-Dhahabī lil-Sīnimā," *al-Jadīd* [February 1, 1979], 12; *Rūz al-Yūsuf* no. 182 [July 22, 1930], 16; no. 227 [June 20, 1932], 28; no. 239 [September 11, 1932], 26, 28; no. 249 [November 21, 1932], 29; no. 251 [December 5, 1932], 28).

56. *Al-Idhāʿa wa-ʾl-Tilīfizyūn* (February 12, 1972), 19. ʿAbd al-Wahhāb was offered 10,000 £E (about $35,000) for his first song film and, by the end of World War II, fees for stars ranged as high as 20,000 £E (roughly $82,800) per film (*Rūz al-Yūsuf* no. 227 [June 29, 1932], 28; Landau, 181). A liberal immigration policy long held by the Egyptian government helped the businesses of commercial performance (al-Tābiʿī, 102–3; Fuʾād, 261).

57. *Rūz al-Yūsuf* no. 275 (May 22, 1933), 18; no. 270 (April 17, 1933), 28. In the latter the writer observed that Fatḥiyya Aḥmad, despite efforts over a period of months, had not secured adequate funding. Umm Kulthūm, never eager to assume risks herself, sought investors. Between 1936 and 1946 film songs accounted for about half of her new repertory.

58. Among the actors with whom Umm Kulthūm worked, Ḥusayn Riyāḍ, Aḥmad ʿAllām, and Mukhtār ʿUthmān were all veterans of Yūsuf Wahbī's troupe. Munassá Fahmī had acted with Salāma Ḥijāzī. ʿAbbās Fāriṣ worked with the ʿUkkāsha brothers. Istifān Rustī acted with al-Riḥānī and Rūz al-Yūsuf in ʿAzīz ʿĪd's production of *Khallii baalak min Emily,* and, along with Ḥusayn Riyāḍ and Mukhtār ʿUthmān, had been in the cast of Sayyid Darwīsh's famous *al-ʿAshara al-Ṭayyiba.* ʿUmar Waṣfī was a competent comedian and veteran of the stage (Khayrī, 78; Kāmil, *al-Masraḥ,* 16, 24; al-Yūsuf, 45, 56; Barbour, 181).

59. *Al-Ahrām* dispatch quoted in *Majallat al-Mūsīqá* no. 12 (October 1, 1936), 619.

60. The students, according to Marsot, "became a corps d'élite in the country, and their importance in social and political life far outmatched their real contributions. The use of students in political agitation, first against the British and then against the monarch and the opposition, caused the years 1935 and 1936 to be dubbed the 'years of youth'" (*Egypt's Liberal Experiment,* 202).

61. *Al-Kawākib* no. 1592 (February 2, 1982), 20–21.

62. Wahba, 57; Majdī Fahmī in *Widāʿan,* 50. For more information about Umm Kulthūm's films and the industry, see Danielson, "Shaping Tradition," 274–75, 277–78.

63. *Al-Majalla al-Mūsīqiyya* no. 4 (June 1, 1936), 206.

64. Majdī Fahmī in *Widāʿan,* 52; Fu'ād, 232.

65. Asmahān's considerable skills in this realm may be heard in recordings of "ʿAleek Ṣalaat Allāh," "Dakhalt Marra" and "Ya Ṭuyuur."

66. Al-Tābiʿī, 35–37, 91–92, 94–95; Fu'ād, 255.

67. Al-Tābiʿī; *al-Mawʿid* (August 31, 1978), 10–13.

68. The figures available for musicians' pay are not completely reliable but offer a rudimentary basis for comparison and suggest what was viewed as standard and extraordinary within the society.

69. *Rūz al-Yūsuf* no. 50 (October 7, 1926), 13; ʿAwaḍ, 80.

70. Ṣiddīq Aḥmad paid 85 £E ($425) in advertising and promotion and 20 £E ($100) theater rental, bringing expenses for the first two concerts to 190 £E ($950) "and he still made money!" (*Rūz al-Yūsuf* no. 50 [October 7, 1926], 13).

71. In 1924–25, Faṭma Qadrī made 80 £E ($400) per month performing in musical theater. Faṭma Sirrī's first role in theater in the early 1920s paid 40 £E ($200) per month, and Naʿīma al-Maṣriyya worked as a singer in musical halls at the same time for 30 to 60 £E ($150 to $300) per month (*al-Tiyātrū* no. 4 [January 1925], 22, 23; *al-Masraḥ* no. 10 [January 18, 1926], 18; *Rūz al-Yūsuf* no. 106 [November 17, 1926], 20; no. 107 [November 24, 1927], 20). More information is available in Danielson, "Shaping Tradition," 281–85.

72. *Rūz al-Yūsuf* no. 365 (February 18, 1935), 30.

73. Umm Kulthūm, "known for the simplicity of her clothes and her lack of concern for appearances . . . after seven years was able to buy 100 *faddāns* [of land] and pay for it in cash" owing to her "abstinence and restraint" with money (*Rūz al-Yūsuf* no. 116 [February 28, 1928], 21. Both her frugality and her purchase of agricultural land rather than urban real estate or other investments were commonly associated with *fallaḥiin.*

74. Fatḥiyya Aḥmad possessed great vocal flexibility and was at first compared favorably to Umm Kulthūm. The recordings of Mary Jamīla, also known as Mary Jubrān, who performed successfully in Cairo during the 1920s, and Nādira, whose career extended from the late 1920s to about 1960, also in Cairo, illustrated virtuosity comparable to Umm Kulthūm's. Mary Jamīla's *layālī* exhibited a strong voice, schooled in the *maqāmāt,* obviously capable of wide range, long phrases, and varied colors. Nādira's *qaṣīda* "Laytanī lam Astaṭiʿ" exhibited a light, flexible voice also capable of wide range and cleanly executed embellishments.

75. Racy, "Musical," 153; Racy quotes Qisṭandī Rizq's formulation of a well-known training procedure and test for a suitably strong voice written during the 1930s, as follows: "Good voices must be trained according to the genuine Arab fashion . . . and must be trained in the maqāmāt and tested from the top of the mosque minarets, as did the late ʿAbdū al-Ḥāmūlī, who trained his voice atop the minaret of al-Ḥanafī Mosque" (154). This story is part of the discourse that links singing with religious practices historically.

76. Al-Khulaʿī enjoined singers to warm their voices ahead of time so that guests would have ample time to listen and return to their homes "relaxed of body

and mind," rather than waiting "half the evening" for the singer to be ready to sing well (*Kitāb,* 90). Singers took breaks during performances, but lengthy intervals between songs were objectionable since the singer was normally the focus of the performance, regardless of the competence of the accompanists to perform solos themselves.

77. *Umm Kulthūm: Qiṣṣat,* 19; an exception may be heard in the commercial recording of ʿAbduh al-Ḥāmūlī's "Arāka ʿAsīya ʾl-Damʿ," in which Umm Kulthūm used a shift between registers to distinguish the male and female speakers in the poem.

78. In al-Khulaʿī's description of voices, clarity or purity appear in over half of the qualities he views as good (*Kitāb,* 26; the list appears also in Rouanet, 2796–97).

79. Al-Khulaʿī wrote that leaning or other forms of bad posture would "bend the throat" thus "weakening" the voice and also hindering clear pronunciation (*Kitāb,* 78).

80. Al-Khulaʿī, *Kitāb,* 26; *baḥḥa* was also part of his description of the *ajass* voice: "loud, but having a pleasant huskiness and grand tone."

81. Al-Khulaʿī described the voice possessed with *ghunna* as "having nasality, sweetness and melodiousness." He distinguished this quality from *al-akhann,* a voice, he wrote, that sounded "as if the nose of its owner were plugged" (*Kitāb,* 26).

82. "Nasality (ġunnah) governs geminate /m/ and /n/, the phonetic phenomena of ixfāʾ, iqlāb, and some contexts of idġām. . . . Although phoneticians would argue that these consonants are naturally articulated through the nasal cavity, the rules of *tajwīd* single out the geminate consonants for nasality, with the result that they are pronounced with an intensified and conscious nasality" (K. Nelson, 21).

83. Sawa, *Music Performance Practice,* 101.

84. Al-Khulaʿī, *Kitāb,* 26; cf. K. Nelson, "In general, the same standards of voice quality apply to both recitation [of the Qurʾān] and singing: reciters are criticized for a blaring, feeble, nasal, dry, rheumy (fī balġam) voice, whereas a strong, clear, and flexible voice is appreciated" (122). Exceptions to the prevailing norm included character actors who sang, such as Zākī ʿUkkāsha, whose voice was described as "screeching." Similarly Zakariyyā Aḥmad was a much-loved singer though his voice was far from beautiful. Audiences loved to hear him, perhaps because his persona as a clever, earthy, populist-minded entertainer was projected in his raspy, inflexible voice; cf. K. Nelson, "occasionally the musicality of a reciter is so effective that his reputation transcends what listeners agree is a weak or raspy voice" (123).

85. Chabrier, 37.

86. El-Shawan, "al-Mūsīḳa," 43–44. Compare Racy: "the extent of audience participation determined the length and the musical quality of a single performance" (Racy, "Musical," 148). The relationship of performer to audience is the subject of Racy's excellent essay, "Creativity and Ambience."

87. Personal communication, Kamāl Ḥusnī, October 13, 1982; also al-Khulaʿī, *Kitāb,* 78–79.

88. Al-Khulaʿī, *Kitāb,* 82, 83.

89. Ibid., 83, 82, 84; personal communication, Kamāl Ḥusnī, October 13, 1982.

90. Cf. K. Nelson, 122.

91. Thus, as a singer known for *qaṣā'id* sung to elite men, Muḥammad ʿAbd al-Wahhāb was the "Singer for Princes." Umm Kulthūm's performances, despite her increasing personal and vocal elegance, were, according to Badīʿa Maṣabnī, generally rowdier and less elegant than ʿAbd al-Wahhāb's (229–30).

92. "Irādat al-shaʿb wa-Umm Kulthūm" (The will of the people and Umm Kulthūm), *al-Kashkūl* no. 57 (June 18, 1922), 6–7. The concept of articulation was expressed using a variety of phrases such as "makhārij al-alfāẓ" and "al-nuṭq al-wāḍiḥ."

93. Further examples of her good diction appear in Danielson, "The Qur'ān and the Qaṣīdah."

94. Muḥammad ʿAbd al-Wahhāb, quoted in Fahmī, in *Widāʿan,* 29.

95. Ṣabrī, 2:302; *al-Mūsīqá* no. 5 (July 16, 1935), 38–39; Fu'ād, 393. As for her colleagues, the writer in *al-Mūsīqá* said that Najāt ʿAlī seemed to have memorized texts but did not understand their meanings. Likewise Ṣāliḥ ʿAbd al-Ḥayy was accused of singing texts "the way he learned them, right or wrong." Setting meaning aside, "correct pronunciation frequently escaped Nādira." The only singers other than Umm Kulthūm who received favorable notice were Muḥammad ʿAbd al-Wahhāb and Maḥmūd Ṣubḥ. The writer credited ʿAbd al-Wahhāb's close association with Aḥmad Shawqī for his learning and Ṣubḥ's to his training in the recitation of the Qur'ān.

96. The two phrases are "Lā tastaṭīʿu juhūdahu ʿaynāki" and "Kāsa 'l-mudāmati an tuqabbila fāki."

97. Other similar examples were the fourth and fifth lines of al-Qaṣabjī's "Khalli 'l-Dumuuʿ" (1930), "Wa-shakat li" from his "Khaaṣamatni" (1930), the first two lines of "il-Shakk Yiḥyi 'l-Gharaam" (1930), and the line "Yā ayyuhā 'l-wajh" from Abū 'l-ʿIlā's "Afdīhi in Ḥafiẓ al-Hawá" (1928).

98. *Al-Masraḥ* no. 26 (May 27, 1926), 15. Note especially the line "Yā zamān al-waṣl."

99. For instance, the *layālī* preceding "Wi-l-Ḥadd Imta" and "Ṣaddaq wa-Ḥubbak." "Kull ma Yizdaad" (line 1) and "Ya ma Amarr il-Furaaq" (at "aṣawwar il-maaḍi") exemplify *ghunna* as a device to heighten the impact of words and sentiments.

100. Racy's careful description of the accompanimental style of early-twentieth-century *qaṣā'id* reflected the practice of the time generally: "In a heterophonic passage the musical elements common to all participating musical lines were usually (a) a roughly similar melodic contour, (b) a similar tempo, (c) an identical emphasis on essential pitches, such as the tonic, the fourth, and the fifth, (d) a roughly parallel phraseology, and (e) comparable dynamics manifested in the accentuation of certain beats (as in the Wāḥidah) and of initial and final notes within particular phrases.

Elements that varied most from one line to another were the melodic and rhythmic details, including the following: (a) introducing additional rests; (b) delaying